WHERE DID OUR LOVE GO?

WHERE DID OUR LOVE GO?

The Rise & Fall of the Motown Sound

NELSON GEORGE

St. Martin's Press
New York

Library of Congress Cataloging-inPublication Data

George, Nelson.
    Where did our love go?

    1. Soul music—United States—History and criticism.
2. Motown Record Corporation.   3. Afro-American
musicians.   I. Title.
ML3537.G46   1986   784.5′5′00973   85–25106
ISBN 0-312-86698-4

First Edition
10 9 8 7 6 5 4 3 2 1

CONTENTS

ACKNOWLEDGMENTS

I don't believe there are "definitive" accounts of anything in history. As the Japanese director Akira Kurosawa demonstrated in his film *Rashomon,* eyewitness accounts of any event can vary greatly. The mind interprets for itself what the eye sees and the ear hears. Moreover, the meaning of a fact or any particular set of facts—facts that are generally agreed to be true—seems to me to be eternally open to interpretation. Whenever Berry Gordy—or Diana Ross, or Mary Wilson —get around to telling their Motown stories, I assure you these chronicles will be no more definitive than any account by a public figure with a mystique to protect or project. Bias would, in all these cases, obviously override objective history.

I, admittedly, have my bias too. What fascinates me is the impact of his family's history on Berry Gordy's values; the music and the people who made it; and the structure of the company organized by Berry Gordy to produce, mold, and stimulate the making of that music. Motown's aggressive non-cooperation with this writer reflected the company's long-standing antagonism to reporters, a stance that I hope hasn't unduly clouded my judgments. One positive result of Motown's attitude is that this book bares no trace of company input or control. The backbone of this enterprise is composed of unpublished interviews with ex-Motowners conducted by myself or other journalists.

The actual research and writing of this book has taken about two and a half years, though I've been studying Motown since the early 1970s, when I was first struck by how remarkable the story of Berry Gordy and his institution was. Over the course of my eight years as a music journalist, talks with these figures were essential to the writing of this book: James Jamerson, Benny Benjamin, Earl Van Dyke, Johnny Griffith, Dave Hamilton, Choker Campbell, Eddie Holland, Brian Holland, Lamont Dozier, Freddie Perren, Marvin Gaye, Diana Ross, Smokey Robinson, Al Cleveland, Weldon McDougal, Cholly Atkins, Sylvia Moy, Joe Jackson, Rodney Gordy, Don Davis, LeBaron Taylor, Thomas "Beans" Bowles, Jack Gibson, Gerry Griffith, Lionel Richie, Mtume, Don Cornelius, Greg Phillinganes, Ray Parker, Jr., Ed Eckstine, Jermaine Jackson, Steve Manning, Marlon Jackson, Tito Jackson, Randy Jackson, Rick James, Reggie Andrews, Ndugu Chancelor, Dick Griffey, Clive Davis, Maurice White, Lonnie Simmons, John McClain, Harvey Fuqua, Regina Jones, Steve Ivory, Harry Weinger, and many others.

In addition, the work of four other writers was invaluable: David Breskin for his conversations with Maxine Powell, Tony Bongovi, and Gene Kee, and for his diligence in unearthing lawsuits; Aaron Fuchs, for out-takes from his interviews with Harvey Fuqua, William Stevenson, Mary Wells, and Mary Wilson for the book *Girl Groups: Story of a Sound;* Randy Wilson for his in-depth research into the life of Flo Ballard and for his talks with Robert Bateman; and *Detroit Free Press* writer Kim Heron's interviews with Esther Gordy and Berry Gordy, Jr.

Back issues of the *Detroit Free Press,* the *Detroit News, Black Music* magazine, *Billboard,* and *Record World,* as well as Peter Benjamin's *The Story of Motown* (Grove Press), *The Rolling Stone Illustrated History of Rock & Roll* (Random House), Geri Hirshey's *Nowhere To Run* (Times Books), and David Morse's *Motown* (Collier) provided important facts. *Rolling Stone, The New York Times,* the New York *Daily News, Cashbox, Variety, Soul, Rock 'n' Soul, Right On!, New Musical Express,* the *Amsterdam News, Essence,* and the *Michigan Chronicle* were all useful. Special thanks to the staffs of the late and surely lamented *Record World* magazine, the *Amsterdam News, Billboard, Black Enterprise,* and *The Village Voice* for their support over the years. Extra-special "yo"s to Robert Christgau, Robert Cornfield, Sheryl Lee Hilliard, Robert Ford, Jr., Russell Simmons, Bob Miller of St. Martin's, Lydia Hannibal, Brian Goodin and family, my mother, my sister and her husband, and the beautiful Ebony George. Oh, yeah, thanks again to Alex, and one wonderful book lady, Patti Romanowski.

FOREWORD

BY QUINCY JONES

The music of Motown Records is a challenge and an inspiration to anyone making pop records. Because, quite simply, the musical achievements of Berry Gordy's company have been monumental. The talented people that flowed through Motown, both the performers on stage and the writers and producers behind the scenes, broke down the barriers between black and white, between the R&B world and the "mainstream," letting everyone see the beauty of black music.

Trying to compete with Motown in the 1960's while I was an A&R executive at Mercury was a study in frustration. Mercury was a major label based in Chicago. Yet just up the road in Detroit this little company was enjoying hit after hit. But they weren't just hits. They were hits with a signature, a sound that denoted quality and soul. What they had up in Michigan was a small cohesive team of writers and musicians who fought for success. The competition, as Nelson George shows, was fierce. But it wasn't competition about ego; it was competition about being better . . . better . . . the best.

The strength of that philosophy is apparent in the creative production flourishes of the Holland-Dozier-Holland team; the cleverness Smokey Robinson brought to songwriting; James Jamerson's revolutionary and still influential conception on electric bass; the intensity of Marvin Gaye and Levi Stubbs's voices; all of these were just a few of Motown's "signatures." All of them challenged their competitors, a group that unfortunately included me, until I wisely moved to Los Angeles to score movies to keep up or get lost in that machine's exhaust fumes. And today, some twenty years since the peak of Motown's "production line," that music still inspires musicians of every color to combine craftsmanship with originality and accessibility.

What Nelson has done in this book, for the first time that I know of, is to have taken the time to get inside the workings of that music; seeing how both the recording process and the personalities of the musicians and producers made magic. Surrounding the music, Nelson has painted a telling picture of the record business in the fifties and sixties, a painting that shows the barriers Motown had to overcome and its strategies used in doing so. Better . . . better . . . the best. It is a credo that Motown's music epitomized.

INTRODUCTION

BY ROBERT CHRISTGAU

Ideally, biographies are written from primary sources. The writer interviews subject, family, and close associates, examines documents and correspondence, and then fans the research outward, gathering testimony from friends and foes and neutral experts. The result is expected to at least aim for impartiality, and sometimes a preponderance of disinterested observers will actually agree that it has hit the target.

That's how it's supposed to work, but even when most of these guidelines are respected, one is customarily ignored: the writer doesn't interview the subject because the subject is dead. Living human beings who are famous or important enough to merit biographies rarely encourage an objective examination of their achievements. Their first-hand biographers are handpicked toadies or dazed admirers; often the biographees will only trade access to his or her exalted presence for an opportunity to "check the manuscript for accuracy"—that is, censor it. So the life stories of living persons are usually either "authorized," a polite way to say biased, or gathered from sources who are willing to talk because they aren't especially close to, or have something against, the principal. This syndrome has been responsible for vast seas of stupid-to-mediocre writing. In popular music, such writing is rendered doubly dubious by the widespread belief that the mean age of its target audience is fourteen.

Strictly speaking, Nelson George's *Where Did Our Love Go?* isn't a biography. It's the history of a corporation, Motown Records, beginning well before its inception in Detroit in 1959 and following its legend closely until 1971, when the label's move to Los Angeles signaled that its legendary days were over. But while Motown became the largest black-owned company in America by selling the creations of other black Americans, all lovingly and searchingly described, the corporation itself was the creation of one man, Berry Gordy, which is why George's story must be Gordy's story. Authorized it isn't. In the grandest and most arrogant tradition of early Hollywood, Motown has always fed the press pap and expected unmitigated subservience in return. That's not how George does things, and as a result he didn't get to talk to Gordy (which doesn't distinguish him from countless more slavish but equally frustrated journalists) or the (mostly white) men who run the company with him.

Unfortunately for Motown, I suppose, this noncooperation proved nowhere near as disabling as the company's flacks and protectors hoped. First of all, as he's already proved in his masterful quickie bio of Michael Jackson, George knows how to use secondary sources. He doesn't just go for the obvious, but finds obscure stuff—local newspaper stories both in and out of Detroit, court cases, old kinescopes. Then, too, as America's foremost journalist of black music, black music editor of first *Record World* and then *Billboard*, as well as a respected critic whose reviews have appeared in a wide range of journals prestigious and otherwise, George enjoys considerable access to the artists who are the other half (or ninety percent) of the story. Some are disaffected now, of course, although quite a few have returned to the fold or never ventured away—unlike the behind-the-scenes personnel who dropped out as Gordy's reluctance to share the wealth became evident. Over the years, George has talked to every one he could get to.

I'm sure Motown won't like the outcome of his research, but that's just vanity if it isn't paranoia. Not only is George's account evenhanded, it's by any reasonable criterion warmly complimentary as well, which for Motown ought to be the ideal combination, because it guarantees high credibility. While George deserves credit for resisting the bitterness of the ex-Motowners who provided their versions of the story, it's clear that one reason he still admires Berry Gordy is that even Gordy's nominal enemies retain not just regard but affection for the man. Of course, one reason for that is the unvanguishable vitality of the music Gordy made happen. The Motown hits (and quite a few of the misses) of the sixties may stand as the most impressive and enduring body of pure pop for now people that rock and roll will ever produce. Individual artists as remarkable as Smokey Robinson and Marvin Gaye and the Temptations and Diana Ross and Stevie Wonder—not to mention composers like Holland-Dozier-Holland

and Ashford & Simpson and the glorious backup band the Funk Brothers
—all put their stamp on the music. But it was Gordy's quality controls,
organizational flair, and unflagging desire to sell millions upon millions of
records that shaped it.

George's narrative moves with grace, dispatch, and attention to detail.
Because he's both a reporter and a critic, he doesn't shortchange history
or art—he keeps his eye on the money and his ear on the music and
explains how they fit together. When he focuses in on one portion of his
tale, be it the Gordy family saga or the sad defeat of Florence Ballard, it's
because he wants to exploit its illustrative value. There is, after all, an
underlying theme here.

For, finally, *Where Did Our Love Go?* is a book about black capitalism. George is no left-winger—he's sympathetic to black capitalism. But
he sees how the paradoxes of power for black people in America undermine their temporary triumphs. People of any color can build an enterprise from a good idea and then move away from what they know best,
with consequences that are disastrous spiritually if not economically. But
in Gordy's case that familiar tragedy of success has an inescapably racial
dimension. He made great music by tailoring black rhythm-and-blues to
the tastes of a notably open-minded generation of white American teenagers, but he knew that if his was to be a true American success story it
couldn't stop there. So, not only did he act like any other boss and treat
the talented people who worked for him like peons, but he ended up
where the American entertainment industry always ends up—in Hollywood. As a result, Motown is now just like any other record company, only
a little smaller. Maybe none of this could have been avoided in any case.
But Gordy's response to his American dilemma certainly accelerated the
process.

In the end, Gordy's stonewall does leave a big question unanswered.
George tells us where Gordy came from and what he did, but he can't
make us feel we understand exactly why he did it. His character, as
opposed to his situation, remains frustratingly enigmatic. Given what
George does tell us, though, we can be fairly sure that even those who
know him best have a lot of trouble getting inside the man. When
somebody is as driven as the prime mover of *Where Did Our Love Go?*,
the quest for motivation is always a chancy one. Just the facts will have
to do. And they're here.

PREFACE

Motown Records is a triumph and a contradiction. It is a testament to the power of black music and an example of how soul-stifling success can be when its fruits are not shared. The myth of Motown is that it is the eternal family, a place where singers and executives, clerks and bass players, shared ideas and energy all for the common good. To a remarkable degree, from the late fifties to the mid-sixties, that myth rang true. Motown was a "family" in the best sense of the word, with founder Berry Gordy, Jr., the undisputed father figure.

We all know his children: Child prodigy "Little" Stevie Wonder; the sepia Barbra Streisand, Diana Ross; the mercurial Marvin Gaye; pop's finest wordsmith and supplest singer, Smokey Robinson; the Miracles; the Temptations; Martha Reeves and the Vandellas; Mary Wells; and all the other offspring. At no other time in record industry history has an independent label been better organized to capitalize on its talent. With the exception of John Johnson's publishing empire (Ebony, Jet), no black business has been as effective in making money. But that is just part of the story. Not all the members of the "family" feel they prospered to the degree they should have. Over twenty-five years after its founding, Motown is as symbolic of dreams frustrated as it is of great music to many of the men and women who contributed mightily to the bottom line.

The contributions of so many of the key gears and important cogs in this music machine have been obscured, often on purpose. So have the personal politics and group dynamics of this optimistic, characteristically sixties endeavor. This book doesn't try to place Motown in the context of the civil rights movement or American social history, though both elements play a part in the tale. The goal here is both more straightforward and intense. This is a picture of how Motown worked, why it worked, and, alas, why it can't work the way it used to. It is an epic story of pride, money, and the harnessing of music into an incredibly durable product. There are no heroes in this book. There are no villains. There are just ambitious people.

WHERE DID OUR LOVE GO?

1·BIG DOGS

On Sunday mornings, white ministers once filled the minds of Southern men and women with images of heavenly Christian salvation and the white man's earthly superiority over Indians and "nigras." But white male slave owners sometimes took black slaves for their sexual pleasure. It was an expression of lust and of power. Though the very institution of slavery was a denial of black humanity, it didn't stop the power of money and possession from turning many whites into sexual hypocrites who acknowledged black beauty through their desire.

Some slave owners ignored the implications of miscegenation and denied, consciously and unconsciously, their role in creating America's bittersweet mulatto culture. In 1870 the Georgia legislature rejected a bill suggested by a black member that would have made "putative [slave owner] fathers maintain their bastard children." Other slave owners—men like Jim Gordy—because of real Christian conviction, genuine affection for their sexual partner, or as part of a general philosophy of helping blacks, took steps to help support their bastard children, though they didn't grant them any claim to their land. As a result, in the 1860s, near the end of the Civil War, down in Oconee County, Georgia, Jim Gordy's black bastard son Berry, the scion of his union with a slave woman named Esther Johnson, learned to read, write, and "figger" as well as any white man.

Berry, who was born in about 1854, had yellow skin—the mulatto badge of honor—and was short of stature, although he had a strong, solid

1

physique. His personality was defined by a stubborn streak, a fiery, often explosive temper, and what his neighbors termed "mother wit," or native intelligence. In his late teens, Berry took as his wife a small brown woman of black and Indian heritage named Lucy Hellum. Over the course of their marriage, Lucy conceived twenty-three times—not unusual for a rural woman of the time, when each child was viewed as a future farmhand— and of that number only nine survived: Sam, Lula, Esther, Mamie, Lucy, John, Joe, and Charlie, and on July 10, 1888, a son who was also given the name Berry.

By his mid-twenties Berry was recognized by his neighbors, both white and black, as a local leader, a "big dog." A shrewd, thoughtful businessman, Berry was respected by blacks and many whites in the community for being self-reliant. He worked for a decade on a local plantation, bending and bowing to make another man's fortune. But by the time most of his offspring were walking, Berry had so carefully budgeted his earnings that in the 1890s, when he was in his forties, he was able to purchase 168 acres in Oconee County and go into business for himself. Cotton was his chief cash crop, just as it had been for his white father, though he supplemented his income by growing corn, potatoes, peanuts, okra, cabbage, collard greens, sugarcane, and various fruits.

Most of his black neighbors were deep in debt to the white landowners on whose land they resided and toiled, and to the shopkeepers from whom they purchased their supplies. Ill-educated by the local government, blacks would have their books kept and their businesses managed by the white men with whom they did business. For a hundred years after the Civil War, well into the 1960s, this system of economic neo-slavery effectively kept many blacks in constant debt. No matter how prosperous a black family was one season, it could never overcome the debts that prevented its economic freedom.

Berry would have none of this. He and his wife Lucy kept every bill, every loan statement, every scrap of paper pertaining to the business. To their neighbors, the Gordys appeared almost fanatical in their desire to account for every dime, as if the accumulation of money and the keeping of records—and not the Good Book—held the key to salvation.

As Berry preached his dedication to business to his children every day, his most attentive student was his namesake, who mirrored his father in many ways. Berry II was short (tagged a runt even by friends), feisty, and always seemed to follow his daddy's lead as closely as possible. While the other Gordy children would play in the fields, little Berry lingered around the adults, supposedly playing by himself, but actually listening closely to what the adults said. As his parents discussed bills and crop prices, he'd be underfoot, quietly itching to join their world.

His interest didn't go unnoticed. When he was ten his father started taking him into Sandersville on Saturdays to sell farm produce, where little Berry's job was to calculate the value per pound of the family's cotton. An awareness of the worth of things and the necessity of keeping one's own counsel about them became part of the young boy's makeup.

His father bought him a law book and encouraged him to study it. The education continued as his father's business expanded. After his initial 168-acre purchase, the elder Gordy bought another 100-acre tract, one complete with a large white house, a general store, and a well-stocked barn. Later he opened a blacksmith shop in town, employing another worker and, on occasions, one of his sons.

Berry II attended grade school, where he learned to read and write. He spent his teen years working on the Gordy property, delaying until he was twenty-two his enrollment in high school. There his shortness led some to think he was still a teenager. At school younger boys would mess with Berry II, teasing him and his brothers about their size. "I never started a fight in my life," he wrote later in his autobiography, *Movin' Up*, "but I never lost a fight. I whupped everybody who jumped me."

When kids beat on his larger but younger brother Johnny, young Berry always sought revenge. In fact, his temper almost led him and his brothers to kill a local tough who had nearly whipped Berry's horse to death. Berry confronted the large black man, a neighbor who resented the Gordy family's "big dog" status, and demanded an apology. After receiving none, Berry reared back and pounded him with a rock. Brothers Joe and Johnny joined in hurling rocks before Johnny finally slammed the man senseless with a two-by-four.

The Gordy family's unity and the depth of the lessons the elder Gordy taught his family were put to the ultimate test in the days following May 31, 1913. At noon, before lunch, the two Berry Gordys surveyed the family property, father showing son idiosyncracies of the plantation that young Berry had never noticed. The elder Gordy had proved himself as a farmer and a businessman, and on this dark, cloudy morning he savored his considerable achievement, sharing that pleasure with his closest son. By the time they reached their back porch the sky had turned black and was filled with lightning. Rain began falling on the Gordys' piece of sweet Georgia soil.

A day later Sandersville's blacks and whites stood by the grave of Berry Gordy as his namesake fell to his knees, tears steaming down his cheeks.

After he'd left him on the porch, a bolt of lightning had struck his father down, killing him instantly. Berry II quickly assumed the role of family leader, organizing his father's funeral.

A few days later, with the family still in mourning, some of the elder Berry's business acquaintances, most of them white, began visiting the house. Since the Reconstruction, it had become customary for white businessmen, playing upon the still strong paternal ties between blacks and whites, to offer themselves as supervisors of the black family's land any time a black father died. They would serve as "administrators," making all of the business decisions relating to the family's land, property, and finances. Berry and his mother, still shocked by the elder Gordy's sudden death, planned to follow tradition and name a white merchant administrator. But luck was with them. On the way to town they stopped at the home of a white woman the family had befriended. After they told her of their plans, she put the situation to them bluntly: any white man you get as administrator will steal your land.

Lucy and Berry II went to the county clerk's office and named themselves administrators, an unusual move that seemed to confirm local speculation that the Gordys' "big dog" days were over. Berry, not quite twenty-five when his father died, was considered an untried "boy" by local merchants. In the months that followed, local businessmen constantly approached him, always seeking his signature on contracts to purchase cars and other items that required monthly payments. Looking into the law book his father had given him, Berry saw that if an administrator failed to meet any of his obligations, his land could be seized as payment. Once he fully understood all the implications of his newfound power, Berry realized why his signature was suddenly so popular. As the bills came in, his father's insistence on careful record-keeping stood him in good stead. Whenever the local white merchants challenged the Gordys over a bill—and they seemed to take every opportunity to do so—Berry and his mother would refer to their records. The Gordys even won a court case based on the evidence their records presented.

As the pressure gradually decreased, Berry turned more of his attention to his social life. Because of his renewed "big dog" status, parents were happy to let Berry court their daughters. Berry would pick up girls for less reputable friends and then, after the "real" date, return them to their houses. Financial standing played as big a part in Berry's love life as in his business dealings. Since he felt that girls from poor backgrounds would not make the best mates, he only took seriously women from other "big dog" families. Not surprisingly, his future wife, Bertha Ida Fuller, was a professional woman—a schoolteacher—and from an established family. Like Berry's mother, Bertha was short, cute, brown-skinned, smart, and quite ambitious.

Shortly after meeting Bertha, Berry was drafted into the Army. Though World War I was winding down, Berry worried that he'd die before he could get married, or that somehow the family would lose its land while he was away. From the day he arrived at Army boot camp in Newport News, Virginia, Berry's only goal was to get out as quickly as possible. He faked bad legs and hopped spastically around superior officers. He reported regularly for sick call. He pretended that he could neither read nor write. Even his right eye suddenly went bad on him. This was decidedly unpatriotic behavior; however, Berry's deepest loyalty was to his family and the land his father had left him to defend. Apparently Berry's ploys worked, because only three months after his induction, he was discharged. His swift exit didn't go unnoticed back home, and local police checked his discharge papers. But it was all legal.

While he was away he had asked his mother to hold the line on their cotton price. The family, despite pressure from other farmers, stuck to Berry's strategy. As a result the Gordys made a killing, earning enough from that one harvest to pay off the mortgage.

In 1918, a year after his discharge, Berry married Bertha; he was thirty, and she was nineteen. Soon after, Berry moved out of the cotton business completely, concentrating instead on edible products such as peanuts, vegetables, poultry, hogs, and cattle. He started slaughtering cattle and running his own meat wagon through Sandersville on Saturdays —payday for most blacks. Over the next few years Berry and Bertha had three children: Esther, Fuller, and George. Berry was making good money and had ideas about opening a market, so that he could sell his produce and meats at one central location. These were good times.

In 1922, Berry made a deal that changed his life, as well as that of his family. A load of timber stumps from the family's plantation was sold for $2,600, an amazing sum for a black man to make on a single deal in Georgia at that time. "If a colored man in the South had that kinda money," Berry observed, "well, everybody likes to talk him outta it." Word of Berry's windfall traveled fast. Several local whites wanted to "help him" deposit it. He quickly became the talk of Oconee County.

The family was worried. In the South of the early 1920s, black men were lynched with chilling regularity by the Ku Klux Klan. In the new century's first twenty years, 1,502 lynchings were reported, most of them in Southern states. To a white mob given enough moonshine, possession of a check for $2,600 could easily appear to be an act of defiance against white supremacy. His father's reputation and Berry's guile had protected the Gordys before. They had always put their faith in figures, records, and pieces of paper. But this particular piece was proving far too precious.

At the same time, Berry's brother John, having found few opportunities in Georgia, decided (like so many other Southern blacks) to try life up North. The promise of city life lured John onto a train to Detroit one Sunday morning before church. That same day at church, Berry's wife Bertha, his mother, and a sister begged Berry to follow John, at least until he cashed the check. Berry felt it wasn't necessary, but he decided to make the family happy. The train had already left, so Bertha's father drove him straight from church to the town of Milledgeville. There he caught a train to Macon and transferred for the long ride past Memphis, around Lake Erie, and up to Detroit, Michigan.

Sitting in the colored section of the train, served by black Pullman porters in their white jackets and shined shoes, and surrounded by families who carried all their possessions in one suitcase and men shouting the blues and picking steel-bodied guitars, Berry was just another black face. It is ironic that Berry had been forced to travel to Detroit because he had made too much money; it was the hope of making more money that lured his fellow travelers to that city's burgeoning car-making machine.

2·MOTORTOWN

1 9 2 2 t o 1 9 5 2

Detroit, Michigan, had once been an important way station on the route of the Underground Railroad, lying on the United States' northern-most border, just a boat ride across the narrow Detroit River from Windsor, Canada, and freedom. Since the early 1800s, Detroit had lured black residents from the Southern states. From 1870 to 1920, Detroit's population multiplied twelve times, as European immigrants and Southern whites and blacks filled and expanded its borders. It was, of course, the prospect of employment on the auto assembly lines—for itinerant laborers, a rare chance at financial stability —that sparked this mass migration to Detroit.

At first, blacks were hardly welcome. Company foremen hired only those with similar national (i.e., European) roots; Ford Motor Company, incorporated in 1901, didn't hire its first blacks until 1914. But by the 1920s, the decade in which Detroit was America's second-fastest-growing city and its fifth-largest metropolitan area, Ford became the auto industry's largest employer of black people, partly because of the labor shortage caused by World War I. This was an important breakthrough, since Ford paid the highest wages of any automaker. In 1914, Henry Ford had introduced an unheard-of five-dollars-per-day wage and a profit-sharing plan. In addition, working for Ford offered blacks the widest range of job opportunities. The periodical *Journal of the Negro Race* wrote in 1947 that "When other manufacturers restrained Negro workers to the drudgery of the shops or to the brush and broom around the plants, Ford employed Negroes to do skilled labor and put them on the production line alongside white workers."

Though white ethnocentricity, Jim Crow laws—restricting the civil rights of blacks—and overall limited employment and housing opportunities would continue to bedevil blacks in the Motor City, they couldn't help but be overwhelmed by the potential for advancement Detroit offered. "You can't imagine the impact that city had," heavyweight boxing champion Joe Louis wrote in his autobiography. He recalled arriving in Detroit from his native Alabama as a young man in the 1920s: "I never saw so many people in one place, so many cars at one time. I had never even seen a trolley, schoolhouses, movie theaters. One thing I knew, Detroit looked awfully good to me."

To Berry Gordy, too, Detroit looked mighty good, but not for the same reasons it did to so many of his black contemporaries. Louis, for example, worked in a Ford factory before becoming a professional boxer. Damned if Berry Gordy was gonna be just another cog in Ford's machine. "I got up there in Detroit and I saw how things was," he wrote years later. "But I wasn't makin' money! I kept lookin' 'round to make money. But I liked it so well; I knew if other people were makin' good money, I was gonna be able to make some." To a man raised from birth to be an entrepreneur, Detroit seemed a simply wonderful place.

A month later, Bertha and the children arrived in Detroit. At first Berry lived on Detroit's East Side with his brother John, but later he looked for housing on the West Side, where a large black community was developing. A white real estate agent named Singleton suggested Berry buy a beautiful, newly decorated home he was offering; as soon as he signed the mortgage he could move in, for only $8,500. But Berry only had $250 available (his share of the $2,600 check, which had been split among the family members). Singleton said that he would accept that, explaining that the rest of the down payment was his commission anyway. He'd just lend Berry that amount and get it back monthly at the same time the mortgage was paid. Berry was then hustled over to 5419 Roosevelt Avenue, a two-story building with shining bright floors and clean, new wallpaper. Seeing that Berry was impressed, the agent suggested that he move in the next day.

When they met the following morning, Singleton appeared agitated. They rushed over to the landlady's house—Singleton said it was important that they make it there by eleven o'clock. Introductions had barely been made when the phone rang, with a call for the agent. From the agent's responses, Berry gathered that the caller wanted to buy the house but had missed an appointment. "If he doesn't buy it, I'll call you right back," said Singleton and hung up. He then turned to Berry, hoping the bait had been taken.

It had. Berry thought he'd made a steal. But he was soon cursing. The new wallpaper would burst, revealing rotting plaster and decrepit walls. A city housing inspector soon condemned the plumbing. One of the sharpest businessmen of Sandersville, Georgia, spent most of his first years in Detroit making payments on a white elephant.

Berry's introduction to the Detroit job market was just as rough. His first job, as a blacksmith at the Michigan Central factory, almost ended in a beating. Berry didn't realize he had been hired as a scab, and had to talk his way out of a confrontation when three angry picketers stopped him after his first day at work. So much for that job. Flipping through the want ads, he noticed that plasterers made good money. It looked simple, so he haunted Detroit's construction sites until someone believed his claim to be a skilled plasterer. That didn't last long; he was quickly discovered when clumps of plaster began falling in his face.

Embarrassed but not deterred, Berry soon talked a black contractor into making him an apprentice plasterer for the princely sum of two dollars a day, a full six dollars below the standard wage. It was rough raising a growing, hungry family on that sum during the Depression. But between their savings and Bertha's eye for bargains, the Gordys survived and persevered. Within a year, Berry was a capable plasterer and a card-carrying union man. Yet he longed to be his own boss.

By the time Berry Gordy, Jr. (actually the third Berry Gordy), was born on November 28, 1929, his father ("Pops," as everyone now called him) had opened the Booker T. Washington Grocery Store (named after the patron saint of black enterprise), owned a plastering and carpentry operation, and was soon to inaugurate a printing shop. He may not have attained "big dog" status yet, but by the early thirties Gordy was on his way to being respected.

Berry and Bertha's philosophy of child rearing was simple and uncomplicated. With the force and persistence of a drill press at the Ford factory, they emphasized in word and deed the same values that had been cherished by the first Berry Gordy: hard work and family unity. The Gordy children were making change at the Booker T. Washington Grocery Store when they were barely tall enough to see over the counter. And at the family dinner table, over corn bread and pork chops, Pops spun tales of life in Georgia and the deeds of the original Berry Gordy, indoctrinating his eight third-generation black Gordys with values they would need to survive. As Pops had already learned the hard way, succeeding in Detroit took wits, toughness, and an ambition that couldn't be sated by working for someone else.

During World War II, when blacks were clamoring for a chance to contribute to the war effort and prove their patriotism, President Franklin Roosevelt set up the Fair Employment Practices Commission to end discrimination in hiring at defense plants. In 1943 there were 185 war defense plants in the Motor City area. Fifty-five of them refused to hire blacks—instead white Southerners, just arriving from the same places the blacks had run from, were given the jobs. The blacks that frequented the Booker T. Washington Grocery Store and used the Gordy print shop for party and wedding invitations expressed a growing resentment toward the "white trash" arriving in Detroit's Union Station. The situation wasn't helped any by the great antipathy between blacks and the police. It wasn't just racial antagonism; it was a class conflict, since many blacks felt they were better educated, and thus more qualified, than the newcomers.

On a hot June day in 1943, on the bridge leading to the recreational facilities on Belle Isle near the mouth of Lake Saint Clair, the tension between whites and blacks almost exploded. A small scuffle was quickly quelled by the police. Later that night, in the predominantly black neighborhood of Paradise Valley, a rumor that whites had started the trouble, hurling a black mother and her child off the bridge while the police stood by and did nothing, began circulating through the neighborhood. Black youths congregated and began taunting, then robbing, white merchants. The police, inflamed by a report of a white woman being raped by a black man, responded by escalating the conflict into one of the bloodiest race riots in American history: thirty-five people were killed, twenty-nine of them black, and seventeen of that number by the police. No whites were killed by the police. The police commissioner would later testify that there was "open warfare between the Detroit Negroes and the Detroit Police Department." He didn't mention that one side had bricks, and the other guns.

The Gordys, though not involved in the riot, were not immune to the anti-black violence that from the forties on would be endemic to the city. Fuller Gordy was harassed and arrested by three white patrolmen just past midnight on July 16, 1949, after the police searched his parked Ford, claiming it looked suspicious because its motor was running. Two women were sitting inside the auto waiting for Fuller, who was inside with his mother. When he came out, Fuller complained because he was given a ticket. The police claimed he and his companions started an altercation.

As a result, he was arrested for disturbing the peace. The charges were thrown out of court, and Fuller later sued for $10,000 in damages. With black policemen making up less than two percent of the force, incidents like this one were typical and, considering the force's reputation for anti-black violence, Fuller was lucky to have received only a few bruises.

The Gordys didn't become embittered. Instead, they channeled their energy into commerce. Like most members of the black middle class, the Gordys took the position that racial advancement could be found in the teachings of Tuskegee Institute's founder, Booker T. Washington, who viewed sweat and labor, along with education, as the only viable tools for the attainment of equality. Pops, of course, had his businesses, and his wife Bertha proved just as ambitious, providing the Gordy kids with a second strong role model. While raising her brood of seven, Bertha studied retail management at Wayne State University and took business classes at the University of Michigan. She graduated from the Detroit Institute of Commerce the same year her son Robert graduated from Northeastern High. In 1945 Bertha was one of three founders of Friendship Mutual Life Insurance Company, a concern specializing in insurance policy sales to local blacks, serving as secretary-treasurer. In her nonworking hours Bertha was an active member of the local Democratic party, making friends—including Governor G. Mennen Williams—throughout Michigan's white power structure.

In the 1940s and early 1950s the most visible Gordy sibling was Loucye, a honey-brown, sweet-tempered young lady whose achievements were emblematic of the family's upwardly mobile yearnings. She was the first woman civilian (and probably first black) to be assistant property officer at the Michigan and Indiana Army Reserves at Fort Wayne, a position that placed her in charge of all vehicles, food, clothing, and supplies used by the reserve unit. An excellent rider, she founded Bits and Spurs, a black riding club at a local Elks lodge, and later taught riding at a school.

Esther was a budding businesswoman who had the same bright, tenacious qualities locals associated with her mother, while Anna and Gwen, though they were interested in money, were so pretty and vivacious that running from men (or was it after them?) took up much of their time.

The oldest boys, Fuller and George, were straight-arrow types, "chips off the old block," who worked diligently at the jobs Pops assigned them in construction and printing. However, the same could not be said for the younger boys, Robert and Berry Gordy, Jr. Their dislike for the manual labor involved in the printing and construction businesses were well known by neighbors. These two preferred dancing at the Club Sedan or playing records in the basement, with Robert singing along in a fairly pleasing tenor. Berry, too, had some interest in music; he even won a local talent show for his composition "Berry's Boogie."

Not that they didn't like money. Berry, Jr., had been hustling around town, doing things like shining shoes on street corners, since he was a kid. At one point in his adolescence a local numbers runner was Berry's hero, because "the cat would pull out four, five thousand dollars, and that's all I wanted," he recalled in 1974. "I said, I'm not going to work on a job for eight hours a day, 'cause that ain't where it's at." He outgrew the attraction for flashy street types, but never lost his desire for big money and his distaste for the nine-to-five life.

In an attempt to harness Berry's restless energy, Pops put him and Robert into the Christmas tree business. "My brother and I would be freezing our asses off, but helping folks search for hours for just the right tree made it satisfying," he related to Maureen O'Brien in 1981. But, for all his holiday spirit, even then Berry put business before sentiment. "As Christmas morning neared, there'd always be a group of people hanging around trying to get the remaining trees for practically nothing. Even though I was just a kid, I knew nothing in life is free and, rather than be forced into selling our trees for a ridiculous price, we'd take them home and have a huge Christmas bonfire."

As a teen, Berry's real passion was for the banging and brawling of boxing. Pops, like his father before him, had encouraged his sons to use their fists when challenged. In Detroit that meant joining any of the amateur boxing teams that flourished in the city. Joe Louis, the greatest heavyweight boxer of his generation, had learned to box in local gyms, and, to the city's blacks, the Brown Bomber's success made boxing seem a glamorous, lucrative escape from poverty.

Robert and Fuller had both boxed before Berry, but neither had his skill or his desire. Berry wasn't big on training; he was cocky and believed his raw talent was enough. Yet in the ring he was a dangerous and tenacious opponent. Working out with other ambitious young men, like the nimble Golden Gloves winner Jackie Wilson, Berry set his sights on a championship belt. Unfortunately, the glory of a heavyweight title or the respect of a middleweight or lightweight championship were quite literally out of Berry's reach. At five feet, six inches, Berry was originally a flyweight, weighing in at 112 pounds. By overeating and working with weights Berry was able to fight as a bantamweight and, later, as a featherweight (when he reached 126 pounds). At sixteen years of age, after fifteen mostly successful amateur fights, Berry quit high school in the eleventh grade to turn pro. This shortfall in his education left him a poor reader for the rest of his life.

Fighting in the preliminaries at the Detroit Olympia earned one $150 and a main-event bout $500. For a championship fight the victor took home thousands of dollars and a national reputation. Berry, his ego overriding his common sense, thought he'd be a champ in no time.

But the reality of professional boxing is that, without a well-connected manager, an Olympic victory, or exceptional talent, the pursuit of a title is often just a bloody treadmill of pain. His first pro fight was a four-round defeat at the hands of the colorfully named Rocco DePhillips, in Chicago on January 6, 1948. On the way back home Berry and coach Eddie Futch (later to work with heavyweight champ Joe Frazier) were almost killed in an auto accident. Most of his next eight bouts were at the Olympia, usually before a swarm of Gordys; Berry won six of the eight fights, drew one, and lost one.

It proved difficult to find opponents in his weight class in the Midwest, so Berry made his first trip to California in late 1948. There he fought three matches with Mexican fighters, losing to Jesse Morales, beating Johnny Rivera, and knocking out Morales in a rematch. Later in the year Berry returned home, where he fought three more times, winning his final contest in a decision over Joe Nelson at the Olympia in 1950.

Gordy's boxing career was stifled by his size. He came up just when Americans were beginning a post-World War II change in dietary habits that made them taller and stronger than ever before. At the same time, Latins and Orientals remained relatively smaller, and they dominated the lighter weight classifications for over thirty years. Until a young black boxer named Jeff Chandler won the bantamweight crown in 1983, no American had held that title since California's Manual Ortiz in 1950.

Despite its frustrations, Berry's boxing career revealed his true character for the first time. He wasn't as lazy or unambitious as some in the neighborhood had thought; he simply hadn't liked the tedious physical labor of his father's business. Berry didn't mind making sacrifices. The man just needed motivation.

He didn't find it in the U.S. Army. Like his father, Berry could think of more important things to do than wear fatigues. Whether or not his father gave him tips on how to gain a quick discharge is unknown; if he did, they didn't work. Berry split his two-year stint between Fort Keep,

Arkansas; Fort Custer, Michigan; and Korea. (His only tangible benefit from his Army years was that he obtained a General Education Development—high school equivalency—degree.)

A few months after his discharge, Berry married nineteen-year-old Thelma Louise Coleman, in Toledo, Ohio. Now twenty-four years old, Berry appeared ready to settle down and raise a family. Between the fight game and the Army, he had surely sown his wild oats. But instead, Berry was about to enter a period of great professional and personal turmoil.

3 · I NEED MONEY

1 9 5 3   t o   1 9 5 9

About two-thirty any afternoon in 1953 you could walk into the Gordy print shop or follow the family truck over to one of their plastering jobs. And you would see that, among all the Gordys, Berry worked hard, carrying rolls of paper to the printing press or mixing the gooey plaster concoctions used to beautify shabby ceilings. Pops wouldn't accept anything less than hard work from his boys. He believed in nepotism, but not as an excuse for inferior workmanship.

For Berry, it was a living. It put a roof over his head and a little cash in his pockets. But this life of bending his back and politely taking orders far from satisfied him. There was none of the challenge or excitement of the ring, nor did it offer any real opportunity for advancement. Printing and construction businesses had allowed Pops to provide well for his family. Still, there was no chance in these crafts to get the kind of quick return on investment that Gordy had seen was possible in the fight game. Berry was miserable; he was trapped by a lack of direction and by the ambition that told him he needed one. In a family that valued achievement and financial growth, Berry was way down on the totem pole. He loved his brothers and sisters, but to be in such a deep rut underneath them ate at his pride.

The working days were long, and afterward his well-conditioned body ached in places even boxing had never reached. Moreover, Berry's spirit was sick, and at night he did his best to cure it. In a suit, his processed hair glistening with pomade grease, Berry, with (and sometimes without) Thelma, frequented Detroit's jazz clubs, shaking his head and tapping his

15

feet to the frantic rhythms and swirling improvisations of bebop jazz. When Charlie "Bird" Parker or Thelonious Monk hit town, Berry always caught their sets, inspired as much by their hip attitude and the jive talk of the players as by the music itself. According to Berry's friends of that period, he was never quite as cool as he thought he was—vestiges of the Gordy work ethic always held him back—but he was far from square. Berry knew enough to go see Billie Holiday one evening at the Flame Show Bar and, despite the obvious toll drugs were taking on her body, found in her sultry delivery and regal presence a quality that would haunt him for almost twenty years.

Berry really made the scene, hitting Baker's Keyboard Lounge, the West Inn, the Minor Key, the Paradise Club, the Chesterfield Lounge, or Club 21, where a slew of superb jazzmen, players who would later bring their invigorating style to New York and fame, were cutting their teeth. Donald Byrd, Yusef Lateef, Tommy Flanagan, Charles McPherson, Hank Jones, Barry Harris, Paul Chambers, Alice McLeod (later to marry John Coltrane), Kenny Burrell, Thad Jones, Elvin Jones, and Frank Foster were a few of the future jazz giants Berry watched grow in Detroit's nightspots.

These musicians and their listeners were part of a sophisticated flowering of Detroit-bred blacks. Unlike the one-room schoolhouses their parents attended in the South, these young people had benefited from formal musical education at Detroit's "Negro" high school, Northeastern, or the integrated arts school, Cass Technical, which during the forties and fifties had an exceptional music program. In Detroit it seemed as if every home had a piano, but while Pa and Ma used it to sing gospel songs like "How Great Thou Art," or an occasional twelve-bar blues, their hip kids were more interested in Charlie Parker's "KoDo" or Thelonious Monk's "Straight, No Chaser." There was a certain snob appeal, a cool aura about playing or listening to bebop then, and Berry loved being "in" with the "in crowd."

Berry was so stimulated by jazz that he decided to turn his passion into a business, as he had with boxing. Using his personal savings, including his Army discharge pay, and a seven-hundred-dollar loan from Pops, Berry opened the 3-D Record Mart, a retail store dedicated to jazz, in the summer of 1953. Considering the many local musicians and clubs around the Motor City, Berry was sure there was enough clientele to support his enterprise.

But for the next two years Berry learned a hard lesson in business. Yes, jazz was "art," as Berry would label it. However, Berry found that the bulk of black Detroiters, men and women who toiled in hot, dirty factories all week, were not the "hep cats" he hung with, but folks who wanted a beat to dance away the blues to, and lyrics that talked about the basics of life. In 1953, black Detroit's favorite performer was not jazz giant Charlie Parker, but John Lee Hooker, a foot-stomping, one-beat-boogie bluesman from Clarksdale, Mississippi. Hooker shared the same values and background as the older black masses of Detroit. His songs catalogued his life, especially the transition from rural to urban living, and, in doing so, created a verbal portrait of life as seen by Detroit's black immigrants. And Hooker's metallic guitar strokes were the perfect stimulant for house parties and gin drinking.

Hooker's blues, and that of other urban bluesmen, was a crude, vital music that didn't move Berry the way jazz, or even the smoother sounds of Nat "King" Cole or Detroit native Della Reese, did. Despite the national attention Detroit singers LaVern Baker and Little Willie John, honking saxophonist Paul "Huckebuck" Williams, and gospel choir leader the Reverend C. L. Franklin (father of Aretha) were gaining with raw, rougher-sounding music, Berry was slow to embrace a bluesier sound.

In 1955, the 3-D Record Mart went out of business. Chastised by popular taste, Berry found himself in a most unenviable position; no business, no job, an equivalency diploma, one kid to feed (Hazel Joy, born in 1954), and another—Betty—on the way. The Ford assembly line beckoned.

By the 1950s blacks no longer saw a gig at Ford as a road to any kind of salvation. Neighborhoods were becoming ghettos as whites moved out of Detroit. Blacks were kept out of the civil service by prejudice, while the auto industry kept blacks poor through low-paying jobs. Black dreams of thirty years before had turned into nightmares. Every day men went to work, fearful of getting crushed under one of the company's relentless production lines. "Everybody talked about it [Ford], they said it was the house of murder," wrote assembly-line worker Charles Denby about Ford in the 1950s. "There was a big rumor all over the city that other men had to take care of Ford workers' sexual home affairs. Everybody always asked about a Ford worker's wife, 'Who is her boyfriend?' . . . Every worker could identify Ford workers on the streetcars going home at night. Every worker who was asleep was working for Ford."

Berry went into that wonderful environment in April 1955, to earn $86.40 a week fastening on chrome strips and nailing upholstery to Lincoln-Mercurys as they rolled by. Again, Berry was unhappy and restless, his pain spilling over into his marriage. Even the arrival of another girl, Terry, in 1956, couldn't rescue a relationship weighed down by Berry's stifled ambition. In 1956 Thelma filed for divorce, alleging that Berry had "an ungovernable temper" and would become "enraged at her over the most trivial thing and refuse to speak to her for long periods." Frequently Berry "stayed out" all night, ran with other women, and was evasive when asked where he had been, according to Thelma. She claimed that, on November 1, 1955, Berry had struck her in the eye "without any just cause or provocations." It should be pointed out that in this pre–no-fault-divorce era, couples often made pleadings simply to dissolve uncomfortable marriages. That might have been the case here. Thelma dropped the original suit for lack of funds shortly after filing, but things didn't get any better between them, so they separated in 1957 and finally divorced in 1959.

It was sometime during their first separation that Berry accidently discovered the key to his salvation. During days at the plant he took to humming melodies and making up lyrics. He had read in a magazine that "you could get your songs written up on sheet music by paying $25," Gordy recalls about his start in songwriting. "I got a song of mine written up called 'You Are You.' I had been inspired very much by seeing a movie with Danny Thomas, on the life of Gus Tod. . . . Doris Day was in it, and I wrote this song for Doris Day after seeing the movie. So I was inspired by her and Danny Thomas of all people." (In an interview with the *Los Angeles Times* on May 6, 1984, Berry amended this, saying that his interest in the music business dates back to the end of his boxing days when he noticed an ad for a "Battle of the Bands" in a Detroit gym. "I had several fights by this time, maybe fifteen or so, [but] I looked at this poster and saw those two young fighters who were twenty-three but looked like fifty, all scarred and beat up. Then I saw the musicians who were fifty and they looked twenty-three.")

At about the same time that Berry's interest in songwriting was developing, sisters Anna and Gwen had landed the photography and cigarette concession at the Flame Show Bar, another lucrative business move by the Gordy family. Like Berry, Anna and Gwen had been seduced by the sound of music, but in a different way. While Berry came to the Flame to hear " the sounds" and to begin hawking a growing collection of songs, the sisters found in the musicians a flamboyance and sensuality that the bourgeois, God-fearing black middle-class men of Detroit simply didn't have. Marvin Gaye later recalled, "Gwen and Anna were glamorous, always dressed to the teeth and interested in beauty."

Though in her mid-thirties, Anna was widely considered one of the "finest ladies in the city." Visiting musicians made sure to introduce themselves, and Anna, a shrewd woman with a Gordy's characteristic business sense, introduced these suitors to her little brother. "He's a songwriter," she'd coo. They may not have wanted to be bothered by the fast-talking little guy, but he was this sweet-looking woman's brother, so they paid attention. Night after night Berry stopped by the Flame with his tunes, and then moved on to maybe the Masonic Hall and the Paradise Theater, places singers, not jazzmen, performed. "I was very broke at the time," says Berry. "I was sort of embarrassed, because when people asked me what I did for a living, I would say, 'I write songs.' Their friends had sons and daughters that were becoming doctors, lawyers, the things that had great status, and my mother and father were always somewhat embarrassed when I would tell their friends I wrote songs. 'I know,' they'd say, 'but what do you do for a living?' I'd say again, 'I write songs,' and they'd ask if I'd made any money yet. I'd say, 'No, not yet, but I will.' "

Don Davis remembers the Berry Gordy of this period very well. Now the owner of Detroit's United Sound Studios and producer of hits by Johnnie Taylor ("Disco Lady") and Marilyn McCoo and Billy Davis, Jr., ("You Don't Have to Be a Star"), Davis was then a teenage jazz guitarist fresh out of Detroit's Central High. "Every time you saw [Berry] he had tapes in his hand, trying to get someone to rehearse his songs with him," says Davis. "He was reaching out to all the studios in Detroit, seeking to get them involved in his projects. He finally got his first recording equipment from Bristol Bryant, a deejay on WCHB who used to record his radio shows in his basement and then take the tape to the station. Berry purchased Bryant's two-track equipment from him to start his own recordings." Even at this early juncture in his career, Davis says, "Berry was a very fatherly type of guy, almost a patriarch. He was the father and everybody else was his kid even if they were older. . . . He was really very serious and determined to do whatever he had to do."

Berry's big break came one evening in the fall of 1957 while hanging out at the Flame Show Bar. There he heard that Al Greene, a local talent manager, was seeking material for a singer named Jackie Wilson. Berry quickly realized that Wilson was the same cat he'd boxed with back in the forties.

At the Fox Theater four years earlier, Wilson had passed an audition to replace Clyde McPhatter as lead singer of Billy Ward and the Dominoes (McPhatter had moved to New York to join the Drifters). Wilson, an athletic, flamboyant performer whose aggressive, spinning stage style rivaled that of James Brown, was an immediate crowd-pleaser. On record, his operatic delivery was a cross between rhythm and blues star Roy Brown's bluesy swoops, and white crooner Al Jolson. It was a tune with the decidedly unsoulful title "St. Therese of the Roses," released in 1956, that gave the Dominoes their first hit since McPhatter's exit. Wilson's natural synthesis of black and white styles was remarkable, while his lean, well-conditioned body and the onstage tactic of opening his shirt to the waist created intense sexual hysteria wherever he performed. The man just oozed star quality.

Berry may not have seemed ready for this opportunity; he was an amateur still looking for structure and melody, but he possessed an instinctual knowledge of just which words in his limited vocabulary would work. He'd learned the lessons of John Lee Hooker well, and all his songs would tell a story, directly and concisely, yet with a distinguishing flair. With the aid of Billy Davis (who for some reason wrote under the name Tyran Carlo)—another struggling songwriter Gwen had introduced her brother to—Berry worked on several songs, including, "Reet Petite," a lively tribute to "the finest girl you'd ever want to meet," which Nat Tarnopol, Greene's junior partner (who after Greene's death became Wilson's manager and later president of Brunswick Records) got Wilson to record. The finished version featured a shuffle beat and brassy big-band horns. Its melody had the stops and starts then popular in rock and roll and R&B (Otis Blackwell's "All Shook Up," recorded by Elvis Presley, is the best-known example), and the song had a yodeling vocal chorus that was answered by horns arranged in a style that would appear on several early Motown hits (e.g., the Miracles' "Mickey's Monkey"). The record's dominant element, however, is Wilson's voice. It communicates a joyful excitement, but excitement tempered by masterful control, as in the wonderful way he stretches out the *re* sound in *reet*. "Reet Petite," released in October 1957, hit number eleven on the R&B chart two months later, re-establishing Wilson's credentials as an important solo artist and marking the inception of a musical relationship between Wilson, Gordy, Davis, and producer Dick Jacobs that would last until 1959.

Two more songs written by Berry and recorded by Jackie Wilson— "That Is Why (I Love You So)" and "I'll Be Satisfied"—were major hits for Wilson, and both are significant in Berry's career, for each possessed elements that would appear in later Motown productions. The lyric of "That Is Why" is full of specifics about relationships, something Berry would later preach. There is an allusion to Shakespeare's Romeo and Juliet in the lyric, a gimmicky use of establishment culture in R&B that many

Motown writers adopted. Two other musical touches, the use of tambourines to bolster the drum beat on "That Is Why" and the blustering
baritone sax played throughout "I'll Be Satisfied," would later become
Motown trademarks.

His three years of writing for Wilson were crucial to Berry's career.
During this period he went from a struggling, unhappy ex-boxer seeking
direction and identity to a status position as the most respected tunesmith
in town. Wilson was the biggest black entertainer Detroit had produced
to date, and Berry was the most visible and aggressive member of his
hitmaking team. Unfortunately for Berry, though, the size of his new-
made reputation in Detroit was many times larger than his income. "One
day I was talking with Berry and he expressed dissatisfaction with having
written hits for Jackie Wilson and having no money [for his work]," says
Don Davis. "He showed me a printout of sales and said how he could put
out two or three records, sell a little bit and still get his money." It was
Berry's unhappy experiences with Wilson that first got him thinking
about record leasing, a process whereby independent producers would cut
records at their own expense and then sell the rights to a nationally
distributed label.

One of Berry's most pleasing new acquaintances, and a major force
in his move toward record leasing, was Raynoma Liles, a small, stylish
woman with strikingly sexy eyes. She and Berry met in 1958, after
Raynoma won a talent contest at a Detroit nightclub. Ray, as her friends
called her, had been a musical child prodigy; she played eleven instruments competently and possessed a flexible soprano voice. At Cass Tech
she majored in harmony, theory, and composition. "The emcee [at the
club] recommended that I go and see Berry, who had some acts," she
recalled. "I went by his place and auditioned with my sister. He watched
and everything, and then said, 'What else can you do?' " Apparently he
soon found out, because two years after divorcing Thelma, Berry married
her.

Though Berry and Ray were married for only a year and a half, their
union would prove critical to Berry's musical growth. Her technical skills
and musical training helped smooth the raw edges of his records, while
Berry schooled her in the business. For a time they would have a professional and romantic partnership similar to that of Pops and Bertha Gordy.
In fact, Raynoma was the first in a series of such liaisons (some romantic,
some platonic) that Berry would be involved in throughout his life. Together, they formed the Rayber Voices and offered their vocal services to
any singers who wanted to try recordmaking and needed a hand.

The Rayber Voices can be heard on almost all the hits of a local singer named Marv Johnson, the first beneficiary of Berry's writing *and* production skills. It was at this time in 1959, when Berry wanted to take a leap into independent production—renting studio time and hiring musicians —that he borrowed seven hundred dollars from his family to make "Come to Me." The song featured Johnson's gospel-influenced, steady mid-range tenor. "The song itself was simple," wrote Joe McEwen and Jim Miller years later, "simple lyrics set to a stock rock chord progression. But to accompany Johnson . . . Gordy added a churchy female chorus for some call-and-response trades, and a bubbling male bassman. Instrumentally, the record was anchored by a persistent baritone sax and tambourine, with a flute break in the middle. The result was a clean R&B record that sounded as white as it did black." It went to number six on the R&B chart in March 1959. Supervising a team of developing songwriters, young men like William "Mickey" Stevenson and Lamont Dozier, Berry sold a series of highly successful Johnson records during 1959 and 1960, including "I Love the Way You Love" (number two R&B) and "(You've Got to) Move Two Mountains" (number twelve R&B), to the large New York–based United Artists label.

Considering these accomplishments, it would have seemed likely that Johnson would have emerged a few years later as Motown's first male solo star. "Marv had a great tenor falsetto voice, though his range was rather limited," Davis says. But, according to several Detroiters, his ego wasn't. "The difference between Marv and Jackie Wilson was that Wilson would kiss all the women, especially the ugly ones, because he knew if he did they'd be with him forever," said one old-timer. "Marv only kissed the pretty girls and that coldness came through in everything he did." The story is told that Marv's ego grew so large that once, when Berry visited him at a New York hotel during this period, Marv asked Berry if he had an appointment. It's not surprising that Berry soon stopped working with Marv. He didn't sign him to Motown until the mid-sixties, by which time Johnson had languished, a neglected has-been. Today he harbors great bitterness toward Motown in general and Berry in particular.

It was while visiting the offices of Wilson's manager one summer afternoon in 1957 that Berry began an enduring professional and personal relationship. It didn't begin auspiciously. In the middle of the room stood a rather unorthodox-looking vocal group: the lead singer was a seventeen-year-old light-skinned black male with light green eyes—the kind girls called "super fine"—and reddish, processed hair. His name was William "Smokey" Robinson (an uncle had tagged him Smokey), and he was backed by Claudette Rogers—a petite, shapely teenage girl—and three rather homely male backup singers. There was frail-looking Ronnie White (a large kid with thick glasses), Bobby Rogers (Claudette's brother), and a nondescript cat named Pete Moore. These kids called themselves the Matadors and they had a nice sound. The lead singer in particular had a real sweet, tender falsetto, and they were singing some interesting songs that Berry had never heard before.

With a girl and guy in the group, Wilson's manager felt the Matadors should have a duet sound in the coy mold of Mickey and Sylvia's 1957 hit "Love Is Strange." "Thanks, but no thanks," was the message. Berry followed them into the hallway, saying, "Hey, I like you and I like your sound. Where did you get those songs?" Smokey replied that he had over a hundred songs in a notebook at home. It seemed that, despite his pretty-boy looks, Smokey was very much a bookworm. He loved school, loved reading—especially poetry—and took pride in receiving high grades at school.

Smokey needed two things Berry could supply. On a purely professional level, Berry's ear for what constituted good songwriting was essential to Smokey's development. After their first meeting, Berry and Smokey sat down with his notebook and dissected the material, with most of the songs landing in the nearest garbage can. "I had songs that went all over the place," Smokey said. "Like in the first verse I might have been talking about 'Oh, I miss you so much now that you're gone' and then in the second verse I might say 'Hey, I wish you would leave.' . . . I was basically interested in rhyme schemes at that time. I thought that if you rhymed something, that was a song. However, he straightened me out a great deal as far as writing."

The friendship that developed out of this meeting also gave Smokey a family connection he treasured. His mother had died when he was ten and his father, William, Sr., a truck driver who was away for long stretches of time, allowed his sister, a woman already saddled with ten children of her own, to raise Smokey. So the size of the Gordys' all-engulfing brood didn't faze him one bit. In fact, that desire to be part of a large group, be it a traditional family, a vocal group, or a company working and growing together, would be one of the constants in his life. Formal music training—at eight he was a reluctant saxophone student—wasn't as important to his developing musical sensibility as was listening to records with his cousins. "You can imagine all the records we had with all those kids," he recalled in the *Detroit Free Press* in 1972. "And our pad was like the neighborhood meeting place. We'd be out looking for our friends, man, and they'd be back at our pad." Though he listened to every type of music he could find and sang in a church choir, he had a special fondness for jazz singer Sarah Vaughan and was influenced by the fluid phrasing that added deeper meaning to everything she sang.

Out of his large circle of friends, Smokey would form several enduring relationships. He met Ronnie White, the paperboy on his block, when he was ten. He grew tight with Pete Moore when he was thirteen. At fourteen, through his friendship with Emerson Rogers, Smokey came to know his brother Bobby and sister Claudette. Together Smokey and these male friends started the Matadors vocal quartet in 1954. Claudette attended rehearsals but didn't become an official member until Emerson left to join the Army in 1957. She was the natural choice, not only because she knew the songs, but because she and Smokey were high school sweethearts, holding hands at every opportunity and talking about marriage. Later Smokey would brag that as a teenager his wife-to-be "had the greatest body in the world." It was at Berry's urging that the group changed its name from the Matadors to the optimistic title of the Miracles. The Miracles would become the key link between Berry's years of hustle and the glory days to come.

On February 19, 1958, the eighteenth birthday of Smokey and Bobby Rogers, the Miracles' first single, "Got a Job," produced and written by Berry, was issued on the small New York label End Records. It was what the record industry called an "answer record," a song recorded in response to another—in this case the Silhouettes' popular "Get a Job." Under the banner of Ron and Bill, Miracles member Ronnie White and Smokey appeared on several Chess singles. (During this period, Berry also recorded his brother Robert Gordy, under the name of Robert Kayli, in a rock and roll–influenced style with "Everyone Was There" on the Carlton label.)

Despite Berry's Jackie Wilson and Marv Johnson hits, Berry claimed an income of only $27.70 a week in 1959—including a royalty check for a thousand dollars he received for writing the Wilson hit "Lonely Teardrops." A financial statement Berry filed in response to ex-wife Thelma's request for additional child support and alimony payments paints a surprisingly sorry picture of this thirty-one-year-old music man. According to the affidavit, loans from his father, some contracting work at Pop's company, and miscellaneous work, brought in an additional $20. His bank account was $100, "approximately." When Berry subtracted his weekly expenses from his income he totaled a net income of $4.85. In contrast, Thelma made $85 working at Kirkwood General Hospital, though her expenses put her in the hole for $67.48. The major reason for her deficit spending was the children. Hazel Joy was being treated for a "severe" skin rash, and Berry IV was recovering from rheumatic fever.

The need for money was slowly pushing Berry toward being more than merely a writer and producer. He was seeing that it was the record labels distributing his music in New York and Chicago that so far had really profited from his efforts. Sometimes they wanted even more than just his records; sometimes they wanted his acts. One of the white-owned companies to which Berry leased a Miracles record tried to take over the group's contract. Berry, realizing that he was in a weak position, called several prominent black deejays from the East and South to Detroit for a Sunday afternoon meeting. He met them at Union Depot, and together they called the company's president, who received their call while sitting by his pool. At first he refused to give up the Miracles' contract. Finally, after they threatened to boycott all of his label's releases ("We were gonna pass the word to all the black jocks that he was screwing brother Berry," remembers one collaborator), the conversation lightened considerably. The company president then said, with a laugh, that it was only a joke. By Tuesday the Miracles were safely back in Berry's hands. For the deejays it was a chance to signal their affection for Berry's aggressive attitude, to cast a vote of confidence in his future—and a rare chance to flex their muscles against the white boys who then controlled R&B. For Berry it was just another hard lesson about power and where it lay in the music business.

This was a lesson his writing partners Billy Davis and sister Gwen had apparently learned before him. In 1959 they started Anna Records, named after sister Anna Gordy, who was a limited partner in the company. Davis and Gwen, who by then were romantically involved, gained the trust of Leonard and Phil Chess, two Jewish South Side Chicago merchants who had noticed the central role music played in the life of the area's growing Negro population. All the Chess brothers had intended to do was to make a little money. But by recording recent arrivals from the South, such as Bo Diddley, Chuck Berry, Howlin' Wolf, and Muddy Waters—blues guitarists using electric instruments—the Chess brothers had, unknowingly, changed the texture of the blues, helping create a primitive form of rock and roll, which would profoundly affect the shape of pop music in the coming decade.

On the strength of Wilson's hits, Chess Records felt that Gwen, Davis, and Anna could create hits using Motortown talent. It is revealing of the attitudes of the Gordy women that when they entered the record business they immediately sought to maintain some control of their product; Berry's sisters had absorbed their parents' lessons about possessions. Instead of simply leasing records to other labels, they started their own, making a deal for distribution with Chess that ensured them a bigger return on sales than record leasing could have given them—as well as giving their music an identity within the industry and with record buyers.

Ironically, Anna Records' biggest hit was written and produced not by Gwen or Billy Davis, but leased from Berry. The staying power of this one song, "Money (That's What I Want)," would rival that of anything to come in Motown's history. The strong, driving rhythm and blues dance tune with a cynical view of romance and finance was written by Berry with Janie Bradford, later a Motown secretary, and performed by a local singer named Barrett Strong. Money, or lack of same, was very much on Berry's mind: "I was broke until the time I wrote 'Money'; even though I had many hits, and there were other writers who had many hits, we just didn't have profits. And coming from a business family, my father and mother always talked about the bottom line, and simple things, and the bottom line is profit. You know, are you making money or not?"

That explains the lyric, one that inspired many memorable covers, including John Lennon's passionate version on *The Beatles' Second Album* in 1964 and the Flying Lizards' weird spoken-word cover in 1979. But Berry's memory reveals nothing about the assurance of Berry's production. With Raynoma and Berry providing the "That's what I want" chorus, Strong sings over a boogie-woogie piano riff, a funky bass-drum groove augmented by gospel tambourine. This tune, like Berry's Jackie Wilson material, would serve as a prototype for early Motown recordings.

"Money" was an artistic triumph, but for Berry it ended the 1950s on a rather bittersweet note. After years of indecision and unrest he had found a way to make a living as exciting as boxing at the Olympia and —physically, at least—much less painful. Yet where was the return on his investment? He had hits. He had a name. He had the respect of the local youngbloods looking to make music. He had gone from spectator to songwriter with amazing ease. It was Smokey Robinson who knew what had to be done, and after a particularly memorable drive in 1959, he sat Berry down, nineteen-year-old disciple advising thirty-year-old mentor, and made a suggestion.

4·SHOP AROUND

1 9 5 9 to 1 9 6 2

Winter, 1959: Berry Gordy is at the wheel of his Cadillac with Smokey Robinson at his side. They are driving from Detroit to a Flint record pressing plant to pick up advance copies of Marv Johnson's "Come to Me." The radio is blasting and each man is commenting on the songs as they come on. It sounds like two professionals talking shop. Yet their businesslike chatter disguises concern.

Snow is falling. The road is slick and dotted with large patches of ice. People have died driving on roads like this in Michigan since old man Ford designed the Model T, and on this day it almost claims these two not-yet-illustrious music makers. Twice the car skids off the road, once barely missing the front end of an oncoming truck. All this for a few hundred copies of a record that they had made, but that now belonged to the United Artists record company in New York City. They might be able to sell those records—off the books—to a friendly local retailer for some much-needed quick cash, or give them to a local disc jockey in exchange for airplay. Somewhere down the line—if United Artists treated Berry and Smokey right—they might see some substantial royalties on sales and airplay. But it hadn't happened before, so there was no reason to be overly optimistic now.

Smokey was frustrated by their impotence in the record industry. It was clear to Smokey that the way to really make it was to stop leasing records to others and to begin marketing and merchandising their music themselves. In short, they needed to follow the lead of Gwen and Anna and start a full-fledged record company.

Berry finally came around to Smokey's point of view. His sister Esther would later say, "It was not his goal to head up a major entertainment complex with recordings, films, and all these sorts of things. He just wanted to be a successful songwriter." At the time Berry had told her, "If I ever get this house and get it paid for, I'll have it made [a reference to a house at 2648 West Grand Boulevard that Raynoma had found to make their base of operations]. I'll live upstairs, I'll have my offices down in the front part, and I'll have a studio out back where I can make demonstration records or masters to sell to record companies." To Esther, "All Motown is is the result of one thing leading to another and Berry Gordy saying, 'I'll do it myself' when he could not get something done to his liking. We had parents who always said, 'Your gift will make room for you. You make a better product and they will buy it.' "

That Berry was a reluctant industrialist is clear from an insightful (though self-serving) story Berry wrote in 1979 for *The New York Times:*

> I began working with a publisher in New York, but the moment came when he owed me $1,000 and was refusing to pay. I consulted a lawyer and insisted that he bring suit against the publisher.
>
> "Look," I was told, "if you sue him for $1,000, it will take you three years or so in court. You're going to pay me more than $1,000 and you're going to end up settling with him for probably $200—it doesn't make sense."
>
> "You mean that he owes $1,000 and I just can't collect it?" I asked.
>
> "That's exactly it," he said.
>
> "What would happen if I started a company for young writers?" I asked the lawyer. "For people in the same position I'm in."
>
> "You'd be undercapitalized," he said, "and it would never work."
>
> In retrospect, I guess that was it. I had just been told I couldn't do something, and I was determined to prove him wrong.

Aside from putting a down payment on the West Grand Boulevard building, Berry formed Jobete Music Publishing (named after his daughters: Joy, Betty, and Terry); the corporation Berry Gordy, Jr., Enterprises; Hitsville, USA; Motown Record Corporation (a contraction of Motor-town), which would issue records under a variety of labels, including

Tamla (originally named Tammy, after the Debbie Reynolds film of that name); and International Talent Management, Inc. (ITM), to guide the careers of his signees.

In conjunction with these moves Berry established policies that set the tone for Motown's business style. Motown would be very strict about who had access to its books. Artists would only be allowed to review them two times a year and no industry regulatory group, such as the Recording Industry Association of America, the organization that awards gold and platinum albums, would be allowed to audit the company's books (a policy that didn't change until the late seventies, which is why none of Motown's hits of the sixties was ever certified gold).

Motown would also establish a policy of cross-collateralization of royalty accounts. So, for example, if an artist signed as a performer and a writer to Jobete, any cost incurred in preparing his records could be charged against songwriting royalties. Berry also made plans to pay his creative personnel a weekly salary—even when they weren't being productive—that would be charged against royalties should they suddenly have a hit. None of these practices was illegal and, for a new enterprise, they were quite cost-effective. But certainly no sharp talent manager would have agreed to all of them, since they placed the power in the management-artist relationships squarely in Motown's hands. Of course with Motown, through ITM, looking to manage all of its own acts, these policies would prove easy to enforce.

In the summer of 1959, the Miracles' "Way Over There" was the first record released on the Tamla label and, if that weren't historic enough, it was also Smokey's first solo production. Every previous Miracles release had been credited to Berry and Smokey, with the older man providing his protégé on-the-job training. This time, after coming off a road trip, Smokey was so sure that the song would be a hit he took the Miracles and a band into the studio himself. "Way" wasn't a national chart success, but by the end of its run it had sold 60,000 copies, most of it in the Midwest, a remarkable number for an unknown Detroit label.

For Berry, the move into record manufacturing proved financially beneficial. In June 1960, Berry was making $133 per week from the music business, had paid $1,300 on a $4,800 red Cadillac, $3,000 on the 2648 West Grand's $23,000 mortgage, and had total assets of $32,600. Yet Berry, who filed this information in response to another child support request from Thelma, claimed liabilities of $32,500. So, according to him, his net worth in 1960 was only $100, an on-paper decrease of $5,000 from

1959. "I have tried to explain to my wife that my financial situation has been a matter of future prospects rather than present profits, but she refuses to believe me," was Berry's prescient comment to the court.

At around the same time that Berry was pleading that his best years were just ahead, he was making the record that would give Motown its first golden success. The song "Shop Around" was written by Smokey with Barrett Strong in mind. Smokey had dashed off the basic elements of this "mother-knows-best" story-song in just ten minutes. However, it wasn't until Berry heard it on piano and offered some suggestions that "Shop Around" took on the qualities of a classic.

"We were at the piano and [Berry] said, 'No, I think that we oughta do this with the chorus,'" Smokey recalled. "That part that says, 'Try to get yourself a bargain son/Don't be sold . . .' and I had some other chords there. He said, 'No, we oughta put *these* chords in there and then, at the end [when the lyric says], 'try the one who's gonna give you true lovin',' he said, 'we oughta break that in there, you know, so that can stand out.'"
It was a brilliant choice, which highlighted the lyric's key message line. In addition, Berry suggested that Claudette—not Strong—sing it, even though Smokey had written the song for a man.

Two weeks after the record's initial release in the Detroit area Smokey was awakened by a phone call.

"Hey, man, what you doin'?" It was Berry.

"It's three o'clock in the morning. What do you think I'm doing? I'm asleep."

"I want you and Claudette to get up and come over here and I want you to call the other guys and tell them to come to the studio right now."

"Why, man?" Smokey asked.

"Because, man, I can't sleep. I haven't slept in three or four days. 'Shop Around' keeps going through my mind. You didn't cut it right. I gotta change the beat. . . . And then it's going to be number one."

This logic impressed Smokey.

"Well, okay, all right."

After waking Claudette he called the other Miracles, all of whom were less than enthused by Berry's timing.

But by four A.M. the Miracles, Berry, and a rhythm section had gathered at Hitsville. Berry hadn't been able to round up a pianist, so he played piano. The session ended in the late morning and the new version was on the market before the week was out.

The differences between the two versions are few but critical. On the original, drummer Benny Benjamin played with sticks and at a slightly slower tempo. The new "Shop Around" featured Benjamin using brushes. On the second "Shop Around," Berry made Smokey sing lead, reviving the song's original mama's-boy angle. In addition, Smokey's light voice, with its air of plaintive yearning, had the adolescent quality Berry had been striving for when he had had Claudette record it.

In early 1961 "Shop Around" went to number one on the R&B chart and number two on the pop chart. That spring, before eight thousand people at the Michigan State Fairgrounds, Berry came onstage and handed the Miracles their first gold record. It was an emotional moment: Claudette, Berry, Smokey, and the other Miracles all hugged and cried and smiled, basking in this first moment of glory.

"Shop Around" signaled Motown's future, yet it was a series of blues releases on Motown, aimed at the same Detroit blues market that had once helped close Berry's 3-D Record Mart, that helped keep the young business afloat. Singing Sammy Ward, a gutsy shouter with much the same vocal timbre as the Reverend C. L. Franklin, cut several sides from 1960 to 1962, some with Sherri Taylor ("Oh! Lover," "That's Why I Love You so Much") and several solo singles, including the raw blues "Big Joe Moe." Mabel John, sister of popular R&B singer Little Willie John, possessed a strident soulful voice like her brother's, which on "Who Wouldn't Love a Man Like That" and "Looking for a Man" made an impression around the Motor City in 1961. During the 1950s, piano-playing bluesman Amos Milburn was notorious throughout black America for his "drinking" songs: "Bad Bad Whiskey," "Let Me Go Home, Whiskey," and the barstool standard "One Scotch, One Bourbon, One Beer." Milburn, a hard-drinking braggart who once sang, in "Roll Mr. Jelly," about raising a dead woman with his penis, cut a single and an album, Return of the Blues Boss, for Motown in 1962. By the end of the year, however, none of these singers was on Berry's roster, apparently having fulfilled their role in generating local cash, but with no future at a place where the emphasis was on youthful singers and songs.

Over the next three years, roughly 1960 through 1962, a community of administrators, musicians, and entertainers began coalescing inside 2648 West Grand Boulevard, motivated by family pride, marital ties, a sense of black unity, the chance to make music, and, of course, the desire to become rich and famous. This was a time of building, of adding pieces to the puzzle and giving unproven talent a shot. Berry literally was shopping around, not sure what would come of his label, but knowing that having it gave him at least a fighting chance against the forces that controlled his industry. One man couldn't beat the big boys at this game, certainly not one black man from Detroit. He'd already proven that himself. "Shop Around" 's triumph showed him that Smokey was right; Berry had nothing to lose and only dreams to gain.

The family came first in Motown's evolving corporate culture. Esther's involvement in the music business had begun back in 1957, when she did secretarial work for Berry and set up tour itineraries for Marv Johnson and the Miracles. In 1959, while enjoying a well-paid patronage job provided by her husband, state legislator George Edwards, Esther volunteered time to Berry's young record company, and a year later she gave up her other business interests to assume a vice-presidency at Motown, where she was put in charge of developing the management company, International Talent Management, Inc. At the same time, Edwards, while serving in the legislature, became Motown's first comptroller. Loucye left her job with the Army reserves for a Motown vice-presidency and the job of organizing billing and collection. Her husband, Ron Wakefield, a sometime saxophonist who'd later tour with several Motown acts, joined as staff arranger in 1963. Berry's brother Robert, no longer recording as Robert Kayli, quit his job at the post office for on-the-job training as an engineer at Hitsville, for sixty-five cents an hour. Older brothers George and Fuller were deeply involved in operating Pops's construction and print shops, and yet Berry's enterprise would eventually pull both of them into what was quickly becoming the most important Gordy family enterprise. Pops, of course, was overjoyed by Berry's blossoming into a money-maker. To him Motown came to represent the fulfillment of the lessons he'd passed on to his children, and that his father had passed on to him. From the beginning he was a constant consultant to Berry, whispering words of encouragement, lecturing about the value of control and discipline in managing his business. The later Motown artists, who often saw Pops as a kindly figure with an uncanny resemblance to the Colonel Sanders of fried chicken fame, never knew just how profoundly his philosophy had affected their careers.

Gwen and Anna contributed, too, by marrying two important Motown musicians—literally bringing them into the Gordy family. Both Harvey Fuqua and Marvin Gaye had shopped around the industry before joining Motown, and the experience they brought was critical to the fledgling organization.

Fuqua, a large yet very gentle man, had started a vocal group called the Crazy Sounds as a teenager in Cleveland. Top local disc jockey Alan "Moondog" Freed had invited them over to the radio station after an impromptu telephone audition, and signed them to his Champagne Records in 1952 after changing their name to the Moonglows. After cutting a couple of sides for Champagne, they split from Freed and Cleveland, winding up in Chicago, where they signed to Chance Records, a label owned by black record man Ewart Abner. Unfortunately, after a couple of local Moonglow hits that failed to make money, Abner advised Fuqua and company that he wouldn't be able to pay them and suggested they walk around the corner to the offices of Chess Records. For about five hundred dollars, Chess bought out the group's Chance contract and the Moonglows were on their way.

With Fuqua providing the deep bass vocals, the Moonglows' first Chess single, "Sincerely," became an instant doo-wop classic in November 1954. In order to double their money they also recorded several sides as (pun surely intended) the Moonlighters, scoring in Chicago with "Shoo-doo-Bedoo," a takeoff on the Chords' seminal rock and roll single "Sh-Boom." At local gigs they'd appear first as the Moonlighters for one fee, change their suits, then come out again as the Moonglows for another. By 1955, however, this trick was no longer necessary; the Moonglows emerged as a premier vocal group, enjoying major national hits with "Most of All" (1955), "See Saw" (1956), and "Please Send Me Someone to Love" (1957).

In 1958, the thrill of stardom began wearing thin. Fuqua, a practical man, was disturbed to see everybody except the Moonglows profiting from their hard work. It was during Fuqua's period of disillusionment that four Washington, D.C., teens who called themselves the Marquees talked him into auditioning them in his hotel room. He was impressed by their ability to reproduce the Moonglows' sound, and he was especially impressed by the voice of a member named Marvin Gay. The Marquees had cut a few obscure singles (such as "Wyatt Earp," in 1957) for Columbia's "race" label Okeh, where Bo Diddley was one of their strongest supporters. And, unlike most groups of the time, the Marquees actually wrote some of their own material.

A few months later, the original Moonglows split up. Determined to keep the name alive, Fuqua returned to Washington, where he found the Marquees and brought them to Chicago. Leonard Chess, impressed by Fuqua's maturity and ambition, offered him a salaried job as a talent scout and a continuation of the Moonglows' recording contract. With his youngbloods in tow, Fuqua continued to record—this time as Harvey and the Moonglows—and in 1958 scored a massive hit with "Ten Commandments of Love."

With a steady job and the option of recording at his leisure, Fuqua should have been happy. Instead, "I started feeling closed in. I was going to the office everyday at ten A.M. and I'd never worked like that before. So I told Leonard I couldn't handle the job. I wanted to be out and free. At the time he had a lease master deal with Billy Davis and Gwen Gordy over in Detroit—Anna Records—so he said, 'Why don't you go there and work in that operation, since you wanna be free. You can come in any time you want to, you can go on the road, you can produce when you feel like it.' It was an ideal situation and I'd be helping to build a new label, so I kept Marvin with me; I sent the other three guys home and went to Detroit."

It made sense. Fuqua had already established a working relationship with Davis, with whom he'd composed the Moonglows' "See Saw" and some other tunes. He knew Gwen through Davis, and had met Berry when he visited Chess's offices to peddle the Miracles' "Bad Girl." But the fact that Fuqua kept Marvin with him is testimony to his keen eye for talent and the growth of a friendship that, in some ways, paralleled that of Smokey and Berry.

Marvin was a tall, smooth-skinned charmer whose cool style was attractive to women. Yet he was insecure about himself, and had many conflicts with his overbearing father, a well-known Pentecostal minister. Reverend Gay was flamboyant and persuasive, yet many in the D.C. area found him a strangely disquieting figure. Along with the fury of his sermons, there was an androgynous, almost feline quality about him that caused whispers in the nation's capitol (it wasn't until 1984 that Reverend Gay's transvestism became generally known). His son, sensitive and clearly possessed of his father's charisma—along with his own special musical gifts (he sang and played piano and drums)—sought to establish an identity outside the church. He wanted to be an athlete, but his father stifled that urge when Marvin was young. By his teen years, Marvin had found a more insidious form of rebellion: singing "the devil's music." In Fuqua, Marvin found a strong, solidly masculine figure who respected and encouraged his talent. Together they'd sit for hours at the piano, Fuqua showing Marvin chords. His pupil took instruction well, but every now and then his rebel's spirit would flare when something conflicted with his views. Marvin's combination of sex appeal and spirituality, malleability and conviction, gave his voice a quiet electricity similar to that of Sam Cooke's, who had had a number-one pop single in late 1957 with "You Send Me" after a career as one of gospel music's biggest stars.

Strangely, Marvin, who by this time had added an *e* to his last name, never recorded for Anna Records. Yet he surely liked the label's namesake, and she liked him. "Right away Anna snatched him," Fuqua told writer Aaron Fuchs. "Just snatched him immediately." When they met, she was seventeen years older than Marvin, but folks in Detroit thought she was a match for any man. Ambitious, haughty, shrewd, and adept at manipulating men, Anna introduced Marvin to Berry, who then used him as a pianist and drummer on his sessions. At night he appeared at nightclubs around Detroit, often accompanied by Fuqua.

In 1960, in the wake of "Money," Fuqua joined Anna Records and, like Marvin, was quickly sucked into the Gordys' extended family. For ten dollars a week he lived with Esther Gordy and her husband, George Edwards. He became fascinated by Esther's efforts to make Edwards a Michigan state legislator, and also by the Gordy family's remarkable togetherness.

Fuqua, in turn, attracted the attention of Berry for a practice that struck him as unusual. In the basement of Esther's home, Fuqua would rehearse hour after hour with the acts on Anna. Berry had never seen anyone spend so much time on the live presentation of an act. Yet here was Fuqua, a large yet graceful man, leading the Originals, a quartet featuring a postman named Freddie Gorman, and his favorites, the Spinners, a group with a real flair for showmanship, through carefully choreographed steps. Berry's curiosity hadn't yet led him to reach out to Fuqua; their conversations were usually limited to "Hi, how ya doing?" despite their recording activities. Berry had to have noticed, however, that Fuqua and sister Gwen were getting mighty friendly. Davis, often on the road promoting Anna Records' releases, was becoming the odd man out. It was then that Berry started asking Fuqua if he could maybe help some of his acts.

But Fuqua was too busy. He cut some sides with fiery R&B singer and close friend Etta James for Chess, and toured with her a bit. Whenever he was on the road, he visited local radio deejays with the latest Anna records, using his reputation as a Moonglow to stimulate airplay. In Detroit he split his time between recording, rehearsing his groups, and hanging out with Gwen Gordy. Davis decided, quite predictably, that it was time to leave the company. With the backing of Chess, he started Check-Mate Records, which lasted a few years before Davis gave up recordmaking for a spot at New York's McCann-Erickson advertising agency, where he works to this day writing jingles.

With Davis's departure, Anna Records died. In its place Fuqua started his own Tri-Phi and Harvey labels in 1961. In that same year Harvey Fuqua married Gwen, with Marvin serving as his best man;

Harvey returned the favor when Marvin married Anna. For better or worse, both men were now Gordys—even if it was the ladies who had changed their last names.

Fuqua was quite adept at ferreting out young talent; in his first three years in Detroit he recorded Johnny Bristol and Lamont Anthony (aka Dozier) at Anna, and Shorty Long, Junior Walker, and the Spinners at Tri-Phi and Harvey; all would be artists of some importance during the next two decades. But, unfortunately, Fuqua was again showing the inability to deal with the nuances of the record business that had led him to quit Chess. Through his network of radio contacts Fuqua could get his songs on the air, but he could never get enough records into stores around the country to capitalize on this radio exposure.

Fuqua's problems were the problems of every small independent record operation of the era, and they serve as a survey course in the difficulties that Motown would overcome through superior organization. Fuqua, for example, would have a hot record in Philadelphia, sell a lot of copies, yet have little luck in receiving the bulk of his money from his local distributor. Meanwhile, bills from the record-pressing plant arrived in a steady stream. Delinquency in paying the plant meant that the next release would only be pressed following cash payment upfront, causing cash-flow problems. That Harvey Fuqua was a black dealing with whites didn't help either. The same industry that allowed Chicago's Leonard and Phil Chess's operation to flourish while, around the corner, Ewart Abner floundered, was now squeezing Fuqua.

It got so bad that Fuqua almost began to fear success. One Harvey release sold 400,000 nationally. He should have been ecstatic. Instead, he found himself with a huge pressing bill that required immediate payment to keep the product flow going. Distributors paid for sales in thirty- and sixty-day cycles that too often stretched to ninety. Distributors were in total control when dealing with small undercapitalized labels, since they controlled the means of distribution and there was really no way to monitor them systematically. The "indie" labels needed the pressers and distributors more than they were needed by them. Moreover, the large labels (Columbia, Decca, Mercury) were handled by many of these distributors as well, and their stars and money gave their records priority.

Fuqua just couldn't make the numbers add up. So when his brother-in-law asked him to join Motown and be in charge of record promotion, dealing with radio stations and polishing his acts' onstage presentations, Fuqua was in no position to turn it down. Bringing the Spinners and Johnny Bristol with him, he came aboard.

While Gordys, old and new, were Motown's first inner circle, Berry brought in a group of Detroit music industry veterans to form the next layer of management. Some of them would later supersede Berry's family in the Motown structure. These were men Berry had met around the city who, like him, were hungry for a chance at big money but hadn't figured out how to get it. Before becoming director of artists and repertoire, or "A&R," William "Mickey" Stevenson had been trying unsuccessfully to get members of Detroit's black bourgeoisie to invest in a Motown-like operation. After cutting R&B and gospel music since the mid-1950s, Stevenson—a show-biz kid whose mother Kitty was a singer—felt it was time for a strong black label. He approached black doctors, lawyers, and businessmen to back him, but they weren't interested in entering what they saw as the hustling, unsavory world of black show business, feeling that the field wasn't respectable or safe enough for them to invest in. Stevenson had little interest in developing a licensing arrangement with any white-owned indie labels; he didn't trust them. He'd watched Berry's rise since his days with Jackie Wilson and had admired his drive and confidence. Moreover, Berry was a black man whose family watched his back. Stevenson had found that, despite all the talk about blacks getting their civil rights down South, it was rare to see blacks—outside the church —giving of themselves in organized effort. Berry knew about Stevenson's ambitions and commitment to black advancement, qualities he accurately perceived would make him a loyal, diligent employee.

Stevenson's position meant that he supervised all musicians, producers, and writers. He assigned producers to acts (subject to Berry's approval), made sure songs were written on time, and produced acts when deadlines had to be met or he couldn't find anyone to take the assignment. But in the early days his most important duty was building Motown's stable of studio musicians.

Like Berry, Stevenson preferred jazz musicians for his sessions, believing that they were both more technically assured and more creative than their blues-based counterparts. The leader of Motown's first road band was Choker Campbell, a pianist and former leader of Count Basie–style big bands at summer resorts. A burly jazz pianist, Joe Hunter, headed the studio band. Dave Hamilton, who would make a vital and largely unknown contribution to Motown music, played the unlikely combination of guitar and vibes. Bassist James Jamerson and drummer Benny Benjamin, both regulars at Detroit's several popular after-hours spots, had worked with Berry on and off since the early Miracles records; in the early sixties, they were just beginning to realize how well they worked together.

Stevenson helped Berry inaugurate a jazz label called Jazz Workshop, and, using it as an inducement, Stevenson got several players under dual contracts as recording artists *and* staff musicians. For Motown, it ensured a reliable, skilled group of players who were always on call. For the musicians, many of whom were bebop fanciers from the fertile East Coast jazz scene, Jazz Workshop held the promise that they would be able to record the music they really loved. So they tolerated playing Motown's "Mickey Mouse music" for session fees of $5, $7, and $10 a single (the union minimum was $52.50) for the often-illusory opportunity to record jazz.

Working under Stevenson as assistant A&R director was Clarence Paul, a long-time comrade with whom he had once recorded duets. Stevenson also had an ambitious secretary named Martha Reeves. Unlike many inside Motown, Reeves had considerable musical training—she had sung religious music at her father's Methodist church and classical music at Northeastern High. In addition, she brought her previous industry experience. With friends Annette Sterling, Rosalind Ashford, and Gloria Williams, she had recorded for Davis's Check-Mate label and had sung background vocals for a number of local singers. All of this made her invaluable to Stevenson. "She would be the one to get the information across," he told Aaron Fuchs. "We had a lot of artists and a lot of records going out. I had the sales department on my back. The executive department on my back. I got artists on one end. The musicians on another. Everybody was constantly coming in and screaming they wanted things. I had to have people around me who knew what was happening, so I didn't have to break down every word. Martha was right in there."

He knew that Martha's diligence wasn't without purpose. She wanted to record again. But Stevenson's attitude was that "she was there to make a living. She'd work little gigs on the weekends on her own, but she was a secretary to me and I liked it that way because she knew the business." Martha hung in there, smiling and waiting for her chance.

For Motown's first and arguably most important white executive, just joining the company was a thrill. "I remember when [Barney Ales] got this job with Motown," recalls CBS vice-president LeBaron Taylor, who was then a deejay at WCHB and a prominent figure on Detroit's music scene in the 1960s. "He was the most excited guy in the world. He said, 'Man, I'm making more money than I've ever made in my life.' He was making a hundred twenty-five dollars a week and they gave him a Cadillac."

Ales entered the record business in 1955, working around Detroit as a representative for Capitol Records, moving on for a year to the then-new Warner Bros. Records before becoming a partner in a local distributorship. In all of these jobs Barney acted as liaison between record labels, radio stations, and distributors in the Midwest, learning all aspects of the business. A tall man with an abrasive streetwise style, Barney Ales was not very different in attitude from Berry, something they discovered when they would meet and talk shop at local radio stations and recording studios. Both loved to compete and gamble, each claiming an edge over the other; Barney once bragged that Berry owed him ten thousand candy bars for losing at Ping-Pong, while Berry said that out of every one hundred contests he and Barney engaged in, Barney won three. They were kindred spirits.

So it wasn't surprising when Barney became an unpaid advisor to Berry and sister Loucye in the billing department in 1959. She knew bookkeeping, but was unfamiliar with the many distributors with whom Motown was suddenly doing business.

They had become such good friends, however, that when Berry offered him a job in 1960, Barney was reluctant to accept it, feeling that they might be too close. When Berry insisted, Barney finally, and happily, accepted. Berry hired Barney as vice-president in charge of distribution, believing his friend's skin color and general competence could convert racist distributors. When some suspected that Ales really owned Motown, he and Berry took it in stride. After all, it was probably good for the business.

Ales and Stevenson were selected for their roles at Motown with definite calculation, but many of the most important folks there "fell into" their jobs. Eddie Holland, for example, started out trying to be Jackie Wilson and briefly succeeded. His "Jamie," written and produced by Berry, was a slick uptempo song on which Berry recycled the writing style he'd perfected on Wilson's hits, while Holland mimicked Wilson's trademark vocal licks. Berry even hired members of the Detroit Symphony Orchestra to achieve the upscale R&B sound of Wilson's New York recordings. It marked the first time Motown interacted with classically trained musicians, and it wasn't without cross-cultural conflict.

Berry remembers fighting with the Detroit Symphony players "because sometimes when I asked them to play a particular riff, they were insulted, because they said the music wasn't right, and you couldn't do this or that. They'd say, 'But you just can't play this chord against that chord,' and I'd say 'Well, it sounds right and I don't care about the rules, because I don't know what they are.' Many of them would play it anyway, and mostly would all enjoy it. After we'd hear it back, they'd shake their heads in amazement. And when they heard it played back on the air and it was a hit . . . I mean, I would get calls from these guys and they would say, 'Hey, you were right. Anytime you need us for a session . . .' "

"Jamie" should have been the break this handsome, articulate, debonair young man needed to grab at stardom. Unfortunately, though, for all his pluses, Eddie Holland was shackled with one unavoidable minus: he didn't like to perform. In the studio he was fine, whether he was cutting demos of Berry's songs or making his own records, but out on the road promoting "Jamie" Eddie was dull and clearly frightened.

After one rough experience before the Apollo Theater's notoriously demanding audience, Eddie decided that his musical future was in the studio. He would cut a few singles over the next ten years, but never again would he perform on stage. Eddie would evolve into a behind-the-scenes power, shunning publicity with a passionate secretiveness, even at the height of his success. What now mattered to Eddie was money. "I saw my brother was making money and that I was looking at my recording bill and I was like forty thousand dollars in debt and my brother has got a royalty check because he wrote the songs," Eddie remembers. "I just said, 'I need to start writing songs.' "

Eddie asked his brother Brian if he needed a partner. It wouldn't have seemed so. For the last three years Brian Holland had been part of a loose production team that, depending on the record, included Stevenson, Robert Bateman, Freddie Gorman, and Lamont Dozier. Unlike his older brother, Brian had gotten involved in songwriting and producing early in his career. He met Berry through Eddie backstage at the Graystone Ballroom when he was just sixteen. Brian had sung with some local groups, but under Berry's guidance began putting melodies to lyrics. In contrast to the talkative Eddie, Brian had a quiet understated manner that made it easy for him to collaborate with others. As a teen, in 1959, he would be impressed by the way New York producers Jerry Leiber and Mike Stoller arranged strings on the Drifters' "There Goes My Baby," perhaps the first R&B record to make use of classical instrumentation, suggesting to Brian a sophisticated R&B sound he'd one day like to pursue. Brian had, in fact, been fascinated with the instrumentation of classical music since watching a Ford Motor Company–sponsored concert as a child. "I was so terribly impressed with all the violins and the melodies that they were playing; it just stuck in my mind because I had never heard that kind of big orchestra [before]," he told Portia Maultsby.

A series of records with the Marvelettes established Brian's credentials. Led by the guileless, unschooled voice of Gladys Horton, this girlish quartet came to Motown after winning a talent show at a high school in the working-class Detroit suburb of Inkster and being awarded a Motown audition. They would become Motown's first successful female vocal group, scoring with "Please Mr. Postman" in 1961. That record, produced by Brianbert (Brian and staff member Robert Bateman) and co-written by Marvelette Georgeanna Dobbins, was in the cooing juvenile girl-group style made popular by the songwriting combines in New York's Brill Building. As with many girl-group songs, the lyric highlighted a girl's yearning for a lost boyfriend, while drummer Marvin Gaye's choppy, popping beat made for great house-party boogying. By late 1962 the Marvelettes were Motown's most consistent hitmakers, with "Twistin' Postman," "Playboy," "Beechwood 4-5789" b/w "Someday, Someway," and "Strange I Know," all reaching the R&B top fifteen.

To ensure the loyalty of this obviously talented young songwriter, Berry raised Brian's royalty rate to a regal one-half cent a song per record sold and bought him a new Cadillac. As with Smokey, Berry cultivated a close relationship with Brian, one the tunesmith later described as "quasi-father-and-son."

Brian and Bateman seemed to be growing into a solid team when Bateman made a move he must surely have regretted later. Emboldened by the Marvelettes' sales, he left for New York and a shot at the big money New York represented.

Freddie Gorman started concentrating more on the Originals than on writing, since he was really more interested in being onstage than in the studio. Suddenly Brian was down to one partner, Lamont Dozier, a taciturn young singer-turned-writer who had turned down an opportunity to work for Berry just a few years earlier. While still a member of his vocal group, the Romeos, he'd visited Hitsville's basement studio and, unimpressed, left to cut some sides for Anna after a brief stay in New York. Once back in Detroit, he followed Bateman's advice and began collaborating with Brian and Eddie. In 1962 the production team of Holland-Dozier-Holland, or H-D-H, as they came to be called, was just coming together.

One of the company's strengths during this period was its accessibility to the black community. Just like Sykes Hernia Control Service, Your Fair Lady Boutique and Wig Room, and Phelps's Funeral Parlor—other businesses on the same side of the street as Hitsville—anybody could walk right on up and into the building. Berry's business was very much the neighborhood record company, and singers, dancers, and musicians of all kinds wandered through its front door. A weekly talent audition had to be scheduled to accommodate the traffic.

Four young chicks from the Brewster-Douglas housing projects called the Primettes, friends of a young male vocal group signed to Motown called the Primes, had been coming by almost every day after school and had finally talked Berry into recording them—though, in 1962, they were still more company mascots than anything else. Berry must have identified with those who wouldn't take no for an answer: he hired a quietly persistent kid named Norman Whitfield after he, too, haunted Hitsville. On several occasions before Whitfield joined Motown, Berry had been forced to order him from the control room. The kid was always staring at something.

"I played tennis and Norman would come out to the Northwestern school tennis courts and just stand there and look," recalls then WCHB deejay LeBaron Taylor. "It got so all the players knew him. 'There's Norman,' we'd say. He'd stand there for hours. Watching. And he never did participate. . . . He just observed everything."

Tall, slender, and reserved, young Norman was as observant around Motown's studios as he was at the tennis courts. Squatting on the steps leading down to Motown's basement studio, "Norman would sit there for a year, man," recalls pianist Earl Van Dyke. "He watched everybody."

When not studying tennis or the session men, Whitfield was paid fifteen dollars a week to listen to records and run what Berry called the quality control department, a term he borrowed from the auto industry, which at Motown "consisted of being totally honest about what [records] you were listening to," as Whitfield told *Black Music* in 1976. "You couldn't be influenced by who the producer was. After you'd awarded the demos a score, they went to the monthly meeting where the creative people would attend, and Berry would bring in some kids from outside, too. Releases were decided by majority rule."

Whitfield wanted very badly to produce for Motown. At eighteen, he'd already written and produced local hits for the little Thelma Records label, including "Answer Me" by future Temptation Richard Street, then leader of the Distants, and "I've Gotten Over You," recorded by the Synetics. Whitfield, though, stayed cool about his ambitions.

While growing up in Harlem, where he'd developed into a top-notch pool player, Whitfield had learned that patience and the ability to size up a situation before acting were valuable assets. Norman's family had ended up in Detroit after his father's car broke down in the Motor City on the way back to New York from an aunt's funeral in California. Sometime around his fifteenth birthday, Whitfield became interested in music. To sustain himself and avoid Detroit's auto factories until he could get a break, Whitfield had shot pool, engaging in marathon contests for cash and the challenge of competition. He knew that Motown was the game to be playing in Detroit and for now he was glad he'd worked his way in.

Like Martha Reeves, Whitfield contributed to the company while waiting for his break, hoping to gain the attention of the boss. Quality control had to be doing a good job in 1962; it was Motown's first full year of consistent national sales, the result of a series of now-classic records. Berry wrote and produced "Do You Love Me?" for the Contours, a state-of-the-art dance record, one that capitalized on the twist beat that had made Chubby Checker a national star. A wild sextet that had problems staying in pitch, the Contours had only been signed by Berry as a favor to Jackie Wilson—his cousin Hubert Johnson was a member. "Do You" was a dancer's delight, highlighted by a clever vocal arrangement and a funny lyric that mentioned all the era's hippest dances—the twist (what else?), the mashed potato, the jerk, and the hully gully. It was disposable pop music of the highest quality, going number one R&B and number three pop.

Equally commercial but somewhat more substantial, were three Smokey Robinson penned vehicles for a chubby female vocalist named Mary Wells in 1962: "The One Who Really Loves You," "You Beat Me to the Punch" (which went to number one R&B), and "Two Lovers" (number one R&B), bouncy mid-tempo songs marked by Smokey's increasingly clever lyrics, which made this nineteen-year-old singer Motown's first significant female star. She'd come to Motown's office just a year before with a tune called "Bye Bye Baby," hoping Berry would take it to Jackie Wilson. Instead, after hearing her a cappella rendition, Berry talked her into cutting the song herself. The session for "Baby" was a real test of Wells's voice, as Berry, unsure perhaps of what he wanted vocally, pushed her through twenty-two straight takes, giving her voice the uncomplimentary sandpapery sound heard on the final version.

Luckily for Wells, Smokey was sensitive enough to know that her malleable voice sounded best soft and soothing. Under Smokey's guidance she sang sweetly, coolly, straightforwardly, sticking close to the melody line and the demonstration guide vocal Smokey prepared for each song. As a result, Wells—in contrast to the deluge of adolescent-sounding girl-group records flooding the market in 1962—sang "Punch" and "Two Lovers" with the flavor of a knowing, worldly veteran of love. Together Wells and Smokey had created Motown's first great producer-singer marriage, a pairing that set high standards for the company's music. Berry had taken a chance on Wells, and it had worked.

To some inside Motown in 1962, the label's least likely hitmaker was Berry's brother-in-law Marvin Gaye, who many felt had already blown his shot at stardom just the year before. After Gaye had played sessions and toured as the Miracles' drummer, Berry let him cut *The Soulful Mood of Marvin Gaye*, a collection of MOR (middle-of-the-road) standards (e.g., "Mr. Sandman") done with a bit of jazz flavor. On it, Gaye and Motown made a conscious effort, the first of several, to reach the chic "supper club" audience by marketing an MOR album. It failed miserably. Berry was a bottom-line man and some felt that failure—especially at a time when so many other eager young singers were hanging around Hitsville —would put Marvin back behind his drum kit.

Then in July 1962, Stevenson and Berry's brother George got an idea for a dance record using Marvin. He wasn't enthusiastic about singing hardcore R&B, but Anna Gordy was used to being pampered, and Marvin's pretty face wouldn't pay the bills. Nor would a drummer's salary. With Marvin's songwriting aid, and the Vandellas on backing vocals, "Stubborn Kind of Fellow" was cut late in the month. "You could hear the man screaming on that tune, you could tell he was hungry," says Dave Hamilton, who played guitar on "Stubborn." "If you listen to that song you'll say, 'Hey, man, he was trying to make it because he was on his last leg.'"

Despite the fact that "Stubborn" cracked the R&B top ten, Marvin's future at Motown was in no way assured. He was already getting a reputation for being moody and difficult. It wasn't until December that he cut anything else with hit potential. "Hitch Hike," a thumping boogie tune that again called for a rougher style than Gaye enjoyed, was produced by Stevenson and Clarence Paul. Twenty years later, "Stubborn"'s thumping groove wears better than "Hitch Hike"'s, yet this second hit was clearly more important to his career, proving that Gaye wasn't a one-hit wonder. It proved, also, that the intangible "thing" some heard in Gaye's performance of "Stubborn" was no fluke. The man had sex appeal.

With these—plus the Miracles' sexy "You've Really Got a Hold On Me"—bolstering Motown, Berry and staff prepared in the winter of 1962 for their most ambitious undertaking to date: launching the Motor Town Revue. The idea of putting most of the Motown roster on the road came out of a series of conversations between Berry, Esther, and another member of the International Talent Management, Inc., office, Thomas

Prior to a television taping, Berry Gordy gives instructions—as he did before any major appearance of Motown acts—to (left to right) Four Tops "Obie" Benson, Lawrence Payton, Levi Stubbs, and "Duke" Fakir. *(Don Paulsen)*

Before they were Supremes these Detroit ladies were known as the Primettes, the sister group to the Primes (aka the Temptations). Barbara Martin (left) would drop out to start a family, but Diane (not yet Diana) Ross (top), Mary Wilson (center), and group founder Florence Ballard (right) stayed in show business. *(Michael Ochs Archives)*

In this early photo, Marvin Gaye looks very much like a preacher's son. *(Michael Ochs Archives)*

Smokey Robinson leads the Miracles through one of their hits: (left to right) Bobby Rogers, Claudette Robinson, and Pete Moore. *(Michael Ochs Archives)*

The Marvelettes look for that
postman at the Apollo in 1963.
(Kwame' Braithwaite)

A rare photo of the Velvelettes:
(left to right) Betty Kelly,
Carolyn Gill, and Sandra Tilley.
(Don Paulsen)

Little Stevie Wonder plays bongos in a shirt Ricky Ricardo might have envied. *(Michael Ochs Archives)*

The youthful Stevie Wonder at the Apollo Theater in 1963. It was during this tour that Stevie would record his first hit, "Fingertips, Part I." *(Kwame' Braithwaite)*

Making small backstage areas homey was a big concern of black stars in the sixties. Here Mary Wells employs a portable record player to add atmosphere to her Apollo dressing room. *(Don Paulsen)*

Lois Reeves, Martha Reeves, and Rosalind Ashford look at photos taken of them at the Apollo following a performance in 1967. *(Don Paulsen)*

Martha and the Vandellas sing out on the Apollo Theater stage, circa 1963. *(Kwame' Braithwaite)*

The "Temptations' Walk," in all
its glory. *(Don Paulsen)*

The Temptations—(left to
right) David Ruffin, Eddie
Kendricks, Paul Williams,
and Melvin Franklin—
surround Esther Gordy.
(Don Paulsen)

Mary Wells. *(Michael Ochs Archives)*

Harvey Fuqua. *(Michael Ochs Archives)*

Junior Walker in the center of his All-Stars: (left to right) organist Vic Thomas, drummer James Graves, and guitarist Willie Woods. *(Michael Ochs Archives)*

"Beans" Bowles. Bowles, a saxophonist and arranger by trade, had been in the Twenty Grand's house band since the early fifties, befriending George Gordy and his sisters at the nightclub. Through them, Bowles began playing sessions for Berry, impressing everyone with his head for business and his ideas on how to enhance live performance. Tall, lanky, and relaxed in action and speech, he wouldn't have seemed the logical person to work with the peppery Esther Gordy Edwards. Yet they'd clicked together at ITM, and the Motor Town Revue was their baby.

Touring revues had been a staple of rock and roll since musician-entrepreneur Johnny Otis had organized the first package in 1950. Subsequently, everyone from deejays, such as Alan Freed and Dick Clark, to stars, such as James Brown and Little Richard, organized shows with as many as ten acts on a bill, each performing one or two songs. Motown saw several benefits to packaging its roster revue style: it was a great promotion for the company, it gave the young Motown performers a chance to learn from and support each other in the frightening world of live performance, and, perhaps most profoundly, it meant immediate cash flow into Motown's bank accounts. Revenues from the concerts were seen as a means to offset slow payment from record distributors. In the company's early days, box office receipts often paid the weekly payroll back in Detroit.

Bowles saw the tours as the start of a series of Motown revues, each featuring a different musical style. There would be a jazz tour, a gospel tour, and eventually a tour mixing acts from each style. Some acts would be paired off later and tour together independently, so there would always be one or more pieces of the pyramid on the road. Eventually—though without jazz or gospel—this plan would be implemented, making Motown the first record label in history to tap directly into the income generated by its entire artist roster and to invest, in many cases at a loss, in building its artists' marketability via touring. It wasn't until the late sixties that record company investment in tours, known as "tour support," became an industry norm.

Following a November 2, 1962, date at the Boston Arena, the Motown special would hit nineteen cities in twenty-three days. The heart of the tour was made up of fifteen dates in the deep South, starting in North Carolina on November 5. The zigzag itinerary took them south to Georgia, to Alabama, back to Georgia, back to Alabama, over to Mississippi, up to North and South Carolina, down to Florida, up to Georgia, and finally back for two shows in Florida. (Though the parents of almost all of the Motown performers had come from the South, for many of the performers the tour offered them their first real exposure to the world their parents had escaped.) After taking Thanksgiving holiday off, the tour made a stop in Memphis on December 1, before starting an important engagement in New York from December 7 to December 16 at the "chitlin circuits' " crown jewel, Harlem's Apollo Theater.

Black promoter Henry Wynne of Supersonic Attractions was instrumental in setting up the tour, taking a chance on booking the entire package at a time when only four Motown–Tamla acts (Mary Wells, the Miracles, the Marvelettes, and Marv Johnson, now signed to Motown) could be considered drawing cards. The Contours attracted some patrons because of "Do You Love Me?" But at that time, Marvin Gaye, the Supremes (the new name for those company mascots, the Primettes), the Vandellas, and Singing Sammy Ward couldn't draw flies. Why should a promoter take—and, worse yet, *pay* for—the whole revue, when he'd make more money with just the top Motown acts, mixing them with groups from other labels?

Esther was a persuasive saleswoman and, as often was her technique with promoters and business contacts in the early days, she kept Wynne on the phone for hours, until he bought the whole tour, *and* at a price considerably higher than he originally intended. Part of her pitch was that this was a chance for him to grow with Motown; his Supersonic Attractions and Motown, two black companies, needed to be working together. Reluctantly, Wynne gave in.

To ensure that all money made by Motown acts was controlled by ITM, Esther Gordy Edwards and Beans Bowles set up a system whereby all monies were sent directly back to Detroit. In a mid-sixties interview, the Supremes once commented that they were making $10 a week on the road. "They were lying," is Bowles's reaction. "At that time they were given a ten-dollar check to buy stockings and toothpaste and stuff," while the rest of their income, say $290—already less management fees—was sent to a bank account in Detroit after each appearance. "We worked that kind of stuff out so they couldn't spend all the money on the road," he says. "They would see all those little do-dads and waste their money. When we got back to the office they would draw on it or they could get advances on money on the road by signing a check. I kept all the checkbooks and I'd write the check and they'd sign it. Plus, remember, they're all children." Aside from the artist, Berry, Esther, or Bowles could sign checks. Looking back, Bowles notes, "That's one thing about Motown— [they] did not take any money. Not like that."

It was a historic tour, but despite Bowles's efforts as road manager it was not the best organized. Forty-five people, including singers, musicians, chaperones for the girl groups, stage hands, and other administrative personnel, squeezed into one bus and five cars for the trek. (Berry stayed in Detroit to supervise the recording of new tracks and to keep an eye on things.)

Bandleader Choker Campbell remembers how nervous most of the performers were, "not knowing what the road was like. They had never been out there before." So the musicians, men in their twenties and thirties, "had to keep things anchored." The musicians' experience was helpful, but sometimes they tried to teach the youngsters, especially the teenage girls, a little too much. On occasion, chaperones found female members of the entourage smoking marijuana or sipping whiskey with these "experienced" men. Rules governing the conduct of female performers were as strict as possible. Fraternizing between the musicians and talent was soon discouraged, a policy that would become institutionalized at Motown. The musicians eventually took to calling the front of the bus, where the performers and management sat, "Broadway," and the back of the bus, where they congregated, "Harlem." The musicians weren't going to be treated like kids. If no drinking was allowed on the bus, they'd sneak a taste out of their hip-pocket flask. If marijuana wasn't allowed, they'd just blow the smoke out the window.

Some of the performers probably could have used the occasional joint, since their nervousness often betrayed them. Bowles will never forget the night that Georgeanna Dobbins of the Marvelettes "walked on [stage] chewing gum, looking like, 'God dog, look at all these people,' . . . Like [she] was doing a church or high school benefit." That lack of professionalism was sometimes reflected in the show's sequencing; Mary Wells, despite having good material, sometimes came off as dull when she followed the Contours' frantic performances. Even at her most animated, Wells basically swayed from side to side. Watching from the wings, Bowles remembers thinking, "These acts definitely need some grooming."

The tour didn't only have problems on stage. In 1962, the wave of boycotts, sit-ins, and freedom marches that had started with the Montgomery bus boycott in 1955 were rocking the South's social foundations. Black and white college students from the North—called Freedom Riders —flocked south in buses and cars not unlike those carrying the Motown crew. Those Michigan license plates stuck out on Southern highways. For the youngsters from Motown it was a shock to be denied food and a place to eat, to be called "nigger," and watched with hate-filled eyes. The more worldly musicians—veterans of many Southern tours—kept their pistols handy.

It was a hectic time for Bowles. Acting as road manager, he collected the money (as much as fifteen thousand dollars a night), watched out for the performers, critiqued the shows, battled to keep on schedule, and traveled a day early to each city to monitor ticket sales and hotel availability. Then, on Thanksgiving Day, 1962, tragedy struck. Bowles was being driven by Ed McFarland, Jr., a driver hired for the tour, to Miami in a white station wagon. It was early morning, the sun just under the horizon, and it was raining. A long truck filled with oranges suddenly loomed ahead of them. McFarland turned the wheel. Bowles doesn't remember what happened next.

When he regained consciousness, he was covered with blood and jammed sideways in the car, its shell collapsed around him like a plaster mold. He could speak, but he couldn't move.

McFarland had been killed instantly.

For forty-five minutes Bowles lay trapped in the car. It was a personal tragedy for Bowles, and almost a financial one for Motown. In Bowles's pocket was approximately $12,000; another few thousand were in his brief case. First on the scene was a state patrolman. "When I got hurt, I told him to look in my pocket and get the money," recalls Bowles. "He asked me if I could reach the briefcase and I pulled it up. . . . I was told by one reporter down there that he was the only honest cop in five hundred miles." Motown got its money back, but the tour was in disarray.

With Bowles laid up in a Florida hospital, Esther flew down to supervise the revue. Musicians had to be paid, hotel rooms confirmed, and entertainers calmed. Esther was nervous, but by all accounts handled the pressure well. The first Motor Town Revue had been a memorable experience, to say the least. Everyone was glad to be back in Detroit that Christmas.

The week before Christmas 1962 a young staff writer at the *Detroit Free Press* named Ken Barnard left the paper's building at 321 West Lafayette and drove up to the mid-Detroit area, looking for 2648 West Grand Boulevard. It wasn't hard to find. How many of the modest two-story houses on that tree-lined street had HITSVILLE, USA etched across the living room window?

The result of Barnard's visit was the first major piece in the local media about Berry's growing operation. The headline was HE SELLS HARD 'N' SOFT ROCK. The subhead read "Berry Gordy—Detroit's Record King."

In the accompanying picture Berry is sporting a head of shiny, wavy "processed" hair, with a part on the left side. His left eye, slightly more closed than his right, bears testament to his boxing career; there are signs of scar tissue on his eyebrow. The story notes that Berry, just turned thirty-three, had enjoyed two million-sellers ("Shop Around," "Please Mr. Postman") and several other records that had sold over a half-million each. "I wasn't a good pianist, but I knew some chords," he said about his musical training. About Detroit performers, he claimed, "The talent here is terrific and was largely untapped when we came along. And the personalities of the performers here seem to be basically warmer than in many other cities."

There were a couple of curious comments in the piece. Barnard writes: "[Berry] mainly records blues, gospel, and jazz numbers and is working into polka." And Berry's remarks about the future direction of music are quite ambiguous: "Taste is turning a little bit toward softer music. The hard 'rock' record is changing subtly. But it seems after a period of buying 'soft' records a loud record will go big. Basically, its a cycle type of thing."

Berry praises his "department heads and all the other people in the corporation" for making Motown successful. Yet, of all his staff, only Smokey Robinson is mentioned by name. Summing up Motown's strengths as it enters 1963, Berry says, "Our rise could have been faster if we had hedged on some verbal contracts or cut corners, but we stuck with integrity, and it's paying off. We've got respect in the business and people trust us. . . . We try to help artists personally with their investment programs so that they don't wind up broke. We are very much concerned with the artist's welfare."

The tone of the story was upbeat and optimistic, and it wouldn't have surprised the average *Detroit Free Press* reader that Motown would continue to grow. But if they'd had any idea of how big Motown would get, or of what it would take to get there, they'd never have finished breakfast.

5·PRODUCTION LINE

1963 to 1967

From 1957 to 1963—the period of Berry Gordy's rise to prominence within the American record industry—black popular music was the industry's bastard child and mother lode, an esthetic and economic contradiction that was institutionalized by white record executives. The major labels—Decca, Columbia, RCA in New York, Mercury in Chicago, and Capitol in Los Angeles—all recorded a few black singers. Capitol had Nat "King" Cole, Columbia had Johnny Mathis, RCA had Sam Cooke, each of whom were known for crooning styles that owed much to the mellow Big Band vocal style epitomized by Frank Sinatra. Not that there was no art in this approach; Cole, Mathis, and Cooke all made many spellbinding, beautiful records. Still, anyone who had heard, for example, Cooke's gospel recordings with the Soul Stirrers, knew that there was a whole world of emotional power he had access to that his RCA recordings rarely tapped. Underneath the glistening strings, Broadway show tunes, and relaxed vocal styles was a music of intense feeling. In the spirit of the Eisenhower era, the major labels dismissed real black music as a curiosity, recording this gutsier style first as "race music," then as "blues," and by 1960 as "rhythm and blues," all on subsidiary lines, such as Columbia's Okeh Records, which were not pushed in the white marketplace. (Harry Belafonte's calypso ditties had in fact received more mainstream exposure and been extremely popular.) Blacks simply weren't considered good enough to sit in the front of the record industry bus with the Sinatras, Comos, and other white angels that men such as Columbia A&R director and television personality Mitch

Miller so steadfastly supported. Like a bastard child, this music was shunted to a corner and left to fend for itself.

Yet, for all the prejudice aimed at blocking its growth, this rambunctious sound was quietly "poisoning" the minds of young white Americans. Its vehicles were small independent record companies, called "indies," usually owned by white entrepreneurs who knew that an expanding market existed for blues, gospel, and rhythm and blues. New York's Atlantic Records, founded by Ahmet and Nesuhi Ertegun, the sons of a Turkish diplomat, built an impressive enterprise, with Ray Charles, Ruth Brown, the Drifters, and the Coasters. Chicago's Chess Records had been catering successfully to black tastes with Muddy Waters and Howlin' Wolf, and to white teens with Chuck Berry and Bo Diddley, since the early 1950s. Fats Domino, a portly New Orleans pianist with a quavering tenor, a bluesy delivery, and access to the Crescent City's unceasing stream of rhythms, had found white and black fans by way of the Los Angeles–based Imperial label. The big labels knew that this music, labeled "rock and roll" by deejay Alan Freed, but really rhythm and blues in disguise, was making deep inroads into the youth market. Sam Phillips, with his Sun Records in Memphis, had taken the logical step of recording white singers, most prominently Elvis Presley and Jerry Lee Lewis, in this rock and roll style, sending a tremor through America's popular culture and tapping black music in ways that the big boys couldn't ignore. Presley's signing with RCA in 1955 could have been the moment that the majors went all the way, acknowledging the appeal of Presley *and* the musicians who had inspired him. Instead, after Presley, more white rock and rollers—and only a few blacks—made the leap. Lloyd Price, once a New Orleans R&B shouter, was suddenly cutting cutesy pop (like "Personality" for ABC-Paramount); most other blacks were left safely in their place on the indies.

During the seven years from 1957 to 1963, black music, performed by whites and blacks, was being either co-opted by the majors through whites in black face (or, in Presley's case, black shakes) or being picked up by adventureous young whites through airplay on rhythm and blues stations located on the AM dial's far right end.

In this environment, success for a black performer was characterized by sales of 45-rpm records in the 100,000 to 300,000 range, a lack of substantial album sales, headline status in a national network of ex-vaudeville houses in black neighborhoods (labeled "the chitlin circuit") and a rapid rise and fall. The indies found it more economical to emphasize hit records over hit singers, and so black music was rife with one-hit wonders and performers who bounced from label to label in search of hits. For all its wondrous musical energy, the world of black music was marked by chaos. When Berry sold one record to Chess, one to United Artists, and one to End, or when he used Smokey Robinson first as part of the Miracles and then as part of a duo (Ron & Bill), he wasn't innovating—he was just surviving in a business that demanded improvisation and flexibility.

Starting in 1963, Motown would change black music's position in the record industry and in American culture. The Motor Town Revue, shortened by now to the Motown Revue, was just a start. Over the next four years that gamble would be overshadowed by artistic and economic triumphs, triumphs made all the more amazing by the fact that Motown was owned and largely operated by blacks.

Until Motown, the history of black-owned record labels had been marked by frustration, cynicism, and unfulfilled potential. Black Swan, the first important black record company, had been founded in 1921 by Henry Pace and W. C. Handy, the latter a Northern bandleader who made his fortune committing blues songs he'd heard in the South to paper. The money he made from blues standards like "The St. Louis Blues" financed Black Swan's operations, including the hiring of famed big-band arranger-writer Fletcher Henderson as music director. While Pace and Handy recorded some "down-home" blues artists such as Trixie Smith, they had a definite crossover philosophy, as their recordings of the Broadway-flavored voice of Ethel Waters and the following ad attests:

> Only bonafide Racial Company making talking machine records. All stockholders are Colored, all artists are Colored, all employees are Colored. Only company using Racial Artists in recording high class song records. This company makes the only Grand Opera Records ever made by Negroes. All others confine this end of their work to blues, rags, comedy numbers, etc.

But, despite its potential (and Handy's dollars), Black Swan didn't last three years in competition with the two major labels, Columbia and Paramount, who had entered the "race" record market in the 1920s.

Don Robey's Duke–Peacock of Houston had no such upscale intentions. This tough former taxi-company owner specialized in the blues, recording Bobby "Blue" Bland, Junior Parker, O. V. Wright, and the late great Johnny Ace, as well as the young Little Richard. In his autobiography *Little Richard: The Quasar of Rock*, Little Richard says that Robey "would control the very breath that you breathed," and claims Robey punched Richard for talking back to him, giving the singer a hernia.

Robey never made big money until he sold Duke–Peacock to ABC Records in 1972. Moreover, Bland, acknowledged master of the blues song, wasn't marketed to white audiences until after Robey had sold his company, thus becoming a victim of a profound lack of vision on Robey's part.

Chicago's Vee Jay Records, which in 1963 was bigger than Motown, took the chances that Duke–Peacock did not. Operated by James and Vivian Carter Bracken (and, later, with the aid of Harvey Fuqua's old friend Ewart Abner), Vee Jay seemed to have everything: solid R&B groups (the Dells, the Spaniels, the El Dorados), gutsy blues (John Lee Hooker did his most polished work for them), talented solo acts (Dee Clark, Gene "Duke of Earl" Chandler, Betty Everett, Jerry Butler), and some extremely popular white groups (the Four Seasons, and the Beatles' first American single, "Please Please Me"). But Vee Jay, in graphic contrast to Motown, was a poorly run family-owned company.

"Vee Jay could have been bigger than Motown," claims one black radio veteran, "but they wasted money." One case in point is the free junket to Las Vegas that Vee Jay sponsored for twelve influential R&B deejays in the early sixties. One participant remembers, "They asked us what we wanted. The guys didn't want free poker chips or liquor. They wanted women." So Vee Jay flew in twelve tall blondes from Oslo, Norway, via the North Pole to Los Angeles to Las Vegas, for a Friday, Saturday, and Sunday of fun. The deejays left for work happy on Monday morning. "They could have been bigger than Motown, but," the participant concluded, "they needed a bookkeeper." Eventually, the costs of maintaining Vee Jay's huge building on Chicago's Michigan Avenue as well as its large roster of talent, combined with the traditional hostility of the white distributors toward a black company, led Vee Jay into bankruptcy by 1965.

What was Motown's edge, the difference that made it work where so many others had failed? It was Berry Gordy, the talent he acquired, both on record and backstage, and the way in which he organized and motivated his personnel. In the fall of 1963 Berry was, at thirty-four, a veteran at songwriting, at production, and at dealing with checks that never came. His once directionless energy was now focused. The examples of achievement set by his father and mother, as well as the family lore about his grandfather, were inspirations to him.

Berry created an "all for one and one for all" atmosphere in this period at Motown that, for all its sentimentality, appealed greatly to young black men and women. It is easy to say that Berry was a "father figure" to his staff, and for some of the company's members—Smokey for one—there may be some truth to that description. But, more accurately, Berry was Motown's "corporate hero," a man who espoused certain beliefs, represented certain values, and made sure everyone around him knew and believed in them, too. He did so by emphasizing his accomplishments, exuding a confidence that bordered on arrogance, and brimming over with a strange charisma.

To most people who met Berry, that quality wasn't always immediately apparent. He spoke in a flat, slightly nasal manner, with a halting cadence that was rarely eloquent. Those who, because of his achievements, expected a bigger man, were often surprised by his shortness. Despite these handicaps, when Berry spoke about something that fascinated him—songwriting, performing, a sales report, or a sporting contest (be it boxing, baseball, or blackjack)—he could be mesmerizing.

Sitting at the head of a table or standing up, suddenly towering over his seated employees at the Monday morning staff meetings, Berry made himself a symbol of what could be attained and the desire it would take to make it. Berry also liked to illustrate his control of the company—by vetoing release of a record that his sixty or so staffers liked, by forcing a reluctant executive to sing the company song ("Hitsville, U.S.A."), or by surprising the loyal composer of that song, Smokey Robinson, into tears by unexpectedly naming him vice-president at a 1962 staff meeting. Berry constantly talked about songwriting, about what was good and bad, instructing and, perhaps not coincidentally, reinforcing the myth of his own rise. Hadn't he been young and hungry once, as they now were? Look at him today. Berry wore expensive if poorly cut suits, had a confident, commanding air, and a rapid, self-important strut. Writing hits for Jackie Wilson had given Berry a reputation, but he'd taken it further than anyone could have imagined. For the young producer-writers—hungry cats like Norman Whitfield and Eddie Holland—Berry was a constant reminder of how successful a song could be. To the artists, he was a magic man who held the power to turn dreams into cold hard cash. To the young blacks in the area, he was a black man employing local people in a town where Henry Ford supplied almost all the jobs.

Though he never spoke about the issue overtly, Berry's rise in the early 1960s linked him with the civil rights movement. (Dr. Martin Luther King, Jr., once visited Motown briefly, and Berry would release his "I Have A Dream" speech, along with a few other civil rights–related albums throughout the decade.) Naïvely, some saw Motown as the entertainment-business equivalent of the National Association for the Advancement of Colored People, or the Southern Christian Leadership Conference. To them Motown wasn't just a job; it was part of a movement.

It was in this spirit that several Motown staffers once volunteered to pick the dandelions from the front lawns of 2648 West Grand Boulevard; in this spirit they gathered on weekends to cement their sense of identity. "In the early days we were a family, man," says pianist Earl Van Dyke. "We had so many good times together. That is the gospel. We had picnics, Christmas parties or we just hung out. There was a closeness there, man." Rodney Gordy, son of Robert Gordy, currently a Jobete staffer, remembers that picnics at Detroit's Belle Isle "would be the whole staff and friends of the staff and musicians and whoever. I think they started off as Gordy picnics and then kind of blossomed into Motown picnics. . . . There would be sack races, playing football, getting drunk and getting drunk and getting drunk. It was good clean fun." The athletic competition could get fierce. Clarence Paul broke an arm and Marvin Gaye fractured a foot playing "touch" football. Motown staffers were no less combative on Fridays at marathon poker games convened weekly at the home of Berry's secretary Rebecca Jowles, where Berry himself was one of the regulars. "We would be there the whole weekend," says Van Dyke, "just drinking, eating barbecue, lying, dancing, playing cards, and just enjoying ourselves."

Looking back today, most black Motown veterans remember this period as a special golden time of laughing, of drinking—and of a warm feeling of blackness enveloping the company. Berry, however, had already learned a very valuable lesson about American business: his black enterprise needed whites inside it to prosper. Because of Berry's skin color, some may have romanticized his motives, but only if they misread his message. He was preaching success in 1963, not black success. Part of the Motown mystique has been that it was black-owned. It was, however, never entirely black-operated.

"First of all I make the money, it's my money," Berry once said to a black reporter who asked him why he hired whites. "I do what I want with it. But black people have shown a lack of understanding of what I'm doing as a general market businessman. They say, 'Why do you hire this white man, or why this or why that?' Because this white man can do what I've hired him for better than I can do it." Or, taking Berry's statement to its logical conclusion, better than any black he could have hired for the same job. Moreover, Berry's use of the phrase "general market businessman" in reference to his use of white employees shows that he felt whites were essential to helping Motown's sales and image outside the black community.

For all his hard work Berry played hard, too. His love of competition and risk, elements that had led him to pursue boxing as a career, manifest themselves in Berry's love of gambling. Ex-staff members say that once Motown was established it wasn't unusual for him to blow $50,000 to $100,000 a day in bets. They speculate that Berry's interest in Motown acts playing Las Vegas, at least partially, stemmed from his desire to be closer to the gaming tables. Representative of Berry's gambling obsession is a story told by Marvin Gaye, Beans Bowles, and others. In his biography, *Divided Soul,* Marvin related that "Berry's such a hardcore bettor that if you were in his office and it was raining, he'd pick out two raindrops that hit the window at the same time. He'd take one, you'd take the other, and he'd bet you ten bucks that his raindrop would slide down and hit the bottom of the window before yours."

Marvin also observed that for Berry power was an aphrodisiac. He thought "Berry was the horniest man in Detroit. . . . You'd think he was working, but he might be freaking with some chick up in his office." The singer, in addition, charged that Berry, like many black men in positions of power, was attracted to white women, as though possessing them was a symbol of their achievement. But Berry didn't flaunt his white liaisons, perhaps quite aware of his image in black America. "He married blacks," said Marvin, "and fooled around with whites."

Beginning with Barney Ales in distribution, whites became actively involved in the financial and administrative aspects of Motown. Ralph Seltzer, a lawyer and a friend of Ales, came aboard as a special assistant to the president, a vague title that gave him broad powers to dabble in all aspects of Motown's operations. Sidney Noveck was an accountant who eventually superseded George Edwards as chief supervisor of Motown and Jobete's books. His brother Harold Noveck, a lawyer, became an important Motown consultant. Ed Pollack, yet another lawyer, filled a number of administrative positions. In addition, Phil Jones and Irv Biegel, two promotion staffers, came in under Ales as part of Motown's expansion to some sixty employees by January 1963. Physically, Motown was expanding as well, adding buildings on both sides of West Grand Boulevard.

The effect this influx of whites had on Motown is captured in this story by Motown bandleader Choker Campbell: "We had been gone on tour ninety days. When we came back everything was in shipping and we brought all these bills and everything. The way my band was booked, each promoter sends a deposit of x amount of dollars before the tour went out. I would always say, 'Give me my band payroll and give me fifty dollars in pay and keep the rest of that money in escrow for me so when I come home I have a nice amount of money.'

"I come back. My car notes are behind two, three months. They're going to cut off my phone. They're going to cut off my lights. But I ain't worried about that 'cause I got to go on by there on a Sunday night and go down [to Motown] on Monday. When I go down there they say, 'Go to Barney.' I said, 'Where?' 'Oh, he's down the street two buildings.' 'Okay, where is International Talent Management?' 'Oh, it's the other building.'

"So I go to International Talent first and picked up a sixty-day tour. It opens up Tuesday at the Mosque Theater in Pittsburgh. That's fine. So next I go to finance to get my money and run downtown and pay my bills. I said to myself, 'Who is this?' When I walked in the door they say, 'Oh, Choker, you're the bandleader, right? I said, 'Right.' All the time saying to myself, 'Who the hell is these dudes?' So I said, 'I came to pick up my bread.' I opened my books. Seltzer came on over. My books tallied with his books.

"So he said, 'Fine, Choker, fine.' I said, 'Well, give me my check.' He says, 'Since you've been gone, Wednesday is finance day. No one gets any money except on Wednesday.' I said, 'Man, what are you talking about? I've been gone ninety days. I got to be in Pittsburgh Tuesday. And you tell me Wednesday is finance day. I want my money now.' And then we had a little problem there, but I got my money, you dig?"

Campbell was able to get Berry to intercede on his behalf, just as Berry would, over the next few years, often have to act as mediator in disputes between his black music makers and his growing white executive group. Over time, this tension would have a divisive effect on the company morale.

Undoubtedly, rumors linking Motown with organized crime coincided with this influx of whites into the company's management. According to legend, the Teamsters union loaned Motown money to pay some bills and never got out of the company. A now-defunct sixties magazine called *Rock* alleged that Berry had lost the company gambling in Puerto Rico and subsequently spent most of his time under house arrest. "Syndicate figures" reportedly tried to buy Smokey's contract in the late sixties; Berry would say that "someone" offered to buy Smokey's contract for one million dollars cash. As a *Detroit Free Press* writer once put it, "Berry had almost as many hit rumors as hit records."

And the rumors have never stopped. It has, in fact, become a record industry truism that Motown is controlled by underworld figures; that they grabbed power at Motown by lending money to Berry when he was caught in a perilous cash flow bind similar to that of Harvey Fuqua's at

Harvey Records; that Berry has been merely a figurehead at Motown, at least in financial terms, since about 1963.

Not an impossible scenario: organized crime has been involved with the entertainment industry since Prohibition Las Vegas was reputedly the invention of racketeer Bugsy Siegel; New York's Copacabana, a symbol of success in mainstream entertainment to Motown in the sixties, was controlled by mobster Frank Costello (according to informer Joe Valachi). Many of the most chic discos of the seventies were created to launder money. In the entertainment industry it is unlikely that even the most honest citizen doesn't come into contact with some "underworld" figure. Owning a club or managing a superstar is a great way to hide money or camouflage any number of illegal activities.

However, despite twenty-five years of innuendos, there has never been any criminal investigation linking Motown to any segment of organized crime. Nor was Motown, a label that during the sixties would receive generous amounts of radio play, ever mentioned in any of the numerous payola scandals that have rocked pop music, particularly R&B, over the last quarter-century. Considering Motown's visibility since 1963, it is hard to imagine that the company has not been the subject of scrutiny from local, state, and federal law enforcement agencies (during this same period, black advancement proponents as diverse as Martin Luther King, Jr., and the Black Panthers were under covert investigation and attack by the FBI). It would have been a brilliant publicity coup for white prosecutors to catch Motown in bed with a criminal organization, and yet, in spite of the whispers, no mob connection has ever been proven.

Leaving aside the question of the validity of these rumors, it's interesting to note that, without any corroborating evidence, they have been so widely accepted. Perhaps it is hard for many to accept the idea that a black-owned company could be as successful as Motown. And in the early sixties, it was even harder to believe than it is today. Another aspect of Motown that has fueled outsiders' suspicions is the clannishness of Berry, his family, and the people who worked for him. Motown's lack of cooperation with the press is legendary. Artists, as we'll see, were trained *not* to give interviews of substance; for years, almost nothing about Motown— from the roles of its executives to the names of its musicians—was general knowledge. Berry's father, Pops, had encouraged self-reliance and togetherness. But Berry, Jr., instilled in his colleagues a suspicion of outsiders that bordered on paranoia. The rumors of underworld connections, though often denied, have never been aggressively attacked through a major public relations campaign, and this has given the company a subtly sinister mystique within the entertainment industry.

But whatever the rumors, the fact is that Berry Gordy wasn't a puppet manager; he was (and is) a powerful and demanding boss. If he gave you a job, you were expected to do it. If he gave you an assignment, you were expected to carry it out. He didn't usually care a great deal *how* it was accomplished. That was your problem. In fact, "That's your problem" is a phrase many former Motown employees associate with him. Or, as he explained his philosophy in 1969, "My point is to let them do their job and not get involved. When there is a situation that comes up and they want my view on it, then I would give them my view." He delegated authority easily, and the better the company did, the bigger the bonuses department heads received. Black people in business are traditionally perceived as doing a poor job of utilizing and motivating personnel. Usually self-made men, suspicious both of white authority and of black deceit or incompetence, black businesspeople tend to keep their hands on the backsides of everyone who works for them, stifling creativity in the process. In contrast, Berry's style allowed his lieutenants great autonomy —as long as they satisfied his demands.

"People had a lot more freedom then than I think the outside people realized," Lamont Dozier recalls. "[Berry] let you do what you wanted to do. You didn't have to get permission other than say, 'I want to go into the studio and I want to cut this.' Nobody looked at what you were doing. When you sent it to him finished, either he liked it or he didn't like it."

Don Davis, a sometime session guitarist on early Motown recordings, remembers Berry lecturing him one day, "saying I wasn't cooperating enough with his producers. He said I was contributing a lot of ideas, 'But those guys down there are running the show.' He meant he had put them in charge and that I should go do what they say."

One of a series of mid-sixties weekly meetings between Berry, sales vice-president Barney Ales, A&R director Mickey Stevenson, and Billie Jean Brown—Whitfield's successor in quality control—to discuss the scheduling of new Motown releases provides a vivid picture of Gordy's management style and the power Ales and Stevenson wielded over their areas. One staffer remembers it as follows:

> The meeting opened with Barney Ales asking, "Where is the record?"
>
> "I gave it to your girl at quality control three days ago," says Stevenson. "You haven't heard it?"
>
> Berry turns to her. "Where is the record on the Miracles?"
>
> She reaches into the pile on her lap. "Oh, here it is."
>
> Berry takes it from her and puts it on his turntable behind

his desk. Halfway through, he takes it off and says to Stevenson, "I thought you made a change."

"She's got the changes on a tape dated two days later." Brown pulls it out. Ales interjects, "Come on. Give me the record. I got to get it on the street."

"You got your record, Barney."

"Thanks. Now where is the record on Marvin Gaye?" Ales asks.

"Well, where is it, Mickey?" says Berry.

"Nobody came up with anything worthwhile."

"You come up with it," Berry demands. "That's your problem."

"Okay," says Stevenson. "I'll have the record on Marvin by next Wednesday."

"Okay," says Ales. "I'll put the release down for two weeks from now." Then looking at his release schedule, he says, "But I don't want it then 'cause we already have the Supremes for then."

Berry moans. "Now Marvin's gonna go apeshit." He turns to Stevenson. "Okay, you have the problem 'cause you should have had the record. You go explain to him why it's not coming out."

Stevenson, trying not to reveal his dismay, says he'll handle it.

After the meeting, Stevenson asks Gaye to write and produce his next record himself, which, despite Gaye's immense musical gifts, Stevenson sometimes finds is like pulling teeth. Instead of asking Gaye directly, he takes him to dinner, and over drinks convinces Marvin to collaborate with him on a new song. A few days later, after the song's completion, Stevenson makes sure he lets Berry know he has completed his mission *ahead of schedule.* Berry may not have cared about the details, but his employees knew he rarely forgot an order.

"I got a surprise for you. I'm gonna have the Marvin Gaye record sooner than the next two weeks. If I go to Barney, you think he'll go on and put out the record?

"That's your problem," Gordy replies. Then he adds, "Let me hear the record first. Then if you can convince Barney, all right." Interestingly, Berry just wants to know if the record meets company standards; whether that particular record gets out or not is not his prime consideration. After Berry gives it his approval,

Stevenson then stops by Barney Ales's house. Before playing it he builds it up, promoting its sales potential. At the end of their talk, Barney, all fired up about it, says, "That record belongs out. Let's put it on the market."

Further insight into Motown production comes from an unlikely source—Neil Young, founder of the pioneering folk-rock band Buffalo Springfield, and member of the late-sixties and early-seventies supergroup Crosby, Stills, Nash & Young. Young's first recording experience was at Motown, with the Mynah Birds, a Canadian band featuring future Springfield bassist Bruce Palmer and a long-haired, freaky-looking, rock-loving black dude named Ricky James. (The Mynah Birds were one of several white rock bands Motown would sign to no avail in the early to mid-sixties.)

> We went in and recorded five or six nights, and if we needed something, or if they thought we weren't strong enough, a couple of Motown singers would just *walk* right in and they'd *Motown* us. A couple of 'em would be right there, and they'd sing the part. They'd just appear and we'd all do it together. If somebody wasn't confident or didn't have it, they didn't say, "Well, let's work on this." Some guy would just come in who had it. . . . And an amazing thing happened—we sounded hot.

Young recalls that they were the only group on Motown playing twelve-string guitars over the Motown beat. But if the music was different, the contract was standard Motown issue. "They had the hugest, *hugest*, most gargantuan contract you've ever seen in your life. Man, we were ushered into these offices, signing these huge publishing contracts. They still have my publishing: everything with the Mynah Birds," he recalled in 1984. However, the music never hit the street. At the time the single "It's My Time," was due out, Buffalo-born James was busted for draft evasion. Motown, fearful of bad publicity, cancelled its release. According to Young, none of the band members saw any income from the deal, since their manager took the money and "OD'd on our advance." Young and Palmer moved to L.A. and started Buffalo Springfield. James kept in contact with Motown, and, despite the bust, would re-sign with the label, not as a folk-rocker, but as a creation named Rick, not Ricky, James.

The A&R department was so active by 1964 that Stevenson down-graded his role as producer to concentrate on being a cheerleader-administrator. (And since the more hits Motown had, the more money he received in bonuses, this can be seen as enlightened self-interest.) But, on a deeper level, he saw Motown as very much *his* company; he recruited the session players and much of the talent, and he saw their triumphs as his triumphs.

Every Friday there would be a parade of writers and producers into Stevenson's office to give progress reports. If the Supremes needed a new song, he'd ask the Hollands and Lamont Dozier, "What's happening, man? We need some more tunes?" If producer Hank Cosby couldn't get studio time, Stevenson would rearrange the schedule to accommodate him. When Smokey complained that he couldn't find Benny Benjamin for a session, Stevenson would be on the phone to Van Dyke, telling him to chase Benny down. Significantly, while all these musical decisions were being made and these assignments handed out, there were, with the obvious exception of Smokey Robinson, never any artists present.

At night Stevenson would prowl Detroit, visiting Hitsville, nightclubs, and often the homes of Motown writers to check on how songs were developing—and they had better be developing, or the writers would catch hell. Even if a tune were coming along, Stevenson would put the pressure on, saying that it wasn't as good as H-D-H's or Smokey's latest effort, and if they didn't get it together he'd get laughed out of the next Monday morning meeting.

For the writer-producers, the feeling was one of constantly being scrutinized; if your music were consistently deemed inferior, ridicule and even dismissal were the consequences. In fact, encouraging this mentality was essential to the company's creative strength. Eddie Holland, for example, convinced his brother Brian and Lamont Dozier to let him join their team by arguing that his presence as lyricist would accelerate their production process, making them more competitive with the other producer-writers—especially Smokey and Berry (who was then still spending a lot of time in the studio).

When an important act needed a hit, Motown would hold a contest to come up with that elusive hit song. The competition was keen. When the Temptations needed a breakthrough hit in 1964, Berry and Smokey battled to see who'd provide it. Driving back from a concert at the Apollo in New York, Bobby Rogers and Smokey composed a song while taking turns behind the wheel. When they arrived back in Detroit, they found Berry gloating. "Hey, look, I have got this great song on the Temptations, man," he said. "I have recorded it and know that it's gonna win the contest."

Smokey challenged him. "No, man," he said. "Give me two days, because I have got *the* song and I think it is going to wash your song away!" Smokey went down to the basement and cut it. A week later the contest was held with Mickey Stevenson, Clarence Paul, Harvey Fuqua, and about a dozen others sitting in judgment. Five records were played and only two got any votes; three people voted for Berry's now-forgotten ditty, and everyone else voted for Smokey and Bobby Rogers's "The Way You Do the Things You Do."

As a songwriter, Berry may have been somewhat chagrined to be so decisively defeated by his protégé. But as Motown's president, he was delighted that "Things" established the Temptations as major hitmakers.

Even the annual Christmas shows at Detroit's Fox Theater were trials by fire. For five shows a day, over an entire week, Motown's top attractions attempted to outdo each other at Berry's instigation. He made it a point of honor that the better acts were placed later in the program. The only way they could be moved back "was if their act was so good that their applause drowned out the name of the following act," decreed Berry. All week long, between shows, while a movie was on, even while the artists were still onstage, Berry, his sisters, and anyone else in the Motown family could offer criticisms and suggest changes in each artist's show. Egos were hurt. Arguments were common. Everyone was forced to sharpen their presentation, which was just what Berry wanted in the first place.

This combative posture did have its dark side. Some writers suspected others of listening at keyholes to their compositions. There was talk of producers buying quality songs outright from low-level Jobete writers and putting their names on them, basking in the credit and collecting the royalties. Clarence Paul would later tell David Ritz that "tunes were stolen all the time, and often credit wasn't properly assigned." Later Beans Bowles would claim he deserved a writing credit on "Fingertips—Pt. 2." Marv Johnson told a Detroit newspaper that he, not Berry Gordy, wrote his hit "Come to Me." Yet in these two specific instances where rip-offs are charged, neither man has filed suit for back royalties.

Overall, this philosophy pushed the cream to the top and left the lazy far behind. Anything you got at Motown as a creative person you had to earn. The more Motown and Jobete grew, the more intense the competition was to get one's song used by hit artists. "The whole thing at the company was about competition," says Norman Whitfield, "and competition breeds giants."

This same spirited, aggressive attitude permeated the sales department. At one point Loucye Gordy Wakefield had to organize Motown's accounts receivable, and she is credited by Berry and Esther with keeping Motown solvent in the days when more records were being ordered and pressed than were being paid for by distributors. But by 1964, and certainly after Loucye's death in 1965, it was Barney Ales's persona and methods that dominated sales. Ales took no crap, demanding respect and Motown's money from the distributors (at Motown's height in the early sixties the label dealt with as many as thirty-three).

"I'd hear him on the telephone," says one Motown vet. " 'Goddamn it, I want that record moved!' he'd say. That record would move, man. He would say, 'What do you mean? I don't want to hear that fucking shit!' " Ales manipulated distributors, threatening to delay or withhold hot recordings in their area, even saying that he'd change distributors in a particular area if payments were late or incomplete.

"You can always get your money when you're hot," says CBS vice-president LeBaron Taylor, looking back at indie labels in the 1960s. "People would say, 'One of these days Motown's gonna be cold and all those returns that they had all over the world will come back.' But it just so happens that they never did get cold." But Taylor acknowledges that even then "there had to be a certain amount of encouraging your distributors to pay. It wasn't uncommon in those days for guys to visit distributors and leave with their checks. And there were a lot of tough guys in the business a long time ago. They used to come in and break a guy's back. Yeah. It wasn't uncommon for you to know people. You might have difficulty collecting money in certain areas and call friends, and say, 'Well, hey, this guy's holding my money. Your friend would place a call and within a certain time you could get your money." In this hard-nosed environment, Barney Ales's abrasive style was perfect.

That's not to say that Motown didn't use milder methods to get what they wanted. As was standard among indie labels at the time (and as is still done widely in the record industry), Motown made extensive use of various "deals," or discount plans with distributors. The basic unit of a deal was 1,300 records; a "half-deal" was 650 records and a "quarter-deal" was 325. If a distributor ordered 1,000 records he got 300 free records or "free goods," 300 records that contractually Motown paid little or no royalties on. But, while 1,300 was the base, the orders for Motown, once the production line was in place, were usually a lot higher. This meant that an awful lot of ready cash was being made available.

This policy left plenty of room for abuse by sales staffers, but, as ex-Motown sales staffer Tom Noonan says, "Berry trusted him [Barney Ales] one hundred percent and Berry is that type of executive where he does delegate and Barney ran sales. It meant he ran it with a heavy hand and without interference."

So, in 1963, a year before the Beatles broke through in America and the British Invasion pushed most American pop out of the Top Forty, Motown was gearing up. There were still some pieces missing and some valuable teams to be formed. It was a transitional year in which the careers of the young veteran Smokey Robinson, the gifted rookie Stevie Wonder, and the patient Martha Reeves would all take center stage.

Since their marriage in November 7, 1959, Motown's favorite love-birds, Smokey and Claudette Robinson, had battled the enemy of all show business couples, the road. Since Claudette was in the Miracles, she and Smokey were never separated for long periods of time, as were couples with only one performing member. Still, even when the two were touring together, Smokey's good looks and romantic voice had female fans pursuing him, with or without Claudette. ("Smokey wasn't henpecked," one musician remembers, "but she sure kept an eye on him.")

Their first major trial came only a few weeks after their marriage, following a New Year's Eve performance at Philadelphia's Uptown Theater. When they returned to their hotel, the Miracles found women wandering the halls looking for parties and musicians. Smokey, who had left his room to visit another of the Miracles, encountered two female fans in the hallway. Full of the holiday spirit and moved by Smokey's pretty eyes, the two pinned him against a wall and proceeded to place their lips upon his face. In a scene that could have been written for Doris Day, Claudette stepped into the hallway and became a surprise witness to the shocking scene.

Claudette slammed the door and started packing her clothes. Kelly Isley, the oldest of the Isley Brothers (with whom the Miracles were touring), ran down the facts of life on the road to Claudette. For the next two hours, he explained to her that the incident would actually strengthen the Robinsons' marriage, since it had shown them the extraordinary depth of trust they would need if their marriage was to withstand the physical and emotional demands of show business.

But that misunderstanding seemed inconsequential compared to the Robinsons' problems in 1963. In that year Smokey and Claudette suffered a series of personal tragedies that could have destroyed a weaker relationship. That fall, while performing at Washington, D.C.'s Howard Theater, Smokey contracted one of the first reported cases of Asian flu in the United States. Every day of the week-long engagement, a doctor visited the Robinsons' cramped quarters in a rooming house across from the Howard. And every night after the last show they'd stop at a local hospital. At one point Smokey's temperature rose as high as a life-threatening 106 degrees. At the end of the engagement Claudette rushed her ailing husband home to Detroit, and then she headed to South Carolina to join the rest of the Miracles, assuming Smokey's role as lead vocalist.

While convalescing, Smokey began getting news from the road that Claudette was losing weight. At first he chalked it up to fatigue. Besides, she never mentioned any problems when she called. But then bassist James Jamerson and Mary Wells, who was rooming with Claudette, called Smokey, imploring him to make Claudette come home. Unbeknownst to Smokey, his wife was pregnant and had been hemorrhaging for the past few weeks. Had Claudette suffered those symptoms at home, a responsible doctor would have ordered immediate bed rest. Instead, Claudette was touring the country, doing exhausting shows every day, all the while never letting on to Smokey that something was wrong. By the time Wells and Jameson called, Claudette had been losing blood for over a month. She hadn't told Smokey because she knew it would force the Miracles off the road, costing its members money and weakening the Motown Revue. Smokey called her and, after some debate, got her to agree to come home. "When she got off the plane, I didn't even know her. She was down to eighty-nine pounds," recalls Smokey. Doctors thought that the baby might be saved, but the strain proved too great, and Claudette miscarried.

As soon as Claudette regained her health, she hit the road again. She became pregnant and miscarried again. And again. And again. Claudette suffered a total of six miscarriages before Smokey finally told her, "You gotta come off the road."

One can only imagine the anguish that filled their hearts. Before they had their first child (named Berry, of course) in 1968, Smokey and Claudette spent five years nagged by the fear that they'd never have children.

Because of this ongoing personal trauma, Smokey's emotions were closer to the surface than most men ever allow. He says that only one song, the beautiful and uncharacteristically straightforward "More Love" (later a major hit for Kim Carnes), was written in direct response to Claudette's problems. "After she had a miscarriage she would always tell me she was sorry she had let me down. I would explain that she had not let me down because she was there, she was alive, I wanted the babies, but I didn't know them. I wrote 'More Love' to let her know how I felt about her. I wrote it as soon as I went home."

It is hard to imagine this painful experience not having a profound effect on Smokey's songwriting. That is not to say that Claudette's miscarriages were the sole inspiration behind his songwriting brilliance; his technique was too sophisticated to result purely from a raw emotional response, but we can't underestimate the deep well of emotions it tapped. The refinement of deep emotion is the springboard to great art, as these songs illustrate: "Ain't That Peculiar" and "I'll Be Doggone," recorded by Marvin Gaye; "Two Lovers," "My Guy," and "What's Easy for Two Is so Hard for One," recorded by Mary Wells; "The Hunter Gets Captured by the Game" and "Don't Mess With Bill" by the Marvelettes; "The Way You Do the Things You Do," "Don't Look Back," "It's Growing," "Since I Lost My Baby," and "My Girl," recorded by the Temptations; and "The Love I Saw in You Was Just a Mirage," "The Tracks of My Tears," "I'll Try Something New," and "Choosey Beggar," recorded by Smokey's own Miracles.

The great theme of Smokey's writing, one that echoed the conflict between the achievements of the Miracles and Motown with his personal turmoil, is the understanding and dissection of love's paradoxes. Sometimes, this is expressed by the words themselves. "My Girl," a song Smokey and Ronnie White composed backstage at the Apollo Theater, is built on paradoxical images: the singer has sunshine on a cloudy day, he is enjoying May weather in the dead of winter, all because of his lady's love. "I don't like you, but I love you," the opening of "You've Really Got a Hold on Me" is simple, too, but it hooks us right away with the singer's confusion and the overriding power of his love. In one sentence we know that the relationship between the speaker and the woman to whom he is speaking is passionate, loving yet quiet. Smokey wrote "Hold" after hearing Sam Cooke's classic "Bring It on Home to Me" in a New York hotel room. Note that while Cooke's original is a soulful, straightforward declaration of the desire for a lost lover, Smokey's special gift for lyrical invention results in something more realistic. A similar idea can be found in "Ain't That Peculiar," when Marvin Gaye muses, "I know that flowers grow from rain/But how can love grow from pain?" In the end, despite a catalogue of conflicting emotions, the listener is left to assume that love will go on anyway, with Gaye confessing that he still doesn't understand how love works, only that it does.

In the exquisite "Two Lovers," Smokey uses some of his most direct lyrics to put us in the midst of singer Mary Wells's seemingly adulterous relationship. In the first verse she sings the praises of a man "sweet, and kind, and mine all mine." In the second verse we find that Wells's other man "treats her bad" and "makes her sad." But by song's end we find she's loving a dude with a split personality; she loves them both, enduring his evil moods for just a little more of his good, true loving. Smokey based "Two Lovers" on his feelings toward Claudette, a Gemini. Smokey says that in the early years of their marriage she "had the power to really make me very happy or very sad with a word or with an action."

For Wells, who served as Smokey's most effective female mouthpiece, sex is a battleground in "You Beat Me to the Punch." Here common words take on several meanings. In the first verse, the word *punch* refers to the fact that Wells's prospective lover, guessing her attraction to him, makes the first move. By the second verse Wells has guessed that his aggressiveness means he is just a "playboy," so she beats him to the "punch" and tells him to take a hike.

Of course, Smokey's cleverness was sometimes used in the service of pure fun. "The Way You Do the Things You Do" is a celebration of style, and Smokey shows his by comparing his lady to a candle, a handle, a broom, and perfume, drawing smiles in the process and perfectly matching the syncopation of the melody. Better still are the series of unexpected comparisons between love and life that open the Temptations' "It's Growing." In the space of four lines, love is like a snowball rolling down a snow-covered hill, love is the size of a fish a man claims destroyed his reel, love is a growing rosebud, and love is an oft-told tale.

Of course, of his countless great songs, Smokey's masterpiece is "The Tracks of My Tears," a song so compelling, so beautiful, so resilient, that even Linda Ronstadt's wooden interpretation couldn't ruin it. As Smokey recalls, "I had that track for a while, but I really couldn't think of anything to fit it because it's such an odd musical progression. Finally, one day [in 1965] the chorus came to me. No one had ever said 'tracks of my tears.' The whole thought of tears was you wipe them away so no one could tell you've been crying. To say that I can't even wipe them away because they've left these tracks, you know, I thought it was a good idea."

The central image is of a smiling, joking guy at a neighborhood party with a pretty woman on his arm. But the singer soon reveals that his smile is like a clown's makeup, disguising the deep pain he feels at the loss of his true love. But the beauty of "Tracks" goes deeper than Smokey's lyrics. It possesses a wonderfully wistful melody (the "odd musical progression") and a brilliant production. For, while Smokey was so supple a lyricist that Bob Dylan once remarked, and not in jest, that he was "America's greatest living poet," it was Smokey's willingness to collaborate with the other Miracles and the Motown musicians that gave "Tracks" an extra dimension. Marv Tarplin's melancholy guitar introduction, a distant parody of circus music, was the song's basis, not Smokey's words. The melody was shaped with the help of another Miracle, Warren Moore, and then Smokey "fit" words to it.

In fact, most of the songs just cited were written by Smokey in tandem with others who provided melodic and rhythmic ideas: Moore also co-wrote "It's Growing"; Bobby Rogers co-wrote "The Way You Do the Things You Do"; Ronnie White contributed to "My Girl" and "You Beat Me to the Punch"; Motown staff writer Alfred Cleveland accidentally came up with the title of "I Second That Emotion" while he and Smokey were Christmas shopping in 1967; "Ain't That Peculiar," "The Love I Saw in You Was Just a Mirage," and Smokey's 1979 comeback hit "Cruisin'," like "Tracks," were all started by Marv Tarplin guitar figures.

Smokey's songs were sparked by stimuli of every kind. "Don't Mess With Bill" and "The Hunter Gets Captured by the Game," two of his wittiest love songs, were composed to accommodate what Smokey called Wanda Rogers's (of the Marvelettes) "little sexy" voice. The romantic "I'll Try Something New," in marked contrast, came to Smokey while watching the Detroit Tigers trounce the Cleveland Indians with his father at Detroit's Briggs Stadium. Smokey wrote the song's lyrics on the back of a crushed popcorn box.

Because of Smokey's ability to collaborate with others and find inspiration in a variety of ways, his songs never sounded formulated. There were certain recurring melodic and lyrical motifs—"My Girl" was obviously a companion piece to "My Guy—but he avoided the kind of musical signatures and clichés that marked the work of many of his Motown contemporaries. Smokey's role as the Miracles' lead singer also influenced his writing. His voice, wrote David Morse, "recognizes no distinction between speech and song; it uncoils from a breathy, intimate whisper into a clear, bright, continuously intense verbal pressure" that was, perhaps, the most effective tool of seduction of the sixties. At house parties, bachelor pads, and, most profoundly, lovemaking sessions throughout America, Smokey's voice was cooing sweetly in the background. On the more rarefied level of musicianship, Smokey's sense of rhythm—an underappreciated aspect of singing—was remarkable. "While other singers land heavily on the beat," says Morse, "Smokey Robinson maintains a subtle, continuous contact with it, a kind of prehensile touching."

Ironically, it was Smokey's own creativity that would, after 1963, make him an inconsistent member of the Motown hitmaking machinery. One never knew what to expect from him, and so his songs and productions were never guaranteed hits. During his peak years as a writer, from 1963 to 1967, others at Motown would rack up more Top Ten hits and larger sales figures. Yet for durability and sheer beauty, no one at Motown would top him.

Berry Gordy was dining in his upstairs office one evening in 1961 when Brian Holland and Ronnie White requested that he come down to the studio. There was somebody he needed to hear. Initially Berry wasn't too impressed. Why had Berry's dinner—legend says it was steak—been interrupted to see some skinny little blind kid sing? But hearing eleven-year-old Steveland Morris sing the Miracles' "Lonely Guy" and play piano, harmonica, and bongos proved to be worth Berry's while. He had Esther make up a contract for Steveland, whom Berry, in one of his more inspired name changes, decided would hereafter be called Little Stevie Wonder.

It was a miracle of modern medicine that Stevie was alive at all. Born four weeks premature, Stevie had been kept alive for a month in an incubator. Too much oxygen was pumped into the incubator, and as a result Stevie developed retrolental fibroplasia, which creates a fibrous membrane behind each eyeball, and would render him permanently blind. Despite his handicap, Stevie was an active, mischievous child who rode bikes, jumped across rooftops, and played "doctor" with his female schoolmates. Though he was born in Saginaw, Michigan, he was raised in Detroit, where his desire to make music asserted itself. He'd bang spoons on the table and sing whenever asked, and more often when he wasn't. By eight he was making noise on the bongos, piano, and harmonica. He went to bed listening to WCBH, admiring the smooth vocals of Johnny Ace and Bobby "Blue" Bland, and the brash blues guitar of B. B. King. For a time he attended the Whitestone Baptist Church, where he quickly moved from the choir to lead singer to junior deacon. The church and Stevie didn't mix, though; his allegiance was more to music than to church dogma and when a conflict arose over his neighborhood performances of R&B material, he left. It wasn't a church pulpit, but the steps of a building in his neighborhood that became Stevie's first stage. With bongos and harmonica the kid would wail on hot summer afternoons. The Miracles' Ronnie White, at first reluctant to respond to his little brother's urgings, was impressed when he finally heard Stevie. So was Brian Holland; and even Berry Gordy's cold dinner was forgotten.

Because of Stevie's age, Esther had to work with the Michigan Department of Labor to structure his contract to the specifications of the child labor law. While at the company Stevie would receive a small weekly allowance; his royalties and performance fees would be administered by Jobete and ITM like any Motown act, but, unlike other Motown acts, his earnings were placed in a special trust fund, one that would be monitored over the years by the state of Michigan, schools for the blind, and his protectors within the company. It was a provision that would have a profound effect on Motown and popular music.

Viewing Stevie as a diamond in the rough not yet ready to record, Berry encouraged him to hang around Motown after school and on weekends. Bassist James Jamerson remembered being called into Mickey Stevenson's office, along with drummer Benny Benjamin and pianist Earl Van Dyke, and told that "management" would like them to take a little time to work with Stevie. They needn't have bothered; Stevie's natural curiosity and prodigious potential were recognized immediately by the Motown musicians. He spent hours playing drums with Benjamin, whom he nicknamed "Papa Zita," and to this day Stevie's drum style bears Benjamin's imprint.

The Motown staff member who had the most dramatic subsequent influence on Stevie, however, was assistant A&R director Clarence Paul. Paul, whose mother was a singer who had reared him in a show-business environment, sort of adopted Stevie, and Stevie, who had never been close to his natural father, accepted Paul as the most important of the surrogate fathers Motown provided. "Clarence is like Stevie's daddy," says Choker Campbell. "They should recognize Clarence as being the man that really guided Stevie the right way." Guitarist-vibist Dave Hamilton agrees, saying, "Clarence shaped Stevie. I remember when Stevie would be over to Clarence's house and Clarence would be teaching him to sing those standard tunes like 'Masquerade,' those tunes that he was singing that the people would be amazed to see a kid his age singing. Clarence was teaching him because he was a hell of a singer himself."

Stevie was fortunate to have this high-level support, because as an adolescent he could be a real pain in the ass. He loved visiting then-A&R department secretary Martha Reeves after school. They'd sing together, tell jokes, and when Reeves was busy, Little Stevie would sneak behind her back to play with the A&R department's tape recorder. He broke four machines trying to figure out their inner workings before, in a defensive measure, Motown bought him one of his very own. Stevie was a natural mimic, sliding from a stuffy English accent to over-exaggerated jive talk to the strident, bossy tone of Berry Gordy. His Berry Gordy imitation was so accomplished, in fact, that Stevie often fooled Motown personnel with phony instructions. Even Smokey, who knew Berry as well as anyone outside the family, was fooled a few times. Another of Stevie's favorite tricks was to ask what someone in another room was wearing and then to call them in and compliment them, saying, for example, "That's a beautiful blue dress you have on and I just love those Italian shoes." Stevie's ability to "see" startled more than one young Motown secretary.

Recording sessions were always in danger with Stevie roaming around Hitsville. Since he couldn't see the red recording light above the studio door, Stevie would bust in, talking in his shrill child's voice, and occasionally ruin a take. For these reasons, plus the hostility some Motown acts felt toward a kid who was receiving special treatment denied to them, Stevie made some enemies.

But at that time Stevie probably wasn't aware of it. He was too busy hanging out with Mary Wells, Smokey, Berry, Martha Reeves, and the musicians, and, after almost a year of grooming, making records. Though "Thank You (for Loving Me all the Way)," recorded by Clarence Paul and Mickey Stevenson in November 1962, didn't sell, Stevie was just proud to be the first thirteen-year-old on his block with a record. "Thank You" is important not just because it was Stevie Wonder's first record, but because its cutesy melody and hokey lyrics set an unenviably shlocky standard that too many of his subsequent records would match.

His second single, "Contract on Love," written by Janie ("Money") Branford and producers Brian Holland and Lamont Dozier, was a minor hit for Stevie, though much of his success can be attributed to Stevie's appearances as part of the Motown Revue. In his brief, explosive performance he'd play drums, piano, bongos, organ, and sing in a piercing adolescent falsetto. Despite his blindness (or perhaps, to some degree, because of it), Stevie's effervescent personality made him the biggest black kiddie star since Frankie Lymon, even without a huge hit.

That position was endangered when the Detroit Board of Education, apparently acting on recommendations from some of Stevie's teachers, announced that he could not be properly educated if all of his free time were spent touring. The young entertainer had already been feeling peer pressure from students and neighbors who accused him of getting "big-headed," attacks based as much on their jealousy, no doubt, than on any change in Stevie's personality. As a result, Motown arranged for Stevie to attend the Michigan School for the Blind at Lansing, Michigan, which meant that Stevie could continue to tour along with a school-appointed tutor. It was another Motown investment in Stevie, and he was grateful. Unfortunately, though, Lansing was 150 miles from Detroit, and so, when

Stevie wasn't on the road or at Hitsville, he was still spending most of his time away from home. Some may have thought of Stevie as the company "mascot," but in a very real sense he became Motown's baby. While Motown was symbolically "raising" its other teenage charges, Stevie would truly be molded by Motown's very adult values, by his relationship to the company and his responses to their demands, not unlike any child responding to a parent. Even when he later rejected the Motown philosophy, his negative response was defined by doing the opposite of what company orthodoxy suggested.

Stevie's first major hit in 1963 foreshadowed his special place at the company, since it was easily the label's most unusual early success. "Fingertips—Pt. 2" was originally an instrumental on *The Jazz Soul of Stevie Wonder*, which Stevie, Benny Benjamin, and Beans Bowles (who solos on it) had played around with while on the road. They had shifted the key from G to C, and they gave Stevie room to improvise a vocal when he wasn't playing bongos or harmonica. "Fingertips" was inserted into Stevie's live show during a stay at the Apollo Theater in late 1961 and it was refined throughout 1962. The hit version was recorded as part of a Motown Revue recording at Chicago's Regal Theater. On a WJBK special, Stevie recalled, "Everybody say 'Yeah' and all that other junk just came out. It was never planned." Nor were the quite audible shouts of "What key? What key?" by bassist Larry Moses. When the Motown announcer yelled "Let's give Stevie a hand," the set was supposed to end and Moses, bassist for the next act, came charging onstage to begin the next set. When Stevie came running and jumping back on, "Larry didn't know what to do," Stevie recalled. "He was standing with his bass in his hand and he said 'What key? What key?' He said a few other things but I guess they didn't get it on tape 'cause he said a few bad words, too." That feeling of onstage chaos and youthful exuberance leaped off the record and sent it to number one on the pop and R&B charts.

The road provided Stevie not only with his first taste of national stardom, but his first sexual adventures as well. "I had a party in my room and Stevie found me," recalls a member of Motown's road band. "We named him 'Hogsog Damby' because we called his movements a hogsog dance. You know he'd be sitting and we'd call it a hogsog dance. So Stevie come by and says, 'Hogsog.' Then he says, 'You're having a party, ain't you? Sounds like a lot of pretty girls in here. . . . Man, I need one, I'd like to get me one of these chicks.' Now at that time Stevie, about thirteen or fourteen, was on an allowance and he's got a tutor [Ted Hull] with him. We got him [Hull] out of the way and I told the chick, I said 'Look here

Stevie wants a little.' I picked the nicest chick in the room. . . . She said
'Oh, mean to tell me I can go out with Stevie Wonder?' I said, 'Yeah.
She said, 'Well, wait a minute now, you know I'm a prostitute. I just can'
do it for nothing. I want to do it, but . . .' I said, 'Here's twenty dollars
Go ahead.'

"She went back down [to Stevie's room]. They were gone about an
hour and she came back and said, 'Wow.' About a half hour later Stevie'
knocking on my door again. 'Who's there?' I asked. 'Hogsog,' he said.'

They let Stevie in and he asked to be led to the bathroom. Once
inside, he asked his benefactor, "You going to do that for me again?" The
musician, a fun-loving but practical man, said, "I ain't paying for your
pussy. You're making more money than I am. You pay for it!" For young
performers and young men, traveling can be an educational experience
For Stevie it proved particularly instructive. Alas, it wouldn't always be
that easy.

Martha Reeves's patience had finally paid off. After she and her
friends in the Del-Phis sang backing vocals on Marvin Gaye's "Hitch
Hike" and "Stubborn Kind of Fellow" it was harder to keep them in the
background and Martha in Stevenson's office. The big break came when
Mary Wells missed the session to record a song called "I'll Have to Let
Him Go." Wells professed illness, though some suspect that she just
didn't like the tune. Reeves and the Del-Phis, like so many would-be
Motowners, were just hanging around, so Stevenson decided not to waste
the studio time. Reeves and company were desperate to cut anything,
even this weak girl-group record written by Brian Holland and Freddie
Gorman.

Since the girls were still under contract to Chess as the Del-Phis, their
record was released as the Vels, on Motown's Mel-O-Dy label. Gloria
Williams sang lead on it but after it flopped, she quit the group to
concentrate on raising her two kids and a civil service job she'd landed
with the city. With Martha now singing lead, and now viewed as a
potentially viable act, Berry formally signed the newly renamed Vandellas.
The name was created when Martha combined Detroit's Van Dyke
Avenue with that of the singer Della Reese. Their first single under their
new name was "I'll Have to Let Him Go," produced by Stevenson, and
it came and went without a trace in the autumn of 1962.

Then they were matched with the then-embryonic writing-produc-
tion team of Eddie and Brian Holland. At this time, according to some
Motown veterans, Martha and Brian Holland were dating. Whether or

not it was true, there is certainly a lot of bright, optimistic feeling conveyed by "Come and Get These Memories," cut in 1963. There is a joyful buoyancy to the melody and to Reeves's vocal that totally undercuts Eddie's lyric of painful breakup. Annette Sterling and Rosalind Ashford's backing voices are beautifully arranged, heightening the tune's hummability. It was a decidedly "pop" record, with Reeves's voice mixed way up front and the instruments buried in the mix. It was a catchy record that reached number six R&B in April 1963.

Though "Memories" was a good start for both the performers and their producers, neither the Vandellas nor H-D-H would achieve national prominence until "Heat Wave" that July. The driving baritone sax riffs and the clever subliminal use of Dave Hamilton's vibes in tandem with the piano add vibrant highs to the track and foreshadow Motown's future sound. The bass line still isn't as clearly defined as it could be, but the basic elements of the Motown sound (and of Berry's early production idiosyncracies) were being mixed successfully. As for Martha, her voice blasted through the production flourishes on "Heat Wave" in a defiant, lustful performance that shows an emotional intensity "Memories" had only hinted at.

Any question as to whether or not this strident, dense approach was what Martha and H-D-H should have been doing was answered by the cool reaction to the next single—the looser, more traditional R&B record "A Love Like Yours (Don't Come Knocking Every Day)." On the other hand, "Quicksand" (or "Son of Heat Wave"), cut in November 1963, was almost as well-received as its inspiration, and Martha's dream of stardom seemed complete.

Reeves's commercial success should have put her on top of the world. Yet even during this time of triumph, Martha felt subtly slighted by all the attention that Berry and H-D-H were giving to the Supremes, a female trio who'd had plenty of releases but no real hits. Reeves had the hits, so why did all the men at the company seem to think that Diane Ross, a thin, big-eyed gal with "airs" about her, was something special? Even at the time of "Dancing in the Street," released in the fall of 1964 —Reeves's greatest achievement—there was talk that the Supremes were going to get a big push. Perhaps Martha's anxiety over that threat was part of what made "Dancing" so powerful—her voice becomes a gut-grabbing celebration of dancing, communicating a guileless joy and a mature passion that allows Reeves's original to tower over the hundreds of covers recorded in its wake.

"Dancing" was not only Reeves's best vocal performance; it would also prove to be Mickey Stevenson's most important on-record contribution to Motown. With Marvin Gaye, for whom he'd already penned "Hitch Hike," "Stubborn Kind of Fellow," and "Pride and Joy," Stevenson had conceived a driving dance record that would be perfect for the summer. Moreover, he took the musical elements H-D-H had used on "Heat Wave" and tightened them up. The tambourines are right on the beat now, the horns, the backing voices of the Vandellas—Stevenson, Ivy Hunter, and Gaye—are arranged more elaborately, and James Jamerson's bass line is much higher in the mix. All the rhythmic elements, including Gaye's piano figure, bolster a rigid beat perfect for doing the jerk or Philly dog. Stevenson, a student of Berry's work and H-D-H's boss, had refined the formula and gotten a better vocal performance from Martha than anyone had before or would again.

By the summer of 1964, Martha and the Vandellas' period as Motown's most important female vocal group was about to end. Vandellas began to come and go. Martha's relationship with Berry and his sisters deteriorated as she complained about this and that, often with a seeming irreverence that enraged Berry. Martha's previous show-business experience made her more demanding, and less accepting of Motown's paternalistic attitude toward its artists. While others went along with the program, Reeves was constantly challenging it. Despite her hits and obvious commercial appeal, Martha had already reached the peak of her career, at least in terms of Motown's efforts to develop her as a show-business commodity. To Motown, she would remain a record seller, and nothing more.

The Beatles had six number-one hits in 1964—"I Want To Hold Your Hand," "She Loves You," "Can't Buy Me Love" b/w "Love Me Do," "A Hard Day's Night," and "I Feel Fine," and five other tunes that made the Top Ten, all of them musical manifestations of an international cultural phenomenon spearheaded by George Harrison, Paul McCartney, John Lennon, and Ringo Starr. They stormed America with a burst of R&B-flavored pop filled with striking imagery and an unexpectedly infectious good humor that unleashed a wave of dormant Anglophilia in "the colonies." In the Beatles' wake came the British Invasion—a wave of self-contained bands, many of whom learned their chops from old blues and R&B records—which overran the American music industry. In the face of Gerry & the Pacemakers, the Rolling Stones, Herman's Hermits, Billy J. Kramer and the Dakotas, the Animals, the Dave Clark Five, Freddie and the Dreamers (who could forget the infamous "Do the Freddie"?) and others, many American styles were literally pushed right

Marvin Gaye, with backing
vocals by the Spinners, performs
at Freedomland in the Bronx.
(Don Paulsen)

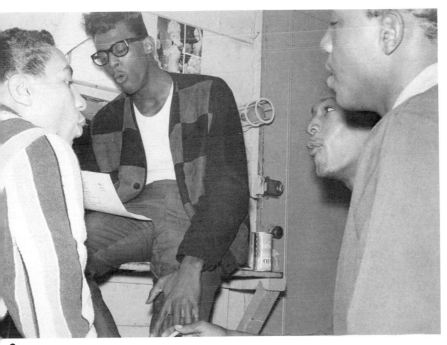

Smokey Robinson teaches (left to right) David Ruffin, Eddie Kendricks, and Paul
Williams "My Girl" backstage at the Apollo Theater in 1964 *(Don Paulsen)*

The Supremes—Florence Ballard, Diana Ross, and Mary Wilson—put their best foot forward in rehearsal for a television appearance. *(Don Paulsen)*

The Supremes share the stage with early rock 'n' roll star Lloyd Price at the close of an Apollo show. *(Don Paulsen)*

Cholly Atkins adds some new steps to the Four Tops' repertoire in the Apollo's basement. Though the steps seem small, notice the attention Lawrence Payton, "Duke" Fakir, "Obie" Benson, and Levi Stubbs give the choreographer. *(Don Paulsen)*

Motown's first female star, Mary Wells, chats with Dick Clark on "American Bandstand," back when it was still shot in Philadelphia. *(Michael Ochs Archives)*

The Temptations, dressed in the height of early sixties style, relax in the "star" dressing room at the Apollo. They are: (left to right) Paul Williams, Eddie Kendricks, David Ruffin, Melvin Franklin, and Otis Williams. *(Don Paulsen)*

The tempting Temptations in their smooth-moving prime. *(Kriegsmann/Ochs Archives)*

The Supremes bounce through "Baby Love," circa 1965. *(Don Paulsen)*

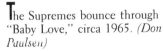

Martha and the Vandellas tape a television version of "Dancing in the Streets" at a Detroit auto factory. *(Michael Ochs Archives)*

Little Stevie Wonder's energy and youth always made him a popular performer. *(Michael Ochs Archives)*

Stevie Wonder in a pose characteristic of his youth: happy and laughing at a piano. *(Michael Ochs Archives)*

The mischievous Marvin Gaye.
(Kriegsmann/Ochs Archives)

Mary Wilson, Diana Ross, Smokey Robinson, and Florence Ballard prepare for a flight, with promotional bags in hand. *(Michael Ochs Archives)*

Backed by Flo Ballard and Mary Wilson, Diana reaches out to ask "Where Did Our Love Go?" in 1964. *(Kwame' Braithwaite)*

Smokey Robinson does an a capella rendition of his latest composition in the always cluttered Motown studio, circa 1964. *(Michael Ochs Archives)*

off the charts. The New York girl-group records, those coy, slick, studio tunes Motown's writers had tried to copy, now sounded dated next to the more aggressive, more masculine Brits. It seemed that young girls would rather oggle the "cute" male musicians of England than identify with female vocal groups.

Yet, in the midst of this profound change in popular taste, four decidedly feminine Motown records would capture the top spot: Mary Wells's "My Guy," and the Supremes' "Where Did Our Love Go?," "Baby Love," and "Come See About Me." They were Motown's only number-one records in 1964, and all four compare favorably with the Beatles' music during that frantic twelve months. Beatlemania swept across the land, but in Detroit, moves were being made that would be just as significant. Mary Wells, seemingly at the height of her career, was already falling. The Supremes were finally ready to exit the Motown incubator and, as a result, would spur the instigation of a crucial Motown division.

"My Guy," a perky love song propelled by a loping, bouncing beat that featured another delightful Smokey lyric ("Like a stamp to a letter, a bird to a feather, we stick together"), was a monster hit, bringing Wells a taste of international acclaim that would prove quite irresistible. Backed by the Earl Van Dyke band, Wells was the first Motown act to travel to England and she did it in high style, touring with the Beatles. She was treated like a queen, as John, Paul, George, and Ringo sang her praises to the English press. When Wells's record went to number one in England as well (it was the first Tamla–Motown single to accomplish that overseas), many observers traced its acceptance directly to the Beatles' aggressive advocacy of Wells, and of Motown in general. Capitalizing on Wells's sudden visibility, Motown quickly matched her with another Beatle favorite, Marvin Gaye, for two Top Twenty duets, "What's the Matter With You Baby" and "Once Upon a Time." The latter was a wistful, melancholy tune credited to Stevenson, Paul (who produced), guitarist Dave Hamilton (an already rare songwriting credit for a session player), and promotion director Barney Ales.

Motown was really working Wells, getting her on "The Steve Allen Show," getting articles placed in all the teen fan magazines, and hiring local bandleader Maurice King to polish her rather stiff stage act—all part of a commitment to her career. But Wells's head was swelling with ambition. Her exposure to the Beatles and their plans to make a film (which would eventually result in *A Hard Day's Night*) opened her eyes to another level of show business where a singer could, with the right management, become a movie star. It was an enticing dream, one Wells could envision coming true when Morty Craft, president of Twentieth Century-Fox Records, approached her about leaving Motown. Egged on by her husband Herman Griffin, once an unsuccessful Motown singer and now a staff writer, and by business adviser Robert West, she also entertained an offer from Atlantic Records. Craft offered her a $500,000 advance for a two-year option contract, quite a large amount of money for a black singer of that era. Still, it wasn't necessarily the money that attracted Wells—the deal clincher was the verbal promise of a film contract. In Charlie Gillet's book *Making Tracks,* Craft recalled telling Wells ". . . if she signed with us she'd get movie contracts and be a real star. That wasn't in the contract, of course, but why should I feel sorry I tricked her. If she's so crazy with overblown ambition she deserves what she gets."

Wells was soon busy looking for ways to escape her Motown contract. She had signed with Motown when she was seventeen years old, and in an attempt to have her Motown contract ruled void, she argued in court "that there is not now and never was any valid contract between her" and Motown, because she was underage when she signed. "Upon attaining her majority [on her birthday of May 13, 1964] notices of disaffirmance and repudiation were given" to Motown. In short, when Wells turned twenty-one, she considered herself a free agent.

It was certainly news to Motown. Brian Holland had hosted a twenty-first birthday party for Wells, where Berry later claimed to have given her a five-thousand-dollar mink stole as a sign of his affection. At that time he didn't know that Wells, Griffin, and West had already propositioned Stevenson and Brian Holland to secretly produce her for other labels.

In the ensuing legal battle Berry testified that he'd spent $300,000, by his own estimates, on training and promoting Wells. Sales manager Irv Biegel noted that Motown had supported Wells in the face of "spectacular failures" such as "Laughing Boy," of which, in an effort to "secure the maximum promotional effort from distributors," Motown had shipped 200,000 copies only to have half of them returned unsold. In short, in spite of the fact that the record went high on the pop and R&B charts, "Laughing Boy" lost money for Motown. Berry testified that he incurred the expense of hiring talent coach Maurice King to enhance Wells's career. But despite the testimony of Berry and a slew of Motown employees that Wells was a Motown creation and had falsely indicated to them that she was going to re-sign with the company, Judge John M. Wise gave Mary her freedom.

It was a genuine embarrassment for the company that one of Berry's discoveries had left in the wake of her biggest hit. Wells's departure might have dealt Motown a mortal blow, destroying Berry's strong-man image and depriving Motown of a consistent seller, if it had happened in 1963. However, the rise of the Supremes during 1964 would soften the impact considerably.

Moreover, the course of Wells's post-Motown career only confirmed the value of the bunker mentality Motown cultivated in its artists. Over the next years at 20th Century and Atco, Wells had six charting singles, but none charted higher than thirty-four. Despite "My Guy," which remained the highlight of her live presentation, Wells was suddenly washed up. Her career, featuring sporadic record releases over the next twenty years, has never recovered.

"I think what happened to Wells solidified the artists that were at Motown to Motown," says ex-staffer Tom Noonan. "They said, 'Wow, look at that. She left and she was a big star and she didn't make it. So there is something here in terms of writers and producers.'"

The Motown mystique led some to murmur that Motown even had used its influence to squash Wells as punishment for her defection. A close friend of Wells claims that through its contacts in black radio, Motown pressured deejays into not playing Wells's later records. But it is unlikely that Motown, then just becoming established and still regarded by most as a small label, would have had the clout in 1964 to stifle Wells's career so completely. If Wells's records had all been great and still were not played, there might be something to this speculation. But the records she made after her years at Motown were inferior, and it didn't take much encouragement for radio stations to avoid playing them.

In the *Billboard* of July 18 and *Cash Box* of July 25, Motown's Barney Ales issued a statement headlined REMINDER IS ISSUED BY MOTOWN that futilely asserted that "Mary Wells is still under contract to Motown," and wasn't free to negotiate with other labels. More interesting was its ending, in which Ales alerted the industry to a group of young ladies called the Supremes "who will have the next No. 1 record in the U.S. 'Where Did Our Love Go?' on Motown." Indeed, that very month the Supremes hit the top spot on both the *Billboard* and the *Cash Box* pop charts.

Ales's comments make it sound as if this achievement was the most natural thing imaginable. Simply a matter of Motown, in its wisdom, switching horses in midstream. At the beginning of a tour with Dick Clark's "Cavalcade of Stars"—a tour Berry and Esther had to cajole the then-hitless Supremes onto for a paltry five hundred dollars a show, the girls received little or no crowd response when introduced. But midway through the tour the audience cheered the Supremes almost immediately, especially for their new single "Where Did Our Love Go?" a quirky, repetitive ditty the girls, Mary in particular, didn't think much of. But it finally gave the girls a hit and placed them on the brink of a stardom no other black act had ever enjoyed.

It was a journey initiated by Florence Ballard, a plump, comely adolescent who resided with her mother Lurlee, father Jessie, and eleven other siblings in a five-room apartment in the Brewster–Douglass housing project. The development was low-rent yet well-kept public housing that served as home for the children of Detroit's post–World War II migration. For all intents and purposes, it was a ghetto, but for Detroit's blacks it was one with hope. The Ballards viewed it as a step up from older tenement buildings on the path to their new homes.

Then Jessie died of cancer in 1959, and those dreams were shattered. Fifteen-year-old Flo sought solace in music, be it Bach and Mozart in class at Northeastern High or doo-wop in the school lunchroom. Her music teachers felt she had wide vocal range and considerable technical polish for one so young. Eddie Kendricks and Paul Williams, members of a male vocal quartet called the Primes, loved her voice and introduced her to a local black entrepreneur named Milton Jenkins, who was then serving as their manager. Flo was soon singing around Detroit with the Primes.

At this point the history of the Supremes gets tricky to chronicle; each of the three principals has told differing versions, as have people who knew them from that period. Jenkins asked Flo if any of her friends could sing, as he planned to organize a girl group similar to those coming out of New York. She recruited Mary Wilson, a slender, shapely girl she'd known since childhood and who, with her mother, brother, and sister had moved into Brewster–Douglass right after its opening. She'd lived in Mississippi until she was eleven and wasn't as hardened by Northern life as her neighbors. Because she was cute and had an upbeat personality, Mary was very popular around the neighborhood, even though she claimed to be shy. As a child Mary may have lacked self-confidence, but it didn't stop her from dressing in a black leather jacket, wrapping a "doo rag" around her head like the slick dudes with processed hair, and slipping into jeans to sing "I'm Not a Juvenile Delinquent" at a junior high talent show.

Along with two other girls, Barbara Martin and Betty Travis, they formed the Primes' sister group, the Primettes. Soon after their founding, Travis's schoolwork took precedence over her singing, and she left. Eddie Kendricks recommended a girl who also resided in Brewster–Douglass,

Diane Ross, one of Fred and Ernestine Ross's six children. He was an assembly-line worker and president of UAW Local 174 and she worked as a domestic for rich white families in the posh Grosse Point area of Detroit.

Diane was a thin bundle of energy who swam, ran track, and sang in church, a "goody two-shoes" who at the same time managed to stay on friendly terms with the projects' many local gang members. She, like Mary Wilson, identified with the high, teeny-bopper voice of Frankie Lymon, singing "Why Do Fools Fall in Love," as she says, "where there was an echo and singing 'ahhh, ahhh' like when [Lymon] used to do the high part. That was one of my favorite songs." Though Diane's voice was noticeably thinner than those of the others, her perky personality came through when she sang. The Primettes decided they wouldn't have one lead singer, but would alternate between Flo and Diane, depending on the song.

Working with the Primes at sock-hops around Detroit, the girls developed confidence and showmanship, surprising themselves by winning first prize at the 1960 Detroit/Windsor Freedom Festival talent contest. Ross, already pushy, got them an audition at Motown through her neighbor Smokey Robinson in 1960. Opportunity, however, can never compensate for lack of poise or professionalism. Berry Gordy and Richard Morris, a minor producer-writer at the company, showed them the door, telling them to get more experience and maybe come back after they finished high school.

Another label, the feisty Lupine, which favored hardcore rhythm and blues, liked their juvenile style and used them to back up Eddie Floyd and the then-unknown Wilson Pickett on recordings. These future soul stars were just starting their solo careers after singing with local vocal groups. The Primettes themselves cut two singles on Lupine, both featuring Mary Wilson on lead. Though the records failed, the Primettes continued on, excited by their first small taste of stardom. Mary's family was supportive, as long as her school work didn't suffer. Diane's father was somewhat skeptical about show business, though her mother was supportive despite Diane's poor marks in music courses at Cass Tech.

It was outside school that Diane shined. She gave permanents for seventy-five cents a head, sewed clothes for a fee, and cleaned tables and fetched catsup after school in the basement restaurant at J. L. Hudson's department store, making Diane the first black busperson in the store's history. Even then, Diane Ross was a hustler who wanted to be somebody, and one suspects that if it hadn't been achieved through music, she would have found something else. Or, as an acquaintance of Diane's from that period says of her, "I have to tell you one thing about Diana Ross—I say it in her defense all the time—when she was poor, living in the projects, she was just as snotty as she is now, so her fame didn't make her snotty."

Flo's circumstances and attitude were very different. She considered the Primettes her group, even when she didn't sing lead, and she banked her future on making it. The result was a concentration on performing that, to her mother's consternation, overwhelmed everything else in her life. Unfortunately, schoolwork was among the things she neglected. Flo got caught up in pursuing this dream and dropped out of school in her senior year.

In 1960, the Primettes became regulars on the Motown scene, partly because the Primes had been signed by William Stevenson, and partly because the girls went to Hitsville after school every day they could. They would tell Stevenson, Clarence Paul, Brian Holland, Berry, and anybody else who'd listen for thirty seconds that they were ready for stardom. They clapped hands and sang on records when they were asked and volunteered to even when they weren't. After much internal discussion, "the girls," as Berry affectionately called them, were signed.

Once that was settled, Berry had them select a new name and Flo picked the Supremes ("At least I get credit for something," she'd later remark sarcastically). And so, on January 15, 1961, Florence Ballard, 17, Mary Wilson, 16, Diane Ross, 16, and Barbara Martin, 16, signed to Motown as the Supremes.

"I Want a Guy," released in late 1961, featuring Diane's high-pitched lead vocal, generated no interest. Shortly thereafter Martin, choosing romance over uncertain finances, got married and split. "Who's Lovin' You," the A side, written by Smokey (and recorded by the Jackson 5 in the seventies), made no impression in 1962, but the B side did. "Buttered Popcorn," credited to Berry and promotion director Barney Ales, picked up airplay around Detroit. It was a funky dance tune for which Flo provided the lead vocal. Ales, who obviously had a vested interest in the record's success, wanted to switch his promotional push to it. But Mary Wilson told Aaron Fuchs in 1982 (later recanting the story) that Berry refused to let Ales put a full-scale selling campaign behind it.

The decision not to promote "Buttered Popcorn" reflected Berry's decision to make Ross's untrained voice the sound of the Supremes. Mary and Flo reluctantly agreed to go along with Berry's decision, though both felt they were natural lead singers. Mary justified her supporting role by telling herself, and anyone who would listen, that singing background was as important as singing lead. Flo had a tougher time silencing her pride. She felt that, if given a fair chance, she might well win the job back. Looking back, one can see that the choice proved crucial to the Supremes, and to Motown's future. But back in 1962, no role at Motown seemed chiseled in stone, and so Flo could hope that things would change.

Certainly, Ross's voice proved to have no great appeal for record buyers in 1963 and early 1964. While the Marvelettes and Mary Wells prospered and Motown grew, the Supremes floundered. "Let Me Go the Right Way," produced and written by Berry and released in November 1962, dented the *Billboard* chart for six weeks, only reaching ninety, which suggests that it charted more as a result of Motown's enticing stations to play it than because of real sales. Smokey was called in to produce the Supremes' next song, "Breath-Taking Guy," but this tune didn't do the job either, dying at number seventy-five.

It was a dispiriting time for the Supremes. Flo, sensitive and insecure, was often depressed. Diane resisted suggestions from her family to give it all up. Though Diane was probably the most devoted of the three, there must have been times when she gave quitting a passing thought.

In this period the Supremes were often used as promotional items to induce good relationships with R&B deejays. As Jack Gibson, then Motown promotion director, explains:

> Motown didn't need any payola because Berry had so many acts available. Any act that wasn't working had to visit any deejay on the weekend we wanted them to. Let's say a jock had sock hops on Friday and Saturday nights. He wants Mary Wells, but he's told she's working the Apollo, but we got this girl group, the Supremes, with this hot record. Just play it three or four times an hour and let everybody know they're coming.
>
> The girls would be put on a bus to, say, Pittsburgh. Using my credit card I'd fly there before them, set up their rooms, and meet them at the station. Diana would say to me, "Why do you have a separate room?" I could see it coming. "I don't like to sleep with Flo 'cause she snores and Mary likes to sleep with the window open." She was persistent even then and she'd talk me out of my room.

But it would be the weekend's only victory for Diane. She would spend the rest of the weekend giving as many as eighteen performances in two nights. "We'd tell the jock if you make some money give them [the

Supremes] some and a ticket back to Detroit," says Gibson. "So the jock would go to various bars and get fifty bucks from each place to bring them in. Eight shows, fifty a bar, means four hundred dollars. That's just Friday to cover expenses. The next night's money is all his. We'd pick the Supremes up in a limo and drive them from bar to bar, where they'd sing over the record and then go to the next place and change in the bathroom."

This wasn't even the chitlin circuit; it was a tacky low-class version, something like what many one-shot disco acts would endure in the 1970s. But it was a road many of Motown's lesser acts would travel during the rest of the decade. Many wouldn't withstand the ignominy of it and would disappear into obscurity or grow bitter over being used as musical surrogates.

Instead, characteristically, Diane grew more determined. When the Supremes were the Motown Revue's opening act, Diane picked up the infuriating habit—at least to other acts—of "appropriating" bits of their stage act for the Supremes. More than one performer complained about Diane using his or her onstage patter or stealing a favorite step. She did anything she could to attract attention, and it worked. Berry was attracted by Diane's ambition, her willingness to learn (and listen), and her perky, debutante manner, qualities reminiscent of his wife Raynoma.

At Berry's suggestion, H-D-H began working with the Supremes (though some old hands speculate that a short-lived romance between Brian Holland and Diane played a part). Whether motivated purely by commerce, lust, or some combination of both, the teaming of H-D-H with the Supremes would prove one of the most creative production marriages in the history of popular music.

The Supremes' first record with H-D-H was "When the Lovelight Starts Shining Through His Eyes," a moderately successful harbinger of hits to come. It managed to reach number twenty-three in January 1964, the Supremes' highest-charting record to date and one close in feeling to the classic records to come. The melodic hook is strong, emphasized by the stacking of voices and instrumentation, and the rhythm has a sharp metallic sheen. "Lovelight" misses because the verses are strictly dullsville, a weakness that would haunt even some of H-D-H's best records. (The flip side is of historic interest because its title, "Standing at the Crossroads of Love," would be reworked three years later in the considerably more successful record "Standing in the Shadows of Love," by the Four Tops.)

The Supremes were happy to have a hit, albeit a minor one, though the girls weren't crazy about the material H-D-H was providing them. Mary, for one, was jealous of Martha and the Vandellas, claiming that Reeves was getting material that was more mature and womanly. As she recalled later:

> They were giving us sort of teeny-bop songs like "Where Did Our Love Go?" We didn't want to record that at all. They said, "Trust us, it'll be a hit." We said, "Yes, but it sounds like a kid song. It's not like Martha and the Vandellas' "Dancing in the Street." It's "Baby, baby." Very childish, right? Eddie [Holland] said, "Just trust us, it's going to be a hit." I was the main one saying we'll do it, but my God.

It's not surprising that Mary wanted to record "Where Did Our Love Go?" She almost ended up singing the lead vocal. In a debate that took only a few minutes, but would have a profound impact on the lives of all involved, Eddie voted for Mary to sing lead, while Brian and Lamont held out for Diane: As Eddie remembers:

> Well, I wanted Mary because at the time Mary had a softer sound and I knew the song required a soft sound. And I had never heard Diana sing soft before. So my natural instinct was to try Mary on it. I felt anybody [that] could sing the song soft and sensuous would have a hit on it. But they said, no, that Diana could sing softer, just drop her keys. Most of the songs that Diana was doing were in a somewhat higher register. So Brian and Lamont just dropped the keys and she sounded good.

Who knows what would have happened if Eddie hadn't been out-voted, and Mary had sung "Where Did Our Love Go?" Would Motown have been forced to push Mary or use both Mary and Diane as lead singers? Eddie Holland won't speculate, saying that there was no question that Diane Ross and no one else should have been the Supremes' lead singer. "She had a very unique sound—once you hear her you know it's her, you see," he says. "She doesn't sound like any other singers. That is one of the key things. Her ability is to have her own sound and she has a very sensuous sound. So if you take a person who has a distinct sound that's separated from other singers' sounds and then they have a sensuous sound that generates a lot of appeal, then they have it. And that's the key to her."

"Where" 's number-one status in July 1964 meant that from now on the Supremes would be Motown's top priority. Berry quickly had them sign a new contract, with visions of Mary Wells no doubt dancing in his head. In August, Mary, Flo, and Diane signed a document Motown labeled the "Second Recording Agreement." One can't say that they renegotiated their contract, since none of the three was represented by a lawyer. Motown had them sign the deal that Motown wanted, and what Motown wanted was total control with a minimum of risk—in fact, this contract would become a model for all future Motown contracts.

During the first year of the four-year agreement, each Supreme agreed to record a minimum of three masters for the sum of $12.50 "as a non-returnable advance against all the advance royalties." The standard royalty for Motown sessions was 8 percent of 90 percent of the wholesale (not the higher retail) price for all albums and singles, a payment, it should be noted, that was divided among the three members. So, actually, they were each paid 2.4 percent per record. Motown reserved the right to substitute for members within the group, so that if a record was issued under the Supremes title, but for some reason one of the Supremes wasn't present at the session, she received no money. Motown was not obligated to make any records by an artist during the life of the contract.

Here we should also make note of Motown's accounting system, an integral part of keeping the label solvent in the early days (and later a source of conflict.) When an artist, be it the Supremes or Marvin Gaye, signed with the Motown they were also made part of Jobete Music. So along with controlling their live appearance income, Motown received money from their signees in every manner a recording artist can be profitable. Such obvious conflicts of interest are rare now, but for black acts of the era, whether they were signed to Atlantic, Sun, Chess, or any of the other black-oriented indie labels, some form of this arrangement was standard. Cross-collateralization of these accounts, taking profits from songwriting to pay off debts for unprofitable recording sessions, was a great way to cut overhead and maintain cash flow. Quite clearly this wasn't nearly as helpful for the acts, who anticipated certain earnings on records, only to find royalties had been charged to pay for these "hidden costs." In this respect Berry Gordy was not a black business innovator but, with obvious forethought, maintained the unbalanced relationship between black artists and record companies whites had already established.

After Flo had picked the Supremes' name, Motown claimed it, stating that "In the event you withdraw from the group, or for any reason cease to participate in its live or recorded performances, you have no further right to use the group name for any purpose." (Motown was always passionate about controlling artist's names, even if they recorded under their given names. Beans Bowles, who signed as an artist to Motown in 1962 had to negotiate to get the rights to his name back when he left the company.) Loucye Wakefield, Berry's sister and then a Motown vice-president, signed the contract for the company.

It was during this summer of change that the name Diane Ross disappeared, replaced by the more theatrical and sophisticated *Diana Ross*. It was one of many calculated image-making moves that in 1964 would change the Supremes from a diligent, rather juvenile trio into the epitome of upwardly mobile, adult bourgeois charm.

The key to transforming the Supremes, and all of Motown's acts, was Artist Development, a wing of the organization that operated on an ad hoc basis prior to 1964. Artist Development's goal was to vanquish the unsophisticated, gum-cracking manners and attitude that so annoyed Beans Bowles during the first Motor Town Revue. Harvey Fuqua was given the assignment of supervising the schooling of Motown acts. He was aided initially by his wife Gwen and her sister Anna, both of whom had studied modeling and cosmetology. However, it wasn't until they brought their teacher, Maxine Powell, proprietor of the Maxine Powell Finishing and Modeling School, into Motown full-time that Artist Development was institutionalized.

A fixture in Detroit's black community since the opening of her school in 1951, Powell had met the Gordys in the mid-fifties after hiring the family print shop to prepare programs for a Las Vegas–style talent and fashion show. Esther got involved in organizing it, getting her husband George named master of ceremonies in the process. When he ran for the legislature, Powell supplied office space in a ballroom she owned.

The more time Powell spent around the Gordys, the more impressed she was with their drive, their business sense, and their camaraderie. As she told writer David Breskin, "It seemed that if one Gordy would stick his finger in your eye all the other seven might stick their finger in the eye and never ask why." When Berry started to find success in the record business, he asked Powell's opinion on some of his acts. It was nothing formal at first; just a friend helping a friend. But as time went on she found herself caught up in the family enthusiasm for Berry's record company, and, in 1964, when the expense of managing her ballroom and modeling school were getting out of hand, she was urged by Gwen to close shop and join Motown.

At a meeting that summer it was decided that Fuqua would run the in-house grooming operation, with Powell coming aboard as a special consultant, and it was her idea to call the division Artist Development. Later, the Supremes, the Temptations, the Miracles, Stevie Wonder, Martha Reeves and the Vandellas—the whole bunch—would hear Powell say that they were being trained to perform in only two places: Buckingham Palace and the White House.

That sounded extreme to some of the acts, but to Berry, Fuqua, and the old heads at Motown like Beans Bowles it was just the attitude they wanted to instill in their young charges. For all Berry's demands for quality songs and hit records, he was preaching that real longevity for the acts lay in reaching crossover (i.e., white) audiences with stylish live shows. Besides, with his own ITM acting as manager for these acts, he intended for them to make money, hit records or no hit records.

Lightening up a bit, Powell would mention playing the Copacabana, the Latin Casino, and the Elmwood Casino, noting those were the kind of places a Frank Sinatra played. Her talk was full of Dale Carnegie self-help jargon, with phrases like "Discover yourself" and "Your best friend is your self-image" rolling from her lips. But her message was uplifting for kids whose idea of classy dining was a meal at Hudson's department store cafeteria.

On a more practical level, Powell helped train Motown acts in the art of the inoffensive interview. Apparently, some early acts had said things in interviews that Berry hadn't liked. So Powell asserted, with Motown's wholehearted support, that Motown was a wonderful opportunity and a trailblazing institution. After all, Powell reasoned, even your mother and father make mistakes, so why mention anything "negative" for reporters to "misunderstand." And that became the Motown way.

Unacceptable or unsophisticated onstage deportment was one of Powell's pet peeves. She encouraged the Spinners' Bobby Henderson not to hunch over when he sang. She cautioned the singers not to protrude their buttocks on stage, feeling that it was like telling the audience to kiss their ass. She was also fanatical about acts not standing with their legs wide open. If you had to do a naughty step (which wasn't really necessary anyway, she felt), it must be done pleasantly and not draw undue attention. She thought that Marvin Gaye was a fine actor onstage—when he wanted to be. Too often, however, he was distracted and would rather have been doing something else. Technically, Marvin's only problem onstage was that he would close his eyes when he sang, another Powell no-no. Smokey liked to get down low and shout out a song, and so she worked with him on how to look graceful while doing it. She also felt that Smokey grimaced a touch too much onstage. It was one thing for him to be emotional, but why look sick doing it?

These were the kind of idiosyncracies and flaws Powell would work on eliminating when Motown acts came in to see her in Detroit. On the road, she acted as a chaperone for Motown's girl groups, primarily the Supremes. When an establishment show-business star like Joey Bishop stopped in after a show, it was Powell who greeted him at the door, offering a drink and small talk as he waited for the girls to finish changing. In those early days, when money was still a bit tight around Motown, Powell would improvise outfits for the Supremes, by going to a bridal shop, perhaps, and buying a jacket and matching strapless dress, then splashing it with rhinestones. When shoes wore out on the road, the Supremes and Powell would pick up pairs of white pumps for $5.95 and then tint them to match their dresses. Back in Detroit, Powell would go to Hudson's or Saks looking for sales, buying dresses two or three sizes too big for the girls because they were marked down, then altering them to fit.

Despite Powell's versatility, or perhaps because of it, when Berry felt Diana needed some extra-special grooming he went outside the company. Away from the envious eyes of Motown's other acts, he sent Diana to the John Roberts Powers School for Social Grace in downtown Detroit, a predominantly white operation that had a reputation in modeling circles for turning out quality products. The coaches at Powers felt Diana had potential; her huge eyes, warmth, and enthusiasm made her an able student. But she had some problems. For one thing, she wore much too much perfume. It was said at Powers that if Diana walked in a building five minutes before you, you'd know it; her perfume would still be hanging in the air. She favored a sickeningly sweet scent called Jungle Gardenia that, alas, smelled like it sounded. Although she had studied dress and cosmetology at Cass Tech, her choices of colors were often poor. She wore long "Minnie Mouse" false eyelashes on stage that the Powers people didn't object to, since they were grooming her for offstage poise, but her natural eyelashes were really quite beautiful.

During her five months at Powers Diana made a lot of progress, but her coach was never able to convince her to give up her three-inch-long blood-red false nails. Diana loved them and wasn't crazy about her own considerably shorter real nails. On that point she was stubborn. Powers's philosophy toward Diana was that they weren't teaching her to perform onstage, but off. So they'd spend hours showing her how to sit, how to stand in a crowd, how to put on a coat, and how to suppress the giddy laughs that bubbled out of her whenever she talked of the places she'd been or the famous people she was meeting. Success excited her and talking about it never bored her.

Perhaps because the Powers instructors weren't part of the Motown operation, Diana revealed feelings to them that would have freaked out the folks back at Hitsville. Diana often alluded to conflicts within the Supremes. Diana loved Mary. They both aspired to elegance and shared a petite, very feminine beauty. Moreover, Mary seemed content to let Diana be lead singer, something for which Diana was grateful. But Florence was a different story. With tears in her eyes, Diana told her instructors of how paranoid Flo could be sometimes. (For example, Diana said, Flo resented the time and money Motown was spending on Diana, and it upset her.)

Still, the overall impression of Diana, the Supremes, and Motown at Powers was of smart, well-motivated people on the move. Back on West Grand, the internal Artist Development department was growing, and in 1965 several new faces were added that made it possible for Motown to control every aspect of live performance. Cholly Atkins was hired as staff choreographer. Maurice King came aboard as the musical director of Artist Development, with arrangers Johnny Allen and Gene Kee working under him. All were essential to making Artist Development into an all-encompassing, Hollywood movie studio–inspired image machine.

When Harvey Fuqua flew down to Bermuda to recruit Cholly Atkins into the fold, the choreographer was working in Bermuda with Gladys Knight and the Pips, one of the many groups that swore by his "vocal choreography," a phrase that described the elaborate stage movements he devised that came to be as strongly identified with black music as gospel shouts. During his six years on staff at Motown, from 1965 to 1971, he refined his concept into a high-gloss commercial art.

Atkins's show-business story began in his native Buffalo, New York, where "I was always dancing, doing a soft shoe during our physical education class, participating in a school play. My first formal professional dancing was as a singing waiter at a place called Alhambra-on-the-Lake near Buffalo. I was doing it to collect some money in the summer." He befriended another waiter at the club, William Parton, and together they started singing and dancing as the Rhythm Pals, a nightclub act. During the early thirties they played clubs throughout the Northeast, gaining experience and a taste for bigger things.

In 1936 the Rhythm Pals went West, working clubs that dotted the California coast and appearing as extras in a number of films. Some were major studio productions (*San Francisco* with Clark Gable, *The Charge of the Light Brigade* with Errol Flynn), some were black musical shorts then being churned out by independent companies. For the next twenty years Atkins made a nice living traveling the world as an entertainer, teamed for most of that time with the great tap dancer Honi Coles in the legendary team of Coles & Atkins. By the mid-fifties Atkins was based in New York, sadly watching the rock and roll phenomenon blast apart the show-business traditions he had been reared on. The cool, respectfully hokey, self-consciously "classy" adult show-business styles of Atkins's generation were giving way to sweaty, raunchy, rambunctious, youth-oriented attitudes.

It was during this transitional period in American popular culture that Atkins found himself sharing the Apollo stage with untrained vocal harmony groups off the street corners of New York and, unexpectedly, discovered a new career. "As time went on," he remembers, "I'd show members of the different groups a few steps if I liked them. They were looking for a way to distinguish themselves from the crowd. Pretty soon word got around about what I was doing." Soon both the Shaw and William Morris agencies were asking him to work with the Heartbeats, the Cleftones, the Cadillacs, and others. By 1962 Atkins had given up the road and purchased studio space in the building now known as the Ed Sullivan Theater on 53rd Street and Broadway in New York. On Wednesdays and Saturdays he held classes, charging ten dollars an hour, and taught the cream of the harmony groups how to move in time. It got to the point where almost every group up at the Apollo was moving to Atkins's choreography.

Atkins had begun an on-again off-again relationship with Motown back in 1959, when the Miracles had enlisted his help after "Shop Around" had become a hit. So when Fuqua reached out to him, Atkins was well aware of the company and the significance of what Berry was trying to do.

"The company was all black at that time and I very much wanted to see it grow," he recalls. "I felt that I could help. I'd known Harvey since I did some work for the Moonglows and he wanted people he was familiar with. At that time we were very conscious of the black movement and to be part of something destined to become a first and contribute to the future of black artists was an opportunity." In addition, Motown gave

Atkins a steady salary ("The money was very good"), freeing him from the hassle of hustling up work.

Once relocated to Detroit, Atkins worked almost nonstop to meet the acts' insatiable need for new steps to match their new releases. "Semi-annually I had to revamp every act's show for when they went on the road," Atkins says. "Every time the company released a new single, that had to be integrated into the act. So whenever they were free I'd have them back in the studio working."

Though some later criticized Motown acts for a certain cookie-cutter sameness, Atkins insists:

> I let the punishment fit the crime. I let my clients' talent dictate to me what to do with them, and that basically stops anybody from looking like somebody else. You go with the degree of talent you have to work with, and you try to get the best out of that. We all have certain moves, the standard things . . . the level to raise the arm, how far to step forward, how far to step back. Everybody's doing the same thing at the same time, but they're doing it in their own way so you let them retain the one thing that they will think is very important, their individualism.

For all his talk of "individualism," Atkins was in wholehearted agreement with Berry and Powell that Motown acts should view Las Vegas and the "smart supper clubs," the places in which Atkins had plied his trade for so long, as their real goal. Today Atkins's words reflect the philosophy of integration that underpinned the Artist Development department:

> I get a big bang out of servicing my clients and becoming involved with them, because they have made a transition in coming from one type of show business, which is black. On the other side is another type of show business, like with TV and smart supper clubs. I've had all the experience in the world in those fields, so I take R&B artists and teach, educate, and prepare them for that transition from the chitlin circuit to Vegas.

One of Atkins's first assignments was to tone down the Miracles' stage show. The reason Atkins was asked to do so reflects how Artist Development was used as a powerful tool of image building:

The company felt there was so much going on that it was distracting from Smokey. So they discontinued the choreography. They didn't want the other guys to move around meaningfully, but just sway and be there to sing the background, then everybody would notice Smokey. But that didn't really work. It didn't set too well with the guys even though they went along with the program for a while.

It was Atkins who worked out the Miracles' best-known routine, their pantomime to accompany "Mickey's Monkey," where the four dancing Miracles did the "Monkey" dance, complete with banana peeling, tree climbing, and a see-no-evil move with their hands over their eyes.

The Primes (later renamed the Temptations) had a reputation as the flashiest Motown stage act, one earned in large part before Atkins joined Motown. Atkins felt they all moved well, but in many ways "were still very crude, and a couple had a hard time remembering their steps." There was a subtle rivalry between Atkins and Paul Williams, because as the group's best dancer and a former choreographer, Williams was particularly critical of any of Atkins's suggestions he didn't like. Because of their overall height—each was over six feet—and undeniable flair, the Primes/Temptations were crowd pleasers, but Atkins always felt that Gladys Knight and the Pips, a future Motown act with whom he'd worked with since 1963, was the best stage act to record for Motown.

Atkins's job became more difficult as certain Motown acts became successful. With success came laziness, complacency, the feeling that they didn't need to work hard. The Four Tops were cooperative, though they would eventually go back to the unflashy moves of their jazz days; Marvin Gaye ("He could have been the new Sam Cooke") was moody and reluctant to take Atkins's suggestions; the Spinners, with no hits to support, were like demons in Atkins's studio and could do the Temptations' show as well as the Temptations; the Supremes sought and received Atkins's most feminine, delicate moves, and the swaying hands, demure shakes, and back and forth turns Atkins designed for the Supremes—though to some degree caricatures of femininity—set a standard aspired to by every girl group to this day.

While Powell was in one part of Motown's Artist-Development building working on an act's look and Cholly Atkins was busy designing choreography, Maurice King was helping tie it all together. As musical director and assistant Artist Development director, King was involved in translating Motown hits into performable tunes, arranging pop standards for the voices of Motown singers, and integrating the entire package into a stage show that would work as well at the Apollo as it would at the Copa. It was an already difficult job, made even tougher by the fact that Berry insisted on having final approval over every onstage twitch and enjoyed making changes at the last minute. As King told the *Detroit Free Press*'s Kim Heron:

> He [Berry] liked to come in and have the show run down and sit back and scan every number and give it a rating of one to ten, then have a production meeting. He didn't change every number, but the ones he did would require substantial change if it is to be performed as he sees it. Usually the way he wants it done turns out very well, but I never thought he gave us enough time. In one of those meetings I said, "Mr. Gordy, I'd like to know one thing. Is it possible that you could review our shows a little earlier? Look at the rundowns, make the corrections and give us at least a couple of days to correct it?" You know what he said to me? "Well, no," he said. "I like to see you guys work under pressure. You work better under pressure."

Berry wouldn't have put the pressure on if he didn't think King could handle it, and the veteran bandleader definitely could. Like Atkins, his experience in show business prefigured the rhythm and blues era, and he brought a mature perspective to the stage shows of Motown's youthful acts. Born in Greenwood, Mississippi, and subsequently a music major at Tennessee State University, King had moved to Detroit in 1939 and used his formal musical training, a rarity among black musicians of the era, to pick up arranging gigs. King's first big break came in 1945 when he was named manager-chaperone-musical director for the International Sweethearts of Rhythm, a sixteen-member all-girl jazz big band composed of six whites, six blacks, two Mexicans, one Chinese, and one American Indian. They toured Europe and the United States from 1945 to 1949, entertaining troops in the postwar era abroad and battling Jim Crow laws in the American South (some white band members darkened their faces with chalk to avoid chants of "nigger lover" when they traveled).

The notoriety King earned while traveling with the Sweethearts led him to his most important pre-Motown association in Detroit. On April 21, 1950, the Flame Show Bar opened with Maurice King and his Wolverines as the house band, a spot they'd occupy for the next eleven years.

"It was not a plush supper club," King recalled. "It didn't profess to be. It didn't serve food, but it was the most lively, most friendly and comfortable place with the best entertainers in the city." As a result of his Flame gig King worked with all the nation's black acts, people such as Della Reese and Dinah Washington, performers who walked the line between jazz, blues, and the jumpier dance styles that were emerging out of swing and evolving into rhythm and blues. King grew adept at arranging all these styles (his band backed Elvis Presley when he first played the Fox Theater) and developed a reputation as a man who knew the intricacies of a "classy" show. Reese, Johnnie Ray, LaVern Baker, ventriloquist Willie Tyler, and Gladys Knight and the Pips all befriended King and sought his advice.

King's tenure at the Flame ended in 1961; subsequently, he worked at several local clubs and advised young acts, including several Motown signees, on their stage shows. Berry had, in fact, hired him specifically to work with Mary Wells. As King told Kim Heron, "I was taking them to one of the private studios I rented in the city and he asked me why should I knock myself out doing all this. 'Come into the company and teach everybody.'"

Aside from his official duties, King also served as Motown's unabashed cheerleader, often calling Artist Development "Motown U" and Berry "the dean." Where most of the musicians at Motown, even those who were treated very well, kept their distance from the corporate hierarchy, King was a company man all the way, and it didn't always sit well with the other players. A rival bandleader called King "a politician musically. Let's say it like that. Now whoever the winner is, right or wrong, that's where he's going."

So even though King grew close to the Spinners—he'd work with them into the eighties—he never criticized Motown for relegating them to the status of opening act for Motown's big names. During their eight years signed to Motown the Spinners released eight singles; their first three years at Atlantic they had thirteen singles released. King was sympathetic to the Spinners, but defended Motown. "But there was a plan," he told a Detroit reporter. "And Motown delivered the baby. They were breaking ground and you had to do it right." This attitude—infuriating as it was to some of his contemporaries—allowed King to fit in nicely with the positive pronouncements of Powell and Atkins. Clearly Artist Development was more than a place to learn a few steps. The acts were inculcated with a philosophy of noble striving, loyalty, and acceptance of traditional show-business entertainment values.

King's best known contribution to Motown was the insertion of an ambiguously pro–civil-rights monologue into the Supreme's performance of the *West Side Story* show stopper "Somewhere." Ross talks about a little stream that starts at the top of a mountain and works its way down to the sea. Bathed in a bright white spotlight, music murmuring in the background, Ross, in her breathy, optimistic voice, says, "Certainly we can do that too," and then adds, "Free at last . . . free at last." It was socially conscious bullshit and at first Berry didn't like it. Wasn't this a little too heavy for the Supremes? Apparently not. It worked like a charm, drawing cheers from sentimental nightclub audiences and even shaking up President Lyndon Johnson who, after hearing the monologue at a Los Angeles show, went out of his way to meet Ross and to tell her, "It's going to happen. Little by little, we're getting there."

The Temptations would have said "amen" to that. For almost as long as Berry had been writing songs, members of the Temptations had been bouncing around Detroit, displaying great voices, dancing real flashy, and selling no records—until 1964's "The Way You Do the Things You Do," which climbed to number eleven on the pop chart. As mentioned previously, that song had resulted from an internal Motown songwriting competition in which Smokey had bested his mentor Berry Gordy by a wide margin according to a vote among company creative personnel; now, later in the year, they were the focus of another one-sided battle over who would write and produce their music.

After years of waiting patiently, Norman Whitfield had finally become a Motown producer after taking Beans Bowles's advice and working with some of the company's lesser acts. He responded with "Needle in a Haystack," regarded today as a minor girl-group classic, and the Marvelettes' bubbly, fast-paced "Too Many Fish in the Sea," both songs with lyrics provided by a moonlighting Eddie Holland and an unusually gritty musical setting for Motown. These songs and others earned Whitfield a long-awaited shot at working with the Temptations. Whitfield had fallen in love with the group's harmonies when he saw them playing around Detroit as the Primes. So Whitfield, playing can-I-top-Smokey, cut "Girl (Why You Wanna Make Me Blue)" for the Temptations, a driving mid-tempo song, featuring Eddie Kendricks's wispy falsetto, that reached number twenty-six on the pop chart.

Unfortunately for Whitfield, in the competitive atmosphere at Motown, that promising start wasn't enough. Smokey was as charmed by the Temptations' sound as Whitfield was, and from 1965 to 1966 would win vote after vote, over Whitfield and Motown's other producer-writers, to produce for them. To Whitfield, Smokey personified the "in" group clique against which Whitfield often found himself battling. Smokey was a sweet guy, but he was also Berry's best friend and a vice-president, and Whitfield made it his personal goal to usurp him as the Temptations' producer. It would force Whitfield to refine his craft and to seek out a new lyricist, since Eddie was now writing solely with Lamont Dozier and Brian Holland.

Looking back at 1964, the Temptations' Melvin Franklin would observe, "I suppose Norman took time to find himself, so to speak." And the same could be said for the Temptations. On stage they were slick, sophisticated purveyors of urban doo-wop, yet the roots of all five of its most famous members were in the deep South. Eddie Kendricks and Paul Williams grew up together in Birmingham, Alabama, while Melvin Franklin was reared in Montgomery. Otis Miles, aka Otis Williams, was from Texarkana, Texas, and David Ruffin came from the small rural town of Meridian, Mississippi. But the road they all took to the Motor City was different.

Eddie Kendricks and Paul Williams quit school and left Birmingham in 1956, two wide-eyed seventeen-year-olds hoping to be stars like Clyde McPhatter and Little Willie John. Kendricks and Williams drew on savings to get as far as Cleveland, where both had relatives. They scrambled for a while, working as busboys and sleeping in bathtubs, before meeting a music hustler named Milton Jenkins. Jenkins heard the duo crooning at a basement party and invited them to come to Detroit, where they moved in with him. But an increasingly homesick Kendricks was concerned, because things just weren't happening fast enough. He went back to Birmingham and it took some powerful convincing by Williams to get him to come back. In fact, Kendricks still might not have made it back if he hadn't "kinda borrowed" fifty dollars from his brother Robert. Back in Detroit, Kendricks joined Williams in organizing the quartet called the Primes, who engaged in organized group vocal battles at clubs and house parties. It was at one such doo-wop battle, according to Kendricks, that they faced and bested Otis Williams and the Distants.

The Distants had cut a few sides at that point, but nothing of national importance. Otis, a resourceful Montgomery, Alabama, native, who had changed his last name from Miles to Williams, was struggling to keep the Distants together. Street-corner harmony groups were revolving doors, and it wasn't unusual for one to go through innumerable name and personnel changes in a few short months. Singers were everywhere; you could pluck them off any corner, and that's how Melvin Franklin became the Distants' bass singer. Sometime after bass voice Arthur Walton had decided he'd had enough of the Distants' low pay and tacky gigs, Williams heard fifteen-year-old Franklin harmonizing on a corner with some friends. After Williams assured Franklin's mother that performing wouldn't interfere with his studies—even though Williams himself had dropped out of high school after a teacher told him singing distracted from schoolwork—Franklin joined the Distants.

By 1958 Kendricks, the two Williamses, and Franklin were hanging out with a tall, good-looking ladies' man and sometime second tenor named Eldridge Bryant. After several groups (the Questions, the Elegants) featured some combination of these vocalists, they finally came together as the Elgins, and then as the Primes in 1959. By this time Jenkins was out of the picture. With Paul Williams providing the steps, the Primes built a reputation around town for their spirited live performances. They were making fifteen dollars per man by now, which, considering that they had not had a hit record, wasn't bad. Sometime in 1960 they met Berry Gordy and recorded for a short-lived Motown-affiliated label called Miracle (What was Berry thinking of when he put the slogan "If it's a hit, it's a Miracle" on the label?) They cut a single, the horrible "Oh Mother, Oh Mine," and the promising dance tune "Check Yourself," with Paul Williams on the fiery lead vocal. When El Bryant began ego-tripping, finding hanging out with the ladies more enjoyable than singing, the group asked David Ruffin, a singing drummer the Primes had met playing at an Ann Arbor nightclub, to come aboard.

David was a pure gospel singer with a raspy, hard-edged voice and a stage presence that got turned on at the strangest times. One night when Bryant was still with the group, David came onstage, took the microphone from Paul and, to the crowd's delight, did a frantic Jackie Wilson imitation. This Meridian, Mississippi, native had previously cut for Anna Records, first as a member of the Voice Masters and later as a solo, but with no success. In 1962 Ruffin had made "Mr. Bus Driver, Hurry" and "Action Speaks Louder Than Words" for songwriter Billy Davis's Check-Mate Records. The latter is remembered by R&B oldies fans as a pretty powerful no-holds-barred piece of secular gospel. Again, no sales. But musicians around Detroit knew he had star potential.

It wasn't long after Ruffin's impromptu performance that he replaced Bryant, and the lineup was finally set. Paul Williams was the baritone and initially the chief lead singer; Otis Williams sang baritone and second tenor; Franklin, of course, was bass; and Kendricks provided high tenor and lead vocals. With three lead singers they took to billing themselves rather generously as the group with "five lead singers."

But just because the Temptations (they changed their name at Berry's behest) were musically in harmony didn't mean that everyone was happy. Despite their onstage unity, the Temptations were really two pairs of friends and one outsider with his own agenda. Kendricks was four years older than Franklin and often treated the bass singer like a kid, which irritated Otis Williams, who regarded Franklin as a younger brother. Aside from that problem, Kendricks and Franklin just butted heads on general principle, since both were very strong-willed and sure of themselves. Sometimes it seemed they disagreed just so they wouldn't have to admit the other was right. Paul Williams was tight with Kendricks and tended to side with him in any internal disputes, though both he and Franklin played peacemaker whenever possible. Ruffin was Franklin's mother's first cousin, so they'd known each other since their childhood. Franklin liked Ruffin and was in awe of his ability to mesmerize audiences with his singing. But he wondered whether David really had the compromising temperament a team player needed. Was David really just using the Temptations to ignite a stalled solo career? In those days David denied it, but as guitarist Dave Hamilton put it, "David had his own personality and his personality was a little bit different than their personality because they would stick together. They were pretty tight. . . . David, I don't think he laid with them like that because he was David. Man, you know, David is going to be David."

From 1962 until late 1963 the Temptations released a string of what were, by Motown standards, unsuccessful singles. Only the first, "Dream Come True," a sparsely arranged gospel harmony record that made number twenty-two on the R&B chart, even smelled like a hit. Mickey Stevenson would describe this period as a time the Temptations "were woodshedding," getting prepared for Motown's big push. That might just be hindsight talking, but certainly Motown was watching the group and investing time in its growth. The story is told that after a Motown Christmas show at the Fox Theater in 1963, Berry stood in the lobby asking fans which of the Motown acts they'd liked the best. The overwhelming response was the Temptations, who, unlike the Miracles, Mary Wells, and Marvin Gaye, had generated only sporadic local sales.

"Those cats put on a show," says Hamilton. "Them guys, they worked. They worked hard. They sweated, you know, they'd be wringing out with sweat. Then they weren't making no hell of a lot then, 'cause the different places where we would be playing, hey, sometimes man you wouldn't want to stay. We stayed because we had to, you know, but some of them places was a mess."

They played as hard as they worked, and Beans Bowles gave them several lectures about not driving and drinking, about getting the proper sleep after gigs instead of hanging out all night, and about stretching money, not burning it. Alas, the boys weren't always listening. For a trip from Detroit to Atlanta they chose to borrow a Cadillac rather than travel by bus like everyone else. "When you borrow a man's car, anything that goes wrong is your expense," Beans warned them. "When they went down they had to spend all the money on gas and then the muffler fell off and they had to buy a new muffler. They didn't make a dime."

Both Berry and Smokey had failed to squeeze a hit out of the Temptations until the contest between Berry and Smokey that yielded "The Way You Do the Things You Do" in 1964. Smokey chose Kendricks, the Temptation with the voice closest in texture to his own, for the lead, and it was his creamy smooth falsetto tenor, gliding through a great melody and over a perky rhythm track, that took "The Way You Do the Things You Do" to the brink of the pop Top Ten, finally peaking at number eleven. Unfortunately, as Berry's policy dictated, it was followed by a sound-alike called "I'll Be in Trouble," which deservedly fizzled at thirty-three. Whitfield then had his shot with "Girl (Why You Wanna Make Me Blue)," in 1964, blew it (the record only went to number twenty-six on the pop chart), and for the next year and a half watched Smokey give the Temptations a string of hits.

A lot happened to the Temptations during this period. Out went their processes and in came carefully modulated Afros. In came top hats and tails, open silk shirts à la Harry Belafonte, and suits with tight-fitting jackets. In came "Old Man River" for Melvin to show off his maturing bass and out went cheap hotels, as the Temptations started earning eight thousand dollars a month, a figure that would quickly escalate. Out went many of Paul Williams's "street" steps and in came "the Temptations' Walk," a simple shuffle step that when performed by the temptin' Temptations just looked so cool. Most profoundly, however, out went the "five lead singers" idea, and up front went David Ruffin.

The Ruffin era began magnificently with "My Girl," which in January 1965 became the Temptations' first simultaneous number one pop and R&B single, and their first million-seller. Ruffin got the lead because "the song was a romantic song, a sweet song, so I thought a counterbalance to that would be to use David on lead, who had a rough kinda voice,"

100

Smokey told *Black Music* magazine. This bit of intuition was worth millions to Motown, for Ruffin achieved the effect Smokey had intended, just as he would through five straight singles, all of which went Top Five on the R&B singles chart and to at least the Top Twenty on the pop side. At first, as on "My Girl," "It's Growing," and "Since I Lost My Baby," Ruffin didn't deviate much from the melodies, crooning coolly with much of the charming soul associated with Sam Cooke. His interpretations of the plaintive "Since I Lost My Baby" (number four R&B, 1965) and the delightful "It's Growing" (number three R&B, 1965) are both reminiscent of Cooke's rendition of his posthumous hit "A Change Is Gonna Come." On "Since I Lost My Baby," perhaps the definitive Ruffin performance, he sounds stronger, deeper, and huskier. He starts "Since I Lost My Baby" sounding almost hoarse, then his voice deepens and takes on a husky, world-weary quality that matches one of Smokey's most melancholy lyrics.

Listening to Ruffin, one can easily hear the earthy qualities that would influence whiskey-voiced English rock singer Rod Stewart, who set David Ruffin as his standard of vocal excellence. On the early hits, Ruffin achieves a fascinating marriage of subtlety and power. Music historian David Morse writes:

> [Ruffin's] experience in gospel groups . . . enabled him to bring an unusual earnestness to the singing of secular love lyrics. In fact he can be compared only with Ray Charles in his ability to take the most threadbare ballad and turn it into a dramatic and completely convincing emotional statement. If ever the Temptations teetered on the brink of sentimentality, they were saved from it only by Ruffin's rasping, carefully articulated and deeply soulful delivery.

Though relegated by Smokey to background singers, the vocal arrangements the other Temptations created around Ruffin were quite creative and left a distinctive mark on all of these songs. Kendricks's rising *do-do-do* falsetto riffs are sprinkled throughout "Since" and "Don't Look Back." Paul Williams injects the title in "My Girl" at several key spots, bouncing nicely off of Ruffin's lead vocal. In all of the songs in Ruffin's string of hits, Franklin's bass booms, sometimes injecting a wordless phrase, as on "Since," or just laying a heavy bottom on any number of Temptation harmony parts. With all this talent backing Ruffin's lead, the hit potential Berry and Smokey saw in the Temptations was finally realized, while Smokey's poetic lyrics received some of their most enduring recitals.

Ironically, Smokey's run of success with the Temptations ended with a vibrant, yet decidedly uncharacteristic triumph. "Get Ready" was the group's first number one R&B single since "My Girl," but that was all it had in common with that delicate love song. This driving, funky dance track—listen to bassist Jamerson and drummer Benjamin jam—was, in Smokey's words, "one of the most direct songs I've ever written." In a clever move, Kendricks was given the lead, and his feathery falsetto was a brilliant contrast to the percolating bottom-heavy rhythms. Further emphasizing Kendricks's high tenor was the use of Franklin's bass to "shadow" Kendricks on several lines of the verse, one of those production touches that made Motown's records so special.

"Get Ready" was an attempt to put a little grit in the Temptations' sound, and the black audience bought it. But the record only went to number twenty-nine on the pop chart, a fall from grace with the pop audience that Berry couldn't tolerate from a group that had become so important to Motown's image. And so, at a Motown product evaluation meeting in 1966, the Temptations' production reins were passed from Smokey to Norman Whitfield, marking a most profound shift in power. The Temptations would be the last of the big-money Motown acts, aside from the Miracles, that Smokey would write and produce for on a consistent basis. With the Temptations now under his control, Whitfield—once the quiet, overly observant outsider—would soon emerge as one of Motown's most dependable and visionary creative forces.

All of a sudden, in the early months of 1965, the record industry began wondering just what was happening in Detroit. True, Berry Gordy had been writing hit records since the mid-fifties, and his Motown and associated labels had been fairly consistent hitmakers since their inception. But in 1964, something else began to happen. Motown had a sound. Records such as "Baby Love" and "Baby I Need Your Loving" and "Come See about Me" and "How Sweet It Is (to Be Loved by You)" and "Nowhere to Run" all bore a distinctive, instantly recognizable signature. Drumsticks pounded the skins on every beat, a beat accentuated by tambourine, guitar, and often vibes, while the bass rolled forward like a speeding locomotive. Guitars and pianos and organs all squeezed into a cluttered mid-range while blustery horn charts and weirdly arranged strings lingered in the background. The lyrics were all right; they weren't poetic like Smokey's, but they were strong enough on the chorus (and man, sometimes these songs seemed to be all chorus and no verse), and the words burned into your brain.

It was dubbed "the Motown Sound" by outsiders, a phrase Berry capitalized on by stamping the more innocuous slogan "The Sound of Young America" on his product, beginning with the Temptations' *Greatest Hits* album in 1966, an album that featured liner notes by another popular black entertainer with appeal to all Americans, comedian Bill Cosby. Berry was making his case for the universality of Motown's music and, as usual when it came to music and marketing judgments, he stood on very firm ground.

Motown's sound was now surely the sound *all* young Americans loved. With the exception of the Beach Boys, no other American musical institution would so effectively challenge the Beatles' monopoly of the pop charts. In February 1965, the Supremes, about to enjoy their fourth of five straight number-one singles with "Stop! In the Name of Love," were the flagship, but "the Motown Sound" permeated every level of Berry's operation, giving the company a musical identity and an incredibly commercial sales tool. From 1964 through 1967, Motown records accounted for fourteen number-one pop singles, twenty number-one soul singles, forty-six more Top Fifteen pop singles, and seventy-four other Top Fifteen soul singles. Many of the hits by the Supremes and Four Tops are acknowledged classics, but then so are the Elgins' "Heaven Must Have Sent You," Kim Weston's "Take Me in Your Arms (Rock Me)," Junior Walker and the All Stars' "(I'm a) Road Runner," and the Miracles' "Mickey's Monkey." The impact of the "Sound" is clear when you consider that every one of the songs just mentioned—a mere sampling of the music—has been successfully re-recorded by artists from all parts of the musical spectrum. The Motown sound was magical, it was fun, and it was lucrative. It was the sound of men who loved what they were doing, though to this day they still don't agree on just how it was done. All that is certain is that they made great music.

It was three-thirty A.M. on a hot mid-sixties summer night in Detroit, and Hank Cosby had an idea. He wanted to cut some tracks for Stevie Wonder's next album and, as was his practice, had picked this quiet time between night and morning to record, a time he felt was special for making music. Sitting in the studio with engineer Lawrence Horn, he watched as the "Funk Brothers" assembled below him in the studio. Nobody outside Detroit knew all the players by name, but they may have been the best band in America.

Earl Van Dyke, tall, angular, shrewd, worldly, and laconic, sat behind the Steinway piano, playing some "jazzy" chords. To his right, holding his Fender Precision bass, was James Jamerson. In his large, pliant fingers, the instrument looked like a toy. His perpetual scowl—his "game face" —was in place as cigarette smoke curled mysteriously around his head, adding to the intensity of his darkly handsome features. Behind Jamerson and to his left, in the corner of the room behind two screens, drummer Benny Benjamin smiled, rubbed his slicked back, greasy hair, then tapped out a jazz rhythm on snare and hi-hat. Benny was in good spirits and had amazed everyone by getting there (almost) on time. "Papa Zita" often found it difficult to find the studio on time, even when he had, like Van Dyke and Jamerson, just left the Chit Chat Lounge twenty blocks away.

There were a couple of other Funk Brothers in the room, such as guitarist Robert White, who sat quietly in a chair under the control booth's window. But it was Van Dyke, Jamerson, and Benjamin who were the key men, the men Stevenson was counting on to turn whatever chords and lead sheets he gave them into pulsating commercial music. They were Motown's backbone, the men who played the music that made America dance.

The Funk Brothers, with the exception of a couple of European tours, stayed in Detroit at Berry's request, playing local clubs, always on call for last-minute sessions. Financially, it wasn't a bad gig. The regulars were all under contract to Motown, which guaranteed them a steady income that, when augmented by unauthorized moonlighting, could earn them each as much as $100,000 a year.

By 1965, Motown was recording in New York and Los Angeles with regularity, and songwriters signed to Jobete on both coasts used local rhythm sections on their demos. Tapes of songs written and produced by Detroit staffers were often sent to New York for overdubbing of certain parts, or to get a different feel on certain tracks. Ace New York session drummer Bernard "Pretty" Purdie claimed he played on many demo sessions that Motown later released as singles with no changes. Motown's rigorous touring schedules led many acts to hastily record their vocals on the road in rented studios, so that the product flow would be constant; the Supremes and the Four Tops did this often, usually when Motown was anxious to release a single or quickie album to capitalize on a current hit.

Berry knew the worth of his Detroit musicians, as was illustrated by the story Choker Campbell told about him interceding on his behalf with the Motown bureaucracy. However, that didn't mean he paid them top dollar until he had to, and it didn't mean he felt they should be stars. *None* of Motown's albums carried the musicians' credits until the seventies. The musicians were *never* cited by name in interviews with artists, producers, or executives during the sixties. When Motown acquiesced to releasing an Earl Van Dyke and the Soul (Motown didn't feel the word "funk" was right for the label's image) Brothers album, the players were forced to cut instrumental versions of Motown's hits. Compounding the musicians' frustration, all the solos were curtailed to conform strictly to the melody line, so that even on their own album they weren't allowed to stretch out.

In the case of Van Dyke, Jamerson, and Benjamin this seems an extreme waste of talent. Like Berry, they had been seduced by the complex beauty of bebop, that Charlie Parker and Dizzy Gillespie creation, and bebop's harmonic concepts informed everything they played. The families of all three had moved to Detroit during the great black migration to the North, and as children they benefited from the kind of polished musical education unavailable to most Southern blacks. Van Dyke had been taught to read music by the age of seven after his father, a classical violinist-turned-Ford worker ("Wasn't much call for black violinists in those days," says Van Dyke), heard him play *Lieberstrom* on the family piano. Jamerson learned bass at Northeastern High.

As teens they were part of Detroit's great musical flowering of the fifties. At sixteen, Van Dyke was hanging out with jazzmen Barry Harris, Tommy Flanagan, Roland Hanna, Yusef Lateef, and Kenny Burrell, "getting together after school and jamming. Hank Jones would be teaching all us young piano players different tunes. We all started out playing bebop." Van Dyke recalled:

> When I was in my teens I used to play jazz at this place where the musicians hung out. There were different groups in there every week. Barry Harris, the piano player, was the leader of us young guys. As we got older, we started playing in clubs and all the college dances. We'd play at this popular after-hours spot, the Minor Key. At this time I started playing with the heavyweights like Dizzy Gillespie when they hit town. Different musicians from New York would come in and jam.
>
> Detroit musicians back in that time weren't in competition, but just out to help one another. I remember the hardest tunes for me to get were "Cherokee" and "Lush Life." Hank Jones taught it to Barry Harris. Barry taught it to me. I taught it to somebody else.

In later years they'd look back on the fifties as a golden era when they played for their own enjoyment, "learning together, exchanging ideas with no egos involved," as keyboardist and freelance Motown session player

Johnny Griffith recalls. From these all-night (and sometimes all-weekend) jam sessions, the players developed a camaraderie and understanding (they called it "the Detroit way") upon which Motown would later capitalize.

But first came the musicians' baptism into the real world of music. As much as they loved jazz, they quickly discovered that it was rhythm and blues that paid the bills. Van Dyke's first experience on the road came with Emmett Sleigh and his Sleigh Riders. Sleigh was an ex-jazz guitarist who'd gigged with Louis Armstrong, but was in the midst of a nondescript career in R&B. In 1959, Van Dyke graduated to the big time as pianist with R&B star Lloyd Price's big band. On the road he'd bump into James Jamerson, who, at about the same time, had moved from Jackie Wilson to the Miracles. Van Dyke had moved to the band of yet another young Detroit resident, Aretha Franklin, in 1962, when Mickey Stevenson asked if he'd be interested in a job back in Detroit. Benny Benjamin had already been recruited by Stevenson; unlike Van Dyke and Jamerson, he had stayed close to home.

"I remember talking with Jamerson backstage in the Apollo Theater when we had both been offered regular gigs with Motown. He asked me if I was going home, meaning back to work in Detroit. I told him only if they make me the right offer. The right offer in those days was one hundred and fifty dollars a week." Van Dyke laughs. "That was good then." In the beginning, however, the staff musicians ended up rarely taking home more than $135. Still, it was enough to bring them under Motown's wing.

Soon after he came home, Stevenson named Van Dyke bandleader, telling him, "I was the most qualified, but that wasn't true. I don't think I could play more than anybody else there." The job basically entailed "keeping up with the band, and since I had most of the Motown musicians in my band working every night, I was the one who usually knew where they were."

Van Dyke, designated bandleader in 1964, enjoyed a friendly relationship with Berry. "To me he was always fair. I can't tell you much from the artists' side, though I cut some sides. He never treated me like an artist. He always treated me like a musician." It would prove to be an important distinction, as Choker Campbell could testify. The bandleader's job had become available following the departure of Campbell in 1963. Choker organized a sixteen-piece big band, and got the musicians to waive session fees in exchange for a sixteen-way split on any royalties. The bandleader saw this as a chance to record some of the more complex music Motown normally wouldn't allow. The album, cut at the Motown-owned Greystone Ballroom, was titled *Shades of Time*. It was scheduled for release once, then bumped off the schedule to accommodate a Stevie Wonder album and never put back. "I checked for six months and finally I just gave up," recalls Campbell. "That's what made me say 'To hell with the whole thing.'"

According to Van Dyke, "Berry never let anybody bother the musicians," as long as they remained musicians and not artists. And he paid them, too. Van Dyke made $66,000 at Motown in 1965 and $100,000 in 1966, a figure that includes "outside work." "In that time it was rare for a musician to own his own home, but I did. Everybody there was buying Cadillacs. Everybody had some money. If you didn't come out of Motown with some money or some property, it wasn't Berry's fault."

However, it took a while for Motown's pay scale to become so generous. In 1962 Motown was paying $7.50 a side to a musician and, if you were a jazz man signed to Jazz Workshop, like Johnny Griffith, Stevenson might slip you another $10 out of respect. If you had patience, you might clear $80 to $100 a day. The players got their money in cash; the only record of the sessions was a receipt a secretary might make up and sign. The local musicians' union didn't pressure Motown to pay union scale until 1965, though its pay scale was common knowledge among Detroit's black musicians.

Motown's pay scale inspired the rise of Detroit-based Golden World and Ric-Tic Records. After opening Golden World Studio in 1964, Ed Wingate, owner of the Twenty Grand nightclub, founded Golden World Records and then brought in local WCHB deejay LeBaron Taylor and his Ric-Tic label to give Motown competition. He took advantage of Motown's cheapness, luring Motown's talented crew of players over to his sessions with the promise of union scale wages. The musicians bit. Van Dyke, Jamerson, Benjamin, and others sneaked over on weekends to play on Edwin Starr's "Agent Double-O-Soul," number eight on the soul chart (the R&B chart's nomenclature had changed with the times) in 1965, and "Stop Her on Sight (S.O.S.)" number nine soul in 1966, considered by many to be the finest non-Motown "Motown Sound" record ever. The Parliaments, who in the seventies made their reputation fusing doo-wop harmonies, psychedelic guitars, and perversely humorous lyrics, were then a straight stand-up vocal group who scored on Ric-Tic with "(I Just Wanna) Testify" (covered later by Stax soulman Johnnie Taylor), number three soul in 1967. Golden World Studios was considered the best place to record strings in Detroit, something Wingate took advantage of in 1965 with the San Remo Golden Strings, a group composed of some of the same Detroit Symphony players Motown used, who had a Top Thirty pop hit with the instrumental "Hungry for Love."

Once Motown became aware of Golden World's rampant use of its staff musicians, Mickey Stevenson was dispatched to discourage the players. As LeBaron Taylor remembers:

> [He] would come by at any time of the night. We did a lot of recording on the weekends after the players had gigged that evening at the Twenty Grand or Chit Chat. They'd come by two-thirty in the morning and we'd sit up and record all night. Mickey went so far as to camp out. He'd park his car across the street so he could see them come out and he'd say, "You're fined. You're fined. You're fined." But still they never did stop. They were just a little more discreet.

This moonlighting didn't just extend to Golden World, but to other producers who sneaked into Detroit to tap into the Motown Sound. The players remember Burt Bacharach and Hal David visiting Detroit in the sixties to cut tracks with Dionne Warwick. The players also traveled to New York and Chicago for sessions. Their most famous unauthorized record was Jackie Wilson's brilliant 1967 hit "(Your Love Keeps Lifting Me) Higher and Higher," recorded in Chicago under the guidance of Carl Davis and with Jamerson, Van Dyke, and sometime-Motown session player keyboardist Johnny Griffith creating a typically percolating groove that Wilson's voice literally soars over. It is one of the sad injustices of pop history that, because of contractual obligations to Brunswick, Wilson was never able to benefit on an ongoing basis from a sound that his voice and success helped to create.

Despite Van Dyke's positive assessment of Berry's treatment of the studio musicians, his own tenure at Motown wasn't without disappointment. In fact, as soon as he tried to cross the line from studio cat to recording artist, there was trouble. One afternoon in 1963 Van Dyke, Stevie Wonder, Clarence Paul, and arranger Johnny Allen were jamming and came up with a funky instrumental they called "Monkey Talk." With Stevie on harmonica and Van Dyke displaying his bebop piano flourishes, they came up with a Ramsey Lewis-style pop-jazz number. Berry declared it "a definite smash." But there was one problem. Without an artist contract with Van Dyke, Motown couldn't release it. "That's how they got me," says Van Dyke. "I thought they were going to put 'Monkey Talk' out. They never did."

Gladys Knight and the Pips. *(Kriegsmann/Ochs Archives)*

Eddie Holland ponders a reporter's question. *(Don Paulsen)*

Brian Holland relaxes on his couch with Bach by his side. Classical music would play a significant influence on Holland-Dozier-Holland's late sixties productions. *(Don Paulsen)*

Lamont Dozier at home. *(Don Paulsen)*

The teenaged Stevie Wonder assumes a serious pose in this Motown promo picture. Haircut, choice of clothes, and conservative shades show the influence of the Motown charm school. *(Kriegsmann/Ochs Archives)*

A rare photo of Marvin Gaye, keyboardist, taken at Freedomland in the Bronx, now the site of Co-op City. *(Don Paulsen)*

Tammi Terrell and Marvin Gaye meet Tom Montgomery (Tammi's father), Mrs. Esther Edwards, and Nate Gerson after a show. *(Michael Ochs Archives)*

The Four Tops sing "Sugar Pie
(Honey Bunch)" on
"Hullabaloo" in 1965. *(Don
Paulsen)*

Marvin Gaye talks shop with Murray the K at a
rehearsal for a New York concert in the
mid-sixties. *(Don Paulsen)*

A Motown meeting with Gary Smith (in the glasses), producer of the NBC television show "Hullabaloo." Mary Wilson (middle) and Diana Ross go over the script with Berry Gordy and Motown executive Michael Roskind (far left) giving advice. Flo Ballard quietly has a coffee in the back. *(Don Paulsen)*

Mary Wilson loved shopping when the Supremes had free time. She is seen here at New York's Bergdorf Goodman in the mid-sixties. *(Don Paulsen)*

Diana Ross and Flo Ballard wait for a taxi after shopping on Fifth Avenue. *(Don Paulsen)*

A tired Flo Ballard after a rehearsal in New York. *(Don Paulsen)*

Diana Ross. *(Kriegsmann/Ochs Archives)*

The poster for the 1965 Tamla–Motown tour of England shows clearly that the Supremes have superceded the Vandellas in the Motown hierarchy, a fact that would irritate Martha Reeves during the trip. Earl Van Dyke's Six, the backing band, would also cause trouble, going on strike for better hotel accommodations and more money mid-tour.

ASTORIA FINSBU
Manager : W. L. WEBB
6.40 — SATURDAY, 20th MAR
TWO PERFORMANCES ONLY
FOR ONE
DAY ONLY ON THE STAG
(INSTEAD OF THE USUAL FILM PROGRAMM
HAROLD DAVISON and ARTHUR HOWES
TAMLA-MOTO
THE FABULOU
SUPREM
THE EXCITING!
MARTHA
AND THE
VANDELLAS
THE FANTAST
STEVIE
WONDE
SMOKEY ROBINSON
AND THE
MIRACLES
EARL VA
DYKE SI
SPECIAL GUEST STAR
GEORGIE FAME
AND THE BLUE FLAMES
YOUR COMPERE TONY MARSH

Before Van Dyke knew the fate of "Monkey Talk," Stevenson came back to Van Dyke and enticed him to overdub organ on the original rhythm tracks of Motown hits. The result was *Earl Van Dyke Plays That Motown Sound,* sans "Monkey Talk." Though the deceitfulness of Motown's move still rankles him, Van Dyke understands the thinking behind it. "It was a hot record and it had so much piano and harmonica on it that they'd have to push me. I possibly, from that record, would have had to go out on the road with Stevie to do that and they didn't want that. They wanted me in the studio." And despite two subsequent, jazzier albums, that's where Van Dyke stayed, playing the Steinway and Hammond B3 organ, and covering up for Jamerson and Benjamin.

Musically, they were incredibly compatible, and everyone who worked at Motown raves about their teamwork. Jamerson recalled joyfully, "Oh, man, he [Benny] was my favorite. When he died I couldn't eat for two weeks, it hurt me so bad. He and I were really the ones who tightened up the sound, the drum and the bass. We didn't need sheet music. I started to play. He started the beat. We'd look at each other and know whether we needed a triplet, quarter, double time, or whatever."

Jamerson and Benjamin also shared a deep and ultimately fatal attachment to booze. Van Dyke tried to talk to Jamerson about it.

"I said, 'Jamerson, can't you see that its destroying you?'

"He said, 'Yeah, I know.'

"I said, 'Well, why do you drink?'

"And he said, 'Because I like the taste of it.'

"So what could I say?"

Jamerson was a large, imposing man with big hands and a serious, unfrivolous face. Drinking messed with his bass playing and could make him surly, occasionally violent. "He'd get extremely violent and took no shit," said Beans Bowles. "He fought enough. Too much for a bass player." In contrast, Benjamin, a small, wiry man with a quick wit and a fearless tongue, "could hold himself together. The higher Benny was, the better he played," says Van Dyke.

Together, Jamerson and Benjamin raised hell with Motown's production schedules. When the producers would take a fifteen- or twenty-minute break, Benjamin and Jamerson would often lead a contingent of players over to the bar behind the Motown studio. When the break was over, several players, including the drummer and bassist, were often missing. The producers wouldn't know where they were, and bandleader Van Dyke was reluctant to tell on them. It wasn't unusual for fifteen-minute breaks to become half-hour breaks or longer. When management got wise to the bar, the players shifted their drinking to Coles' Funeral Home, right next to Hitsville. It became a tradition for the proprietor, wearing the rubber suit of his trade, to join the boys for a taste among his "customers." Clarence Paul and Norman Whitfield, who made it their business to be close to the musicians, knew where to find them, but many in the Motown hierarchy were never aware of this "players' lounge."

When Jamerson wasn't indulging his thirst for Budweiser, and later, gin, he played some marvelous bass. On some Motown recordings it's hard to hear the piano, the organ, and vibes blend together, the sax solo is bland, and even Benny's drums, buried beneath tambourines and guitars, are sometimes lost in an H-D-H mix. But never, never does anyone forget the bass lines. Part of the reason for the vitality of the bass lines was that the Motown studio was one of the first to record by plugging the bass directly into the studio control board (in the past, bassists had been recorded using the sound coming through their portable amplifiers). But whether it was swaying on "Love Is Here and Now You're Gone," rocking out on "Heat Wave," funky on "Ain't Too Proud to Beg," or loud and demanding on "Ain't No Mountain High Enough," the invention, technique, and drama that emanated from James Jamerson's 1962 Fender Precision bass made him one of the most influential musicians of the sixties.

Despite his jazz background, Jamerson cited some unusual influences. As he once said:

My feel was always an Eastern feel, a spiritual thing. Take "Standing in the Shadows of Love." The bass line has an Arabic feel. I've been around a whole lot of people from the East, from China and Japan. Then I studied the African, Cuban, and Indian scales. I brought all that with me to Motown. There were people from the East in my neighborhood [in Detroit]. I'd run into Eastern musicians who liked the way I played and they'd keep in contact with me.

I picked up things from listening to people speak, the intonation of their voices; I could capture a line. I look at people walking and get a beat from their movements. . . . There was one of them heavy, funky tunes the Temptations did. . . . I can't remember the name but there was this big, fat woman walking around. She couldn't keep still. I wrote it by watching her move.

The Motown producers rarely wrote detailed arrangements for Jamerson. Instead, they'd hand him a chord sheet or have him listen as the melody and lyrics were run down on piano by Brian Holland or Norman Whitfield, and he would build the bass line around what he heard. "I always tried to support the melody," he said. "I had to. I'd make it repetitious, but also add things to it. . . . It was repetitous, but it had to be funky and have emotion." Louis Johnson, one of the eighties' top studio bassists (he played on Michael Jackson's *Thriller* and *Off the Wall*) and member of the Brothers Johnson, credits Jamerson with "bringing the triplet feel on bass to pop. Before him it was unusual for the bass to deviate from that single note, *dum-dum-dum* style. Jamerson broke the mold and made the bass more creative."

Much of Jamerson's flexibility derived from the fact that Berry always emphasized a hard, emphatic beat to anchor the songs. Sometimes the beat was accentuated by handclaps, sometimes tambourine (a Berry favorite), and very often guitarists Robert White and Eddie Willis's metallic downstrokes, as on "Dancing in the Street."

Of course, setting the main tempo around Hitsville was good old Papa Zita. As Stevie Wonder told *Rolling Stone:* "He could play drums. You wouldn't even need a bass, that's how bad he was. Just listen to all the Motown hits, 'My World Is Empty Without You' and 'This Old Heart of Mine' and 'Don't Mess With Bill.' On 'Girl's Alright With Me,' the drums would just *pop!*" As for Benny's personal style, Wonder gleefully recalled, "Benny would be late for sessions. Benny'd be drunk sometimes, I mean, he was a beautiful cat, but . . ."

Benny was chronically late. It was imperative that he come up with a valid excuse, because Motown would dock *all* the musicians if one member turned up late for a session. "One day he came into the studio late for a session just huffing and puffing," recalled Van Dyke. "He was late and we were mad as hell. Benny was about an hour late when he came running in the door. He said, 'Wait a minute. I'm going to tell you all what happened. You know the circus is in town.' We said, 'Yeah.' 'Well, look, they were coming down the freeway and the elephant got loose and blocked up all the traffic.' Now we knew that was a lie because Benny couldn't even drive a car." Another time Benny claimed that he had been sitting on his mother's steps with his ex–old lady's boyfriend (surely one of the most incredible opening lines of all time) when suddenly a car pulled up. As Benny talked to his ex–old lady's boyfriend, someone in the car pointed a pistol out the car window and shot this cat in the chest. And Benny expected you to believe it.

Benny, like many aficionados of booze and drugs, was often short of cash and always borrowing money, usually a dollar or, at most, a "fin" (five dollars). To justify his borrowing Benny told one Motown musician,

"Damn, man, I was riding home on the bus and I had this transfer and I didn't need it, so I opened the window and I threw out the transfer. But it wasn't the transfer, it was my check."

In spite of his vices, Benny had the respect of everyone at the company. A large part of it was for his musicianship, but part of it was for his candor as well. In a company that prided itself on tight lips, Benny's jaw was always working when something happened he didn't like. He particularly didn't like to see artists who felt they were too big for the music or the other musicians. "They always used to fall out with Benny, probably because he used to lip a lot," says Van Dyke. "When someone would give him some lip, he'd say, 'Look, I been down in this snakepit many a day and many a month and many a year. I seen them come and seen them go. And I'm still here.'"

When you looked at it, Benny's reference to the studio as a snakepit wasn't far from wrong. It was down in the ground, the musicians were piled almost on top of each other, and the battles for success waged there were often venomous.

Just as the personalities of the musicians helped shape Motown's music, the peculiarities of Hitsville were also crucial to the Motown Sound. Engineers Mike McClain and Lawrence Horn, along with Brian Holland and some of the other producers, had, through trial and error, built the original three-track recording machine into an eight-track by the mid-sixties. The control room had two Ampex eight-track machines near the wall next to the door. Microphone cables hung from the ceiling like bunches of black licorice sticks. Looking over the main eight-track console into the studio, you'd see chairs positioned there for guitar and bass players. The piano was to their immediate left and the drums diagonally across from the piano. In the center of the room microphones hung down where the singers—at least in the early days—sang live in the studio. Side rooms had been built into the wall next to the piano after Berry had purchased the building next door. There vibes, organ, and percussion instruments were usually stationed.

The size of the room played an important part in the recording process. Because there was no room for large amplifiers in the studio, the guitars and bass were plugged right into the console and were heard through the room's one speaker. The guitar players would, before a session, adjust their volume to a preset level they were never to exceed, and a Motown guitar player who was too often found playing in the red section of the meter was quickly out of work. The genesis of this setup was necessity, but the lucky accident of the room's size contributed greatly to the crispness of Motown's sound.

A limiter is an electronic brain that corrects for discrepancies in volume. Without a limiter, if someone sang too loudly, an engineer would have to pull the volume control down or risk overloading the tape. If someone sang too softly, that had to be balanced by raising the volume control. If the engineer and the singer had rehearsed the song previously, the engineer could anticipate the changes in volume, but this method left plenty of room for human error. Motown was one of the first places to use limiters extensively, and because of the many young and untrained vocalists at Motown, the limiter was a crucial safeguard. In contrast, the limiter was frowned on in New York recording circles, where some believed it interfered with a singer's "dynamic range" (or perhaps it made New York's powerful engineers' union nervous).

Motown engineers also utilized "an amazing amount of equalizers," according to a former engineer—sometimes as many as sixteen on an eight-track recording—which gave them a wide range of sonic frequencies. At a typical New York session there would be two frequencies available for each microphone—bass and treble. At Motown there was bass, mid-range, lower treble, middle treble, and upper treble for each microphone, and in the mix room even more equalization was used.

Another current record industry commonplace pioneered by Motown was its extensive use of punch-ins, a technique whereby a singer or instrumentalist can perform over a mistake. Today it's not unusual for even the best singers to have songs with twenty punch-ins, making one technically perfect vocal performance from many that are flawed. This is an easy procedure for the 24-track eighties, but it was tremendously tedious work in 1965 or 1966 on eight tracks. To punch in, the engineer had to synchronize the voice with the music and then play it off another machine's tape head, often resulting in a muffled sound and some tape hum. The problem could be defeated, but only by plodding along for hours.

In the early days, Berry and his young producers would cut tunes all night, searching for the right key or tempo. As their confidence grew, they tried new tricks. A saxophonist, say, would solo through the entire song, but during the mixing, the engineer would drop out his sax except at the break or near the fade. In those days, these changes could only be accomplished by stopping the machine and physically cutting out the piece of tape, as with the editing of film. This was the purpose for the second tape that Motown always made.

The target of Motown's technological undertakings was another, more generally accessible piece of scientific gadgetry called the transistor radio. Born December 27, 1947, at New Jersey's Bell Laboratories, the transistor was to replace the vacuum tube as the key element in radio transmission. As Peter Fornatale and Joshua E. Mills wrote in *Radio in the Television Age*, the transistor made possible the miniaturization of electronic devices. It was first marketed to the public in 1953; "the world's smallest radio—small enough to fit in the palm of the hand," wrote *The New York Times*, and by 1965 more than twelve million transistor radios were being purchased a year. Coinciding with the rise of the transistor radio was the spread of radios in cars. Once cumbersome and subject to interference from the automobile's more essential parts, car radios had through the fifties—and, with the aid of transistorization, into the sixties—become part of what made driving so fascinating to Americans struck with wanderlust. In 1963, the year before the Motown explosion, fifty million radios were rolling around the country in car dashboards. Berry and company were wise in their decision to gear Motown's music toward the transistor radio, for it was through this medium—be it from a portable blaring in a schoolyard or a car radio on a Saturday night drive to a dance—that young America was exposed to records.

In quality control's offices Motown chief engineer Mike McClain built a minuscule, tinny-sounding radio designed to approximate the sound of a car radio. The high-end bias of Motown recordings can be partially traced to the company's reliance on this piece of equipment.

Equally important was Berry's view that judgments on a recording's sonic impact could *not* be made from master tapes, but only from what was on vinyl. Music always sounds great over large studio speakers and on the virgin tape it was first recorded on, yet something is lost in the transfer from tape to plastic. This problem was compensated for by the construction of a disc-cutting machine at Motown in 1963, so that any prospective singles could be transferred immediately to vinyl. Berry demanded innumerable mixes of every Motown release—to move the guitars back, the bass up, to emphasize the vocal on the second verse, and so on. And each time a different suggestion was made it would be mixed on tape and then placed on disc for further evaluation. Twenty mixes were a lot, but twelve was not unusual. Only five? Unheard of, even on the hottest tracks brought in by H-D-H. In fact, the stronger the record, the more options were explored in Motown's search for the perfect frequency.

The mixing process could be so extensive, and the variations so extreme, that the Funk Brothers, a prideful bunch, must admit that on certain records, particularly those by H-D-H, it was difficult for them to pick themselves out of the mix. Of all Motown's producers, it was that trio that took greatest advantage of Motown technology to create records as dazzlingly bright and enduring as any ever produced.

Brian and Eddie Holland and Lamont Dozier had hardly been studio-savvy in the beginning—far from it. The musicians, in fact, had harbored some contempt for them in the team's embryonic stage. Emblematic of the tension between H-D-H and the musicians was the day Brian Holland was in the studio instructing Jamerson to try out some chords and Jamerson, to the delight of the other players, ran down "Three Blind Mice." In those days "They didn't know what they were doing," recalls Johnny Griffith. Van Dyke agrees. "Yeah, they'd come in with about five chords and a feel. . . . We laughed at them 'cause they had no form."

Like Berry when he started, H-D-H were self-trained musicians who relied on numerous takes to flesh out their ideas. They were barely out of their teens, but they were supervising jazz musicians anywhere from five to fifteen years their senior. As Van Dyke recalls ruefully:

> Lamont would always sit at the piano and come up with the same little things. Like every tune he played he would remind you of James Brown. He could take one track and make ten songs up because they all sounded alike. Then you give him something and he'd say, "No, you gave me that on the last tune. Give it something different." He was doing this all the time. But the tune wouldn't be different anyway. He'd say, "I'm going to stop calling you 'cause you play the same shit on all my tunes." I'd say, "Well, your shit sounds all alike."

Eddie Holland acknowledges, "They used to play a lot of games with the different writers over there and used to have fun doing that because they realized that a lot of the writers weren't familiar with the chords and different things like that." But Eddie vehemently denies it happened to him or his co-workers. As he remembers:

> They tried it on Brian and he called off the chords they were playing. When they saw that he could call chords off, tell them what to play and what chords they weren't hitting, then they quickly changed their attitude. I used to watch them go through these changes, so with him that was not the situation, 'cause he knew what he wanted them to play.
> Brian used chord sheets because he would arrange things in his head on the floor. You see he would arrange and tell them what to do, what to play. Now take a James Jamerson, who was extremely creative with that bass, Brian would give Jamerson the

115

basics of what he would want Jamerson to do, Jamerson would innovate. So if he came up with a figure that Brian liked because of his ability to innovate then Brian would say, "Hey, man, that's fantastic. Play that." But often, too, Jamerson would overdo it, because he was just that good, that Brian had to say, "No, no, no. Don't give me all that. Simplify that." So all the direction still had to come from the producers in the case of Brian and Lamont.

At first the simplicity of H-D-H's work put off the musicians. But then, the musicians also mumbled about the cheapness of Eddie, who, unlike Norman and Smokey, wouldn't give the musicians bonuses for playing on his hits; Eddie's attitude was that they were already being paid for doing their job. Even Berry would later characterize Eddie as "money hungry," which he said was "general knowledge." Unfortunately for the players, Eddie wasn't just H-D-H's most articulate member, but also its de facto leader. His eye was on the dollar bill to a degree that many of the creative personnel at Motown would come to later, and it was a posture that would eventually cause friction at all levels of the company.

But "tight" or not, it was soon clear that these kids, with their well-coiffed processed hair, their Blye knits, and their pretentious god-damn pipes, had a real insight into the taste of the buying public. They may not have been versed in Miles and Monk or very proficient instrumentalists, but they did possess an innate gift for melody, a feel for story song lyrics, and an ability to create the recurring vocal and instrumental lines known as "hooks."

Brian, Eddie, and Lamont loved what they were doing and worked around the clock, making music like old man Ford made cars. Eddie says:

> We handled it in many ways just like a person would handle a nine-to-five job. Brian and Lamont would get together, work out the melodies. I would come over and stay in contact with the melodies and ideas, so I could stay in tune to the feelings of the music and what direction we all wanted to take these songs. So we'd go through the process, knowing we didn't have that much time. I would take the basic melodies on tape, listen to them and jot down the ideas on each tune as they were rehearsing. Then once they cut some tracks I would work through the day, through the night, wake up in the morning, just constantly chipping away at it, so to speak.

H-D-H completed two or three songs a day, according to Lamont Dozier, by working at them bit by bit. "We would have parts of songs, like hooks or maybe parts of a verse, so that by the end of the day we would have something accomplished. I guess that was primarily the reason for the success we had in such a short time." Whereas Eddie did words and Brian did music, Lamont did a bit of both, collaborating with each Holland brother on their specialties. Song ideas came from anywhere and everywhere. The genesis of Martha and the Vandellas' "Jimmy Mack" was Lamont's attendance at the 1966 BMI awards dinner, where the trio had, as usual, scooped up a slew of honors. There Lamont met the mother of a young songwriter who had been killed in an accident after writing a hit. "When they called out his name there was something, along with the way his mother picked up the award, that kind of moved me . . . and that name seemed to spring up and fit well with the music we were writing at the time."

Looking back, Lamont is proud of the way in which H-D-H responded to the pressure of Motown's relentless release schedule. "You know when you needed it the most," he says, smiling, "it happened." "It's the Same Old Song" was written to head off a Columbia release of old Four Tops material unearthed to capitalize on the sales of "I Can't Help Myself (Sugar Pie, Honey Bunch)." "I think we came up with it in a couple of days and it was cut and the following Monday it was on the radio," Lamont says.

Because of their nonstop touring, time in the studio with the top ten Motown acts was scarce, while the demand for product was unending, and this led to a lot of songwriting on the run. Before going on a national tour in 1966, Berry wanted the Four Tops to have a new single ready. This last-minute order found Eddie working on the lyrics for "Standing in the Shadows of Love" right up until Levi Stubbs walked into the studio. Another example of writing against the clock is "I Hear a Symphony." The track had been completed and a demo vocal was in place when Eddie's phone rang at three in the morning. It was Brian telling him that Berry had heard it, liked it, and wanted it completed and ready for release immediately. "So I got up at three and wrote that song until eleven o'clock to get it to Diana," Eddie says. "I was still writing the lines in while I was teaching it to her."

All of the musicians' bitching and moaning over the sketchy chord sheets was, from H-D-H's viewpoint, missing the point of the music. As Brian says:

117

You see chords only fit in, you know, like a puzzle. But the key thing was always the melody. We might change a chord here or there to fit the melody, or for whatever dramatic reasons. [We made sure the melodies came] first. From there you take chords, chords only help dress them up, like sugar-coat it or make them a little dramatic. It was not a set pattern for chords necessarily as much as it was just to help dress the melody.

The music of H-D-H went through several stages, the results of their ongoing maturation as craftsmen. On a song such as "Heat Wave" (1963), the melody and lyric ride over a rhythm track clearly derived from the interplay of the musicians among themselves. That record is imbued with the spirit of a lively, fun-loving musical ensemble. It is not a producer's record; it's a *band* record, though H-D-H gave it structure. By the time of "Baby Love" and "Where Did Our Love Go?," Brian and Lamont, the team's musical technicians, had developed a repetitive composing style that limited the musicians' room for improvisation and gave the producers greater musical control. Wrote David Morse: "They ruthlessly cannibalize old songs for spare parts; verbal phrases, thematic ideas, musical figures, accompaniments, even saxophone solos are shuffled together and reworked from disc to disc; every song is a collage." And so "Baby Love" picks up its title and melody from the chorus of "Where Did Our Love Go?"; the Isley Brothers' "This Old Heart of Mine" recalls the Four Tops' "Shake Me, Wake Me (When It's Over)"; and the title of "It's the Same Old Song" seems (though according to H-D-H it isn't) to be an inside joke about that song's resemblance to "I Can't Help Myself".

Says an ex-Motown engineer:

This is what they [H-D-H] did. They'd record music tracks and conceptually they might have an idea of who'd be right for it, but they really didn't know. They had basic instruments: the rhythm section, the horns, the strings. Brian or Lamont would take those tracks and edit them into the musical sequence that he thought the record should follow, and Eddie would try to write lyrics to it. They would do this four or five times until they got the perfect song. And then they'd go out and try to get different artists, and whoever had the best thing got it.

Through the mid-sixties, H-D-H's compositions and arrangements grew more ambitious. Within the framework of the three-minute single, they would make the most classically influenced pop records since the heyday of Phil Spector's early sixties "Wall of Sound," in which Spector had fashioned extravagant, symphonic mini-suites around the adolescent voices of girl groups such as the Ronettes and the Crystals. Johnny Griffith calls songs like "Reach Out I'll Be There," "Standing in the Shadows of Love," "Bernadette," and "Seven Rooms of Gloom"—all released between late 1966 and mid-1967—songs full of dramatic pauses, swelling instrumental passages, and unexpected rhythmic changes, H-D-H's "classical period." Brian Holland had been listening to a great deal of classical music, and studied the dynamics of tension and release so important to the form. As the records grew more complex-sounding, the time Brian took to record them grew. "Reach Out," for example, took almost two hours to cut, a marathon session by Motown standards circa 1966.

H-D-H also introduced some progressive studio techniques to Motown sessions. On several sessions, the electric bass of James Jamerson—though he would later deny this—was accompanied by Clarence Isabel on upright acoustic. Each would play two different lines, one a "pulsating" and the other a straight "running" line, intensifying the characteristically dynamic rhythm tracks. Oscillators, an electronic gadget that was something of a precursor of the synthesizer, were used extensively by H-D-H as catchy "ear candy" to enhance the Supremes on "The Happening," "In and Out of Love," and, most prominently, on the eerie introduction to "Reflections," all in 1967.

Most of H-D-H's most elaborate productions featured the voice of the Four Tops' lead singer Levi Stubbs. No accident. With Stubbs leading Lawrence Payton, Renaldo "Obie" Benson, and Abdul Fakir, the Tops were easily H-D-H's favorite Motown act. Unlike most Motown performers, the Tops were all seasoned performers who'd made their first recordings back in 1956 on Chess. Detroit natives all, they, like Berry Gordy, had been influenced by Detroit's active jazz scene in the fifties, and had built a following in nightclubs around the area by interpreting jazzy big-band material. It was, in fact, their live presentation that was their bread and butter, although they did sides for Red Top, Riverside, and Columbia Records in the early 1960s. Prior to signing with Motown in 1963, the Tops had been touring with Billy Eckstine. When Motown approached them about joining the label, the Tops' wives, all former showgirls, weren't too crazy about their husbands giving up lucrative nightclub work for the hit-and-miss life of recording artists. And, at first, the ladies' concerns seemed well founded as a vocal jazz album, *Breakin' Through*, on the Jazz Workshop label, flopped.

Then H-D-H embraced them, falling in love with Stubbs's rough-hewn, melodramatic lead voice, and built records like "It's the Same Old Song" (number five pop in 1965) and "I Can't Help Myself (Sugar Pie, Honey Bunch)" (number one pop in 1965) around it. With the recordings of H-D-H's "classical period" the H-D-H/Four Tops team simply made magic. "He would feel that type of thing and he'd able to sell it because he's basically a dynamic singer anyway," Eddie says. "He's very forceful in his attitude. We knew that, so we wouldn't have given those songs to someone else to sing."

H-D-H's proficiency won them awards, respect, and money. They should have been happy. Yet bubbling under the surface was the uneasy feeling that, considering all the capital they were generating, all the acts they had helped make marketable live commodities for ITM, and the musical identity they had given to Motown, maybe they should have been getting a bigger piece. It was a situation Eddie began to ponder and discuss with Lamont and his brother even as the hits kept rolling in.

In March 1965, the Tamla–Motown Revue traveled to England to celebrate the consolidation of its first major foothold in the international market. The push had begun exactly two years before, when Barry, Ales, and Esther spent several weeks in Europe, stopping in London, Belgium, Germany, and Holland to investigate international distribution, publishing, and management deals. At the time Motown had only one European distribution agreement, that with Oriole Records in the U.K., one of several short-lived business liaisons Motown would have there in the early part of the decade. Labels like Fontana and Oriole didn't provide the consistent promotion required to establish Motown in what was then the world's second-largest record-buying nation. The Beatles and the whole slew of Mersey Beat bands, along with the bluesier Rolling Stones and Animals, had pushed most American pop off the charts. It was even tougher for black American singers. The Beatles and Stones may have cut their teeth on Little Richard and Muddy Waters, but with home-grown stars so plentiful, the British were understandably parochial. The Motown trio's excursion had been only moderately successful, yielding a distribution deal with EMI and arrangements for some U.K. touring by certain Motown acts, notably the Mary Wells–Beatles match in 1964. Yet even when "My Guy" went to number five in the U.K., Motown had no corporate or musical identity there.

It was the Supremes who sparked the label's rise in England. In search of the key to Britain, Berry invited David Godin, then president and founder of the U.K. Tamla–Motown Appreciation Society, to Detroit in early 1964 to talk about how to break through. "The problem was that we had no way of knowing which of their artists would be the first to hit the jackpot in this country," Godin told Britain's *The Face* magazine. "I decided the best thing was to sell a corporate label identity and a sound." While in Detroit Godin had to ask to meet the Supremes because they hadn't been invited to the reception in his honor. Later during Godin's visit, Berry played him "Where Did Our Love Go?," which Godin felt would be a sure hit in his country.

Coinciding with the release of "Where" in England was the rise of Radio Caroline, the first of several pirate stations that transmitted from ships off the English coastline. These stations played music the government monopoly stations of the BBC would not. Godin said, "At the beginning they really had no idea if people were tuning in. To test their listener power they had to pick up records that no one else was playing. They did it with Dionne Warwick and Etta James and the Supremes, and their records started getting in the charts." "Where" went to number two and "Baby Love" reached the top in 1964, making it one of only two American records to go number one in the United Kingdom from 1963 to 1965 (the other was Roy Orbison's "It's Over").

Emboldened by these breakthroughs, Berry took Godin's advice and started Tamla–Motown as one label for the United Kingdom in 1965. Short-term results were disappointing. Only one Tamla–Motown disc— "Stop! In the Name of Love" made the British Top Twenty that year, suggesting that Berry may have been premature. But by 1966, when Tamla–Motown acts began cracking the Top Twenty with regularity, spawning a fanatical following in Northern England (where Motown's music is often referred to as "Northern soul"), Berry's faith in Godin's judgment was justified.

The tour itself—twenty-one shows in twenty-four days—was pivotal in spreading the Tamla–Motown name, though it provided Berry with a rough three weeks. It got press—though certainly not all of it laudatory —so-so concert grosses, one major personality crisis, and a near strike by Motown's musicians. The trouble began when Georgie Fame, a minor figure in the British Invasion, was booked as opening act. Many fans who had come to see the Motown acts were not pleased, shouting "Get off!" as he overran his twenty-minute spot. And a Glasgow writer noted that the Miracles' steps were "reminiscent of production numbers in pre-war Hollywood films."

Writing in the *Western Daily News*'s March 24 issue about the revue's appearance at Bristol's Colster Hall, Tony Crofts observed: "It is no coincidence that while 10,000 Negroes are marching for their civil rights in Alabama, the Tamla–Motown star is in the ascendent." Crofts spent much of his review commenting on Martha and the Vandellas, saying that they "are a typical three-girl group—one vocalist, two chorus, all moving in unison in a sort of sexier Shadows' step [a reference to the backing band of British pop star Cliff Richard]" and "perform purely for their own enjoyment: completely unself-conscious, utterly relaxed, riding the driving Motown beat." Then, almost as an afterthought, he adds: "Likewise the Supremes." Despite what Crofts felt was an artistic success the "Hall [was left] half empty by excessively high ticket prices."

Ron Boyle's report in the *Daily Express* on March 30 was ballyhooed with the headline THE INVASION GOES WRONG, and was illustrated with photographs of different Motown performers that someone had slightly Anglicized with a grease pencil. "To counterblast the Liverpool Sound along came the Detroit sound known to the 'in' crowd as Tamla–Motown," wrote Boyle. "More sophisticated, more professional than the British brand. The punch of the big beat in a velvet glove."

One Glasgow paper gave the Tamla–Motown tour front-page exposure, heralding its arrival with the headline AT LAST, GLASGOW SEES THE GROUPS THAT WERE THE BEATLES' FIRST IDOLS and pictures of the Supremes, Stevie Wonder, and Martha and the Vandellas. A subhead proclaimed "Meet the Man Who Turns 'Unknowns' into Stars." Ramsey Watson's story read: "With all the precision planning of a military operation behind it, the Detroit sound invades the British pop scene tonight and for the first time Glasgow can listen to this half-pop, half-jazz, heavy, haunting, rocking beat that has swept the hit parades of the world. . . . It is the creation of a chubby, boyish-faced Negro, Berry Gordy, Jr." The rest of the story is the basic Berry Gordy rags-to-riches material, featuring one of Berry's better lines about his employees: "Some of these artists would be waiting tables somewhere if there hadn't been a place in Detroit to recognize their talents."

The next day the *Scottish Daily Express* proclaimed BIG DETROIT CHALLENGES LIVERPOOL, stating that "In terms of impact on Britain's pop scene the American influence is becoming stronger with every release from Detroit," a reflection of ignorance as to where this music's roots really were, despite the Beatles' giving credit to Motown and other forms of black music. Reporter Gordon Reed did make the intriguing comment that, in England at least, "The style appeals to twenty-year-olds rather than the teenagers and they listen rather than scream," suggesting a reverence for music British fans usually reserved for artists such as Bob Dylan and Joan Baez. The quotes from the Motown performers in this piece were all brief and, as in some of the other pieces about Motown in England, had a stilted quality (e.g., Stevie Wonder told Reed, "My parents were pretty poor, like all colored folk in Detroit").

At the show in Kingston-on-Thames, the house was only one-third full, even after the local promoter had given away one thousand tickets. For the local paper's reporter, one cause of the show's financial problem was that the performers were too polished, lacking "the rough-edged common touch which is the vital link between the Beatles or Stones and the audience."

But in contrast to the onstage uniformity the British saw, there was plenty of unexpected activity backstage. For this important tour Berry had invited Gordon Van Sauter, a *Detroit Free Press* reporter who'd done a story on Motown in 1964, to travel with them and provide advice on how to deal with the media. Aside from Stevie Wonder's tutor Ted Hull, Sauter was the only other white person among the Motown entourage of forty-one. "I didn't know who the hell these people were, and I certainly knew nothing about their music," Sauter told *New York* magazine. Still, he took a month off from the paper to join the tour as part of his research into black life, feeling civil rights was a "watershed story" after a trip to Mississippi in 1963, and wanting to understand blacks better. However, his duties on the tour were hardly substantial. He helped the Supremes buy and carry forty-two pairs of shoes back to their hotel room. And later in the tour, when Martha Reeves and Berry were at odds, Berry stuffed a handful of money into Sauter's hand, telling him, "Take Martha Reeves and show her some culture." Sauter and Reeves drove up to Edinburgh, Scotland, and looked at castles.

Martha wasn't Berry's only problem. The musicians, led by band-leader Earl Van Dyke, staged a mini-strike the night of the Glasgow concert. The dispute began when Van Dyke's band was asked to cut backing tracks for the Motown acts appearing on a British television show. The musicians had originally been told they'd just be playing to the record. "When we went in," recalls Van Dyke, "I was talking to the English musicians about what was the scale, you know. Everybody nutted on me. So finally I kept enough grumbling going until they told me it was $52.50. . . . They brought in the union man and he straightened it out. So our monies had to be paid through Motown."

Clarence Paul, traveling with Stevie Wonder, helped the musicians get the money. Then Esther Gordy told road manager Beans Bowles to tell the musicians they'd have to give that money back. The musicians refused, complaining that they were being underpaid. Before the tour had commenced the musicians had managed, after considerable give and take, to get their weekly pay for the European tours upped from $150 to $350, the bulk of which was sent back to their families in Detroit.

But being forced to give back that $52.50 struck a nerve. Most were unhappy, dismayed by English food and the damp English weather. So when they played Liverpool Van Dyke said to his co-workers, "Since they want to treat us like that, let's get us some money. So we struck." For two hours before the scheduled starting time Esther Gordy, Pops Gordy, and Bowles all talked to them, trying to change the musicians' minds. Clarence Paul, in a move that would have repercussions later, sided with the musicians and sat with them, advising them on the merit of Motown's offers.

Finally, Berry came into the room. He was smiling. "All right fellas, it can't be nothing but money and you know that ain't no big thing." The musicians wanted more money and Berry told them they'd get it, though no dollar figure was agreed to. But Berry's word was enough. "I know one thing about Berry," says Van Dyke. "When he promised you something, you got it. He didn't back down. He didn't welch. . . . But the thing was to get him to promise to give it to you. So we didn't have any problems." Yet, all these years later, Van Dyke won't say how much his act of defiance earned him, "because I would be stepping on people's feet, like Smokey Robinson and the Supremes. Because we were making more than they were, and Berry made us swear never to let them know. They always paid us separate from everybody else. . . . Then another thing we made an agreement on was we were not going to stay in the same hotels they stayed in." The reason for this was that room and food expenses all came out of their pay. So even though most of the entourage preferred staying in the most expensive hotels, the musicians chose to stay in inexpensive places. Concessions like these gave the musicians a financial superiority over the artists that they savored. Today Van Dyke laughs and says, "Everybody else would be crying broke and we wouldn't allow them on the back of the bus because they talked about us. We weren't shit, you know. So they began to see that shit was reversing. Every time we got on the bus they'd say, 'Did you stay in the hotel?' We'd say, 'No.' They said, 'Where did you eat?' We'd tell them, 'None of your business,' and laugh all the way back to Detroit."

* * *

Was Stevie Wonder "overweight"? That skinny kid? How could he be overweight? Well, what some people at Motown were suggesting with that comment in 1964 was that, in a year when the company was exploding on the charts, there was no need to push a blind, money-burning kid. The intracompany envy spawned by Stevie's special status had grown, and the failure of his post-"Fingertips" singles to generate significant sales allowed his enemies to shoot from the hip. They wanted Motown to write him off as a lucky one-shot and cut him loose. As Wonder told *Musician* in 1984:

> Oh, yeah. Straight out. And probably if I were the president of the company I'd do the same thing. But fortunately it all worked out . . . to everyone's surprise or to some peoples' surprise. Because some people would say things like, "Oh, that boy's gonna really be great. You don't know how talented that boy is." And the others would say, "Yeah, yeah, yeah, uh-huh, sure." They didn't really vibe on me.

This period left a lasting impression on Stevie: he would mention it often during his 1984 tour, and allow the writers for "Saturday Night Live" to use it as the base of a bitingly satiric comedy skit.

It wasn't Stevie's fault that none of his immediate post-"Fingertips" singles were hits; these singles were simply some of the worst material Motown ever cut for a major act during the period. "Workout Stevie, Workout" was a corny attempt to recapture the live feel of "Fingertips" in the studio. The track for "Castles in the Sand," cut in Los Angeles, was a dopey, unsophisticated kiddie love song. "Hey, Harmonica Man" and "High Heel Sneakers" were uptempo stomps with little of the verve you'd expect from Motown circa 1964, though the latter, recorded live, shows Stevie's voice clearly maturing.

And so, by November 1965, the wolves were snapping at Stevie's heels. Luckily, Berry's faith in his boy wonder was about to be rewarded with "Uptight (Everything's Alright)," a number-three pop hit that signaled several changes in Stevie. At fifteen, Stevie's voice had developed an aggressive, masculine edge. His vibrato now belonged to him, no longer to the whims of nature, and he used it to rip through a dance track of breakneck speed. Stevie contributed substantially to the rhythm arrangement, and as a result received his first songwriting credit. Stevie's ability to fuse different styles into a pleasing, commercially viable whole was foreshadowed on "Uptight"—he credited its driving tempo not to any R&B act, but to the Rolling Stones' "(I Can't Get No) Satisfaction." Stevie had toured with the Stones in 1964 and was impressed with how audiences had responded to their driving beat. His fusion of Rolling Stones' drummer Charlie Watts's licks into Motown music is illustrative of his budding genius.

Following Motown policy, Stevie's next single was a stale reworking of "Uptight" called "Nothing's too Good for My Baby." It did well, reaching number four R&B, but prepared no one for his subsequent single, a cover of Bob Dylan's civil rights and antiwar anthem, "Blowin' in the Wind." Away from Motown's studios Stevie liked to arrange his own versions of non-Motown pop music, but unlike the standards that Clarence Paul had taught him, Stevie enjoyed working with songs like Dylan's "Mr. Tambourine Man" and "Blowin'." Clarence Paul encouraged him and collaborated with him on a treatment of "Blowin'" that featured the producer on the high-pitched background vocal. Though Paul's production was overblown, especially in comparison to the spartan acoustic guitar-and-harmonica original, it was still a radical departure from Motown, one that made it into record stores due to Paul's lobbying efforts. Arguing that, because of Stevie's age and the young, hip, white audience that revered Dylan, it was a good career move for Stevie, Paul managed to overcome internal company skepticism.

"Blowin'" did well on the pop chart, reaching number nine. Most importantly, though, the song went number one on the R&B chart, solidifying Stevie's belief that black musical tastes weren't as narrow as most record companies, including Motown, often thought they were. In Stevie's ongoing education, that was a critical lesson; from then on, Stevie would always attempt to lead his core black audience forward, and would never pander to stereotypes.

The success of "Blowin'" didn't silence criticism of the record inside Motown, but this time, Stevie wasn't the only target. Instead, Clarence Paul, was criticized for exploiting his young charge in an attempt to revive his own singing career, the evidence for which was the prominence of Paul's voice on "Blowin'" and his performance of the song with Stevie onstage. According to another Motown staffer, Paul was accused "of trying to ride Stevie's coattail."

Stevie continued to have interesting experiences on the road, but his offstage friendships with the musicians didn't always sit well with the Motown hierarchy. One morning the minions of the Motown Revue gathered on the tour bus, musicians back in "Harlem," Berry up front on

"Broadway," and Stevie sitting unhappily in the middle. There was much nervous giggling in the back as Stevie held his head and moaned about an incredibly intense headache. The night before, the band had introduced Stevie to the joys of marijuana, and in his enthusiasm he had overindulged. It was funny. Then the players got nervous as Berry began to turn around and look closely at the kid. Several people tried to quiet Stevie. Things might have stayed cool if Stevie hadn't turned around and whined, "Man, you guys got any aspirin? I got a big headache from last night."

Outside the bus a meeting ensued in which Berry, in no uncertain terms, told everyone how valuable Stevie was to the company and how much of an investment Motown had in him. It would be someone's ass if anything bad happened to the boy. All involved were embarrassed, but it didn't stop the musicians or Stevie from "hanging out"—if not more discreetly—while touring. For Stevie—who, after all, was still just a teenager growing up in the sixties—drugs were just another thing to be tried, like listening to rock music or meeting the groupies that flocked backstage after a show. All of it was part of his diligent effort to make "Little Stevie" disappear.

Berry Gordy had copyrighted the word *soul* for use on a proposed gospel label, associating the term with the unbridled, impassioned music of the black church. But by late 1965, "soul" was commonly used in the black community, and in black music, with a wider meaning. In general nomenclature, "soul" had come to define a special quality that blacks possessed and whites didn't, a different way of talking, walking, and looking at the world. Musically, "soul" came to mean songs with secular lyrics about love, dancing, and other worldly concerns, sung and arranged with the techniques and, most importantly, the fervor of gospel music. It is hard to say exactly when this particular strain first openly infiltrated popular black music. In the early fifties it was considered sacrilegious for "church music" and non-church forms such as swing, blues, and rhythm and blues to be overtly mixed. But as that decade progressed, men such as Clyde McPhatter of the Dominoes and Drifters, and the Orioles' Sonny Til began exploiting their church roots on secular recordings.

Soul didn't explode into a full-fledged musical genre until a blind former Nat "King" Cole imitator named Ray Charles talked Atlantic Records into letting him try something different. "What'd I Say," "I Got a Woman," and, later, his version of "Georgia on My Mind," put the ferocious devotional energy of the Baptist church into tales of sinning, drinking, and sexual anguish that made him into a national institution, and made soul music a cleansing, cathartic medium for its secular fans. Charles established soul as singers' music, where open, piano-based backing and percussive horn charts provided space for a generation of vocalists —Wilson Pickett, Otis Redding, Carla Thomas, and Aretha Franklin were among the best—to unleash searing, passionate performances. The South, particularly Memphis, Tennessee—and more specifically, a record label called Stax—became the artistic and commercial home of soul. Stax, founded by a white man, Jim Stewart, and run by a black man, Al Bell, either recorded or inspired the era's greatest soul records, and during the mid- to late sixties provided the first dollars-and-cents challenge to Motown's domination of the black music industry. Until Stax began selling soul records by the truckload, blacks in the record industry had had a difficult time competing with Berry. Many imitated Motown, but none could beat it. The soft Chicago soul sound built around Curtis Mayfield's beautiful songs did well, and James Brown's badass funk always sold, but no single artist had ever threatened to challenge Motown.

Stax, however, was well organized, distributed by a company long established in black music—Atlantic Records—and it had its own sound, one that reached blacks as well as whites. Hip whites and progressive blacks were beginning to find Berry's yearning upward mobility and occasionally overbearing production values a bore. Stax was "the real thing," "the hip thing," and what black America was "really all about"—Motown was "Negro music." In an environment where *integration* was quickly being replaced in the mouths of trendsetters by *nationalism, Black Panther,* and *black power,* it wasn't just the glib who looked at the Temptations' tuxedos and said "Uncle Tom."

In 1964 and 1965, records like Wilson Pickett's "In the Midnight Hour," Don Covay's "Mercy, Mercy," Joe Tex's "Hold What You've Got," and Otis Redding's "Respect" and "I Can't Turn You Loose"— all cut in the South and distributed by Atlantic Records—were changing the face of black music. The popularity of soul was a challenge to Motown's upscale sounds and a threat to the black core audience whose loyalty Motown still needed. In response, Berry activated Soul Records in 1965 as a secular label featuring Shorty Long, Jimmy Ruffin, Junior Walker and the All Stars, and Gladys Knight and the Pips.

Long, a diminutive singer-songwriter from Alabama, made the Soul label's most unrefined recordings: "Here Comes the Judge," based on the Pigmeat Markum comedy routine later popularized by Sammy Davis, Jr., on "Rowan and Martin's Laugh-In"; "Devil With a Blue Dress On," a straight blues piano boogie with a casual stroll groove that was later made a rock classic by the white Detroit rock band Mitch Ryder and the Detroit Wheels; and a funny, mid-tempo track about a damn fine party called "The Function at the Junction." Motown musicians felt that this multi-instrumentalist was on the verge of stardom after his diverse *The Prime of Shorty Long* mixed bluesy soul originals with a quirky interpretation of Procol Harum's "A Whiter Shade of Pale." But he drowned in a boating accident in 1969, when he was just twenty-nine years old.

Despite having several hits on Soul, including "What Becomes of the Brokenhearted," a Top Ten pop and R&B hit in 1966, Jimmy Ruffin's career inspired no such optimism. Unlike his brother David, Jimmy was a mediocre stage performer and often had problems remaining in key, though on record his low tenor could be quite affecting when given strong material. Unfortunately, this Ruffin's voice wasn't distinctive enough to overcome the second-tier songwriting with which he was often saddled.

Motown's first "soul" hit came from Junior Walker and the All Stars, a man and a band whose down-home, gritty music and unpretentious manner almost define the term. The band made its living from the mid-fifties through the early sixties playing in bars and clubs in factory towns throughout the Midwest, doing steamy interpretations of B. B. King, Jimmy Reed, and Fats Domino. With Walker on gutbucket tenor sax and gravelly vocals, Willie Woods on guitar, Vic Thomas on organ, and James Graves on drums, they built a following, made a decent living, and gave little thought to a recording career until Johnny Bristol, who was then signed to Harvey Fuqua's Harvey Records, saw them in Battle Creek. Bristol recommended that they look Fuqua up on their next trip to Detroit, and one day in 1962 they arrived at the Harvey Records office. Bristol had apparently forgotten to tell Fuqua about them, which led, according to Fuqua, to the following scene: Walker came in, sax case in hand, and said, "I can play." Harvey thought, "This guy is real country," and told him, "Man, you get out of here." Walker persisted. "I got my band out in the car," he said. "I want to play for you." Fuqua decided to let them come in because, you never know, "They might be angels." Well, they were no angels, but they sure could throw down some funk.

Fuqua cut three singles on them in 1962 and 1963, "Twistlackawanna," "Brainwasher (Part I)," and "Good Rockin' Tonight," all raunchy instrumentals that didn't sell, but set the tone for Walker's recording career. After Harvey Records went under and Fuqua joined Motown, Walker went over to meet Berry. This is Walker's 1965 account of the meeting:

Berry said, "So you want a contract?" I said, "Yeah, I wanna contract." He said, "So you want to record?" "Yes, sir, I wanna record," said I. "Give that boy a contract," says Mr. Gordy. When I got the contract I asked what exactly I was signing. "Can you read?" Mr. Gordy asked. "I can read some stuff but not everything," I replied. And he told me, "Go ahead and sign, we won't mess you around." I trusted him, I signed.

In late 1964, Walker cut his first Motown single, a tune in the earthy tradition of his earlier sides, called "Monkey Jim" and based on one of Walker's many "down-home" expressions. His next single, the first hit on the Soul label, was "Shotgun," the definitive gutbucket sax instrumental of the sixties, a record in the tradition of the great honking saxophonists of the fifties, and as different from the Motown Sound as a process was from an Afro.

Berry and engineer Lawrence Horn are credited as "Shotgun" 's producers. In truth they just turned on the tape, stood back, and let Walker cut loose.

"Shotgun" has the kick of a bull and the greasy feel of a pig's-feet dinner as Walker's wailing tenor sax, Wood's scratchy, bluesy guitar licks, and Thomas's holy roller organ rock over a tough, finger-popping tempo. The bandleader's rough-hewn vocal fits the sound, but to this day no one knows what the lyric means, if it means anything. All we can ascertain is that it relates to shooting something, then to putting on a red dress and high-heeled shoes, then to picking tomatoes, and then to something Walker called "Twine Time":

At session's end even Berry asked, "What are you saying at the end, man? What were you saying at the end?" I was saying "Twine Time." He said, "Sounded like you were saying 'Crying time.' " I said, "No, it's 'Twine Time.' " He said, "Well, it's pretty good, it's pretty good." Then he called me three weeks later and said, "Man, this record is tearin' up."

It sure was, going number one on the R&B chart and, to everyone's astonishment, number four on the pop chart. "Do the Boomerang," a song peppered with instructions on tossing one, went to number ten R&B, while the more straightforward but equally strenuous "Shake and Fingerpop" went to number seven R&B, following "Shotgun" in 1965. "Cleo's Mood," originally released as "Fingerpop" 's B side, was revived as a single as well and reached number fourteen R&B in early 1966. Walker's undiluted soul sax and undisciplined shouts even attracted the attention of H-D-H. While making increasingly complex records for the Supremes and Four Tops, they must have had fun making the looser, decidedly soulful party record "(I'm a) Road Runner." It landed at four on the R&B charts. Walker's versions of H-D-H's "How Sweet It Is to Be Loved by You" and "Come See About Me" went Top Ten soul as well.

In retrospect, the most amazing thing about Walker's run of soulful singles was that not one was produced or written by Norman Whitfield, for ultimately it was he, in collaboration with Barrett Strong—the singer of "Money," who was trying to revive his show business career as a songwriter—who represented the label's prime soul production and writing force. It was Whitfield and Strong who gave Gladys Knight and the Pips "The Nitty Gritty," "Friendship Train," and "I Heard It Through the Grapevine," and, after taking control of the Temptations, made them the most important Motown "soul" group not on the Soul label.

The key to the Whitfield-Strong counterattacks on Stax was that they never sacrificed song structure for grit. On Whitfield records singers were never out of control or so impassioned that lyrics were rendered unintelligible. A classic example of their approach is "I Wish It Would Rain" (number one soul, 1968), a brooding confession of lost love sung with profound regret by David Ruffin, with the other Temptations providing magnificently arranged backing harmonies. To heighten the record's melancholy effect and add that touch of Motown cleverness, Whitfield added seagull chirps, thunderclaps, and the tapping of falling rain to the track. Eddie Kendricks objected to them, feeling the birds detracted from the song and just sounded strange in general. But the other Temps backed Whitfield, feeling that the sounds made "Rain" soulful yet different.

Whitfield, along with Strong, effectively answered soul's challenge to Motown—not by matching the music of Memphis, but by interpreting it with a Motown flavor. And yet, this achievement hardly satisfied him. In 1968, Whitfield—the man who had stalked Smokey and the Temptations—again sought a new sound, one that drew upon the songwriting discipline Berry preached and the changes he was noticing in pop music and society. As he had before, Whitfield watched and waited.

Marvin Gaye had always felt he had three voices: a harsh, impassioned, rough "rock" sound; a resilient, firm, undeniably masculine falsetto or high tenor, often used to dramatize key words in a lyric; and a smooth, cool midrange that was closest in texture to his own delicate, gentle, speaking voice. During the mid-sixties, when Marvin proved himself the most versatile and durable of Motown's male singers, these voices would appear and disappear depending on the song's demands and Marvin's attitude at the moment.

While Marvin possessed an impressive vocal schizophrenia, he also labored under the weight of two distinctly different personalities. There was the "good artist," a devoutly religious, Bible-carrying, Scripture-quoting man who respected his wife and her Gordy relatives, worked beautifully within the context of the Motown system, and contributed profoundly to making material he may have abhorred into hits. This was a malleable team player, whose marriage and loyalty made him an integral part of the family.

Then there was the other Marvin, the one sister-in-law Esther, with characteristic understatement, once described as "difficult." This was the Marvin who hung out with the musicians, strongly identified with their arrogant pride, liked to get high ("I've been open to grass since I was a kid, I've also been open to alcohol, cigarettes, uppers and downers, heroin, cocaine, but I mean, you know . . . I dug all of them, too"), rode his motorcycle around Detroit, bitched about the songs, and called himself "an artist," striving mightily to live up to every affected stereotype the word connotes.

As warm and charming as Marvin could be, especially to the women who sighed at his long eyelashes, smooth skin, and sly, ingratiating smile, there was an impetuous, evil side to him that could flare easily. "I'm an individual and I demand that I be treated as an individual and not as cattle," he'd say, adding, "My position and my independence has gotten me into a great deal of trouble in the past, but I've managed to overcome it because my convictions are honest." To Marvin it may have been a matter of integrity, but to even his friends, like Pete Moore of the Miracles, he could come off as "unusual, bizarre, erratic."

Sometimes, when Marvin went too far, he would have to be brought back into line. One night at the Twenty Grand, with the whole Motown hierarchy front and center, the band hit the introductory chords to one of his hits, he was announced, and . . . no Marvin. They played it again. No Marvin. Berry went backstage and found Marvin languishing in his dressing room with a slight case of insecurity. As a local deejay watched, Berry slapped him and "advised" him in a loud voice to proceed with his performance. Marvin proceeded.

It was just one of the little dramas that these two intensely creative and completely different men played out over the years. Where Marvin was languid and worked only when inspired, Berry was a businessman and a craftsman, a nine-to-five artist of the dollar bill who had little tolerance for Marvin's flights from responsibility. That they were relatives through marriage heightened the tension, particularly for Marvin, whose enmity toward authority figures started with his father, continued with the Army, and resurfaced with Berry.

After writing an underrated slice of easy-rocking R&B for Marvin in 1964 ("Try It Baby"), Berry's active involvement with Marvin's career waned. Subsequently, a number of Motown producer-writers used Marvin as a vehicle for radically differing concepts.

To Mickey Stevenson, Marvin's romantic appeal and the Motown publicity campaign that promoted it had made him the perfect instrument for furthering the career of Stevenson's wife Kim Weston. Stevenson saw his wife, a dark-skinned woman with a strong bluesy voice and a tendency to put on weight, as his Diana Ross. After putting so many hours into the care and feeding of Motown's creative department, Stevenson viewed Weston's stardom as his payback, the vehicle through which Motown's well-oiled machine could make dollars for *his* pocket. Weston's one significant hit, produced and written by H-D-H, was the uncharacteristically (for Motown) gospel-flavored, "Take Me in Your Arms (Rock Me)," which went to number four on the R&B chart in 1965. But it was her husband, with "Love Me All the Way," a Top Twenty R&B hit in 1963, "Helpless," number thirteen in 1966, and several other releases, who was providing the moving musical force behind Weston's career. Despite Stevenson's efforts, it was only her duets with Marvin, particularly "It Takes Two," a soulful mid-tempo dance song with a memorable vocal chorus written by Stevenson and Jobete staff songwriter Sylvia Moy, that captured the public's imagination.

Motown never could quite get a handle on just what image Weston should project or who her audience would be. Part of the problem, according to Motown employees, was Weston's physique. The sequined, tight tube dresses Motown poured—or stuffed—its female artists into were perfect for Diana Ross's narrow frame. But on Weston, a woman with big hips and an ample backside, the dresses made her curves seem mountainous. White nightclub audiences found this exhibit of black physiology amusing. An ex-Motown staffer remembers, "The white folks would just laugh at her body. They just thought it looked too big. It made it difficult for them to take her seriously." Another part of Weston's problem was that many at the company, including some of Berry's sisters, resented Stevenson using his position to further her career. Taken together these factors, plus Berry's emphasis on Ross as Motown's only female star, ensured that Weston never became any more than a regular opening act for Motown's bigger names.

H-D-H saw in Marvin Gaye's supple vocal shadings a welcome respite from the tightly controlled productions necessary for the Supremes and, to a lesser degree, the Four Tops. "How Sweet It Is to Be Loved by You" is so different in its musical approach from "Baby Love" and "Where Did Our Love Go?" that it could have been the work of an entirely different producer. "How Sweet" has a warm, loose feeling, as a relaxed Marvin flows in and out of the beat with a jazz singer's sense of phrasing. The instruments are all clearly defined, from the rumbling drum intro, to Earl Van Dyke's tinkling piano, to the soulful female backing vocals. Marvin is at his most charming, and the lyric has a mature quality quite different from the adolescent melodramas of the Supremes. Similar in tone and lyric is "Little Darling (I Need You)," another H-D-H composition that showcased Marvin's sculptured voice, with none of the studied quality usually associated with their productions. In fact, the directness of these two songs made them extremely durable properties. In the seventies "How Sweet" (by James Taylor) and "Little Darling" (by the Doobie Brothers) were both substantial hits when recorded in a laid-back Los Angeles style.

In 1967, two teams of producer-writers—one old and one new—and one fine young female singer collaborated with Marvin on seven of the most enduring romantic pop songs of the sixties: "Ain't No Mountain High Enough," "Your Precious Love," "If This World Were Mine," "If I Could Build My Whole World Around You, "Ain't Nothing Like the Real Thing," "Good Lovin' Ain't Easy to Come By," and "You're All I Need to Get By." The old team was composed of Harvey Fuqua and Johnny Bristol. Bristol had originally entered the recording industry as an artist on Fuqua's Tri-Phi records. After Fuqua's company was absorbed by Motown, Bristol was made a staff arranger and Jobete songwriter who occasionally traveled to check on Motown acts' live shows for Fuqua. However, it wasn't until he joined with Fuqua to create for Marvin that his gifts were really utilized by Motown.

Two young New York residents, Nick Ashford and Valerie Simpson, were the new kids on the block. The tall, elegant Ashford had traveled from the town of Willow Run, outside Detroit, to New York to become a jazz dancer in 1963. At Harlem's White Rock Baptist Church one Sunday he met a cute, lively little member of the choir, Valerie Simpson. They became friends and started writing songs together, Ashford providing the lyrics and Simpson, an exceptional gospel pianist, composing the music. They cut three singles for the small New York indie Glover Records in 1964 and a year later joined the staff of Scepter Records, a label known for its fine girl group, the Shirelles, and the state-of-the-art pop records made by Hal David and Burt Bacharach for Dionne Warwick. In 1966, after Ray Charles's version of their "Let's Go Get Stoned" went to number one on the soul chart, Motown approached them about joining Jobete.

Their first trip to Hitsville was memorable, as Simpson told *The New York Times:*

> The bus driver took us to these tacky little brownstone buildings with a homemade sign in the window that said "Hitsville." We couldn't believe it. We said, "We want the main office at Motown," and he said, "This is the only Motown I know." But once you got inside that little house, you knew they were the hottest thing going.

Their contributions to Motown were marked by a sophisticated musical sensibility that fused gospel's inspirational power and wonderfully colloquial lyrics with dramatic song structures that, considering their affinity for ballads, rarely grew overly sentimental.

The singer was a petite, utterly sexy lady named Tammi Terrell, who would overshadow Mary Wells and Kim Weston, Marvin's previous duet partners, and set standards Gaye's later coupling with Diana Ross wouldn't match. Born in Philadelphia as Tammy Montgomery, she recorded her first sides as a fifteen-year-old for Wand Records of New York, after Luther Dixon, their top producer-talent scout, discovered her at a talent show. Not much happened with those records, and for a time she attended the University of Pennsylvania, where she studied psychology. She returned to performing, by traveling with James Brown's revue on the chitlin circuit during the years when he was truly "the hardest-working man in show business." Tammi cut one single for Brown's Try Me label and reportedly became romantically involved with her boss. According to her friends, Tammi's relationship with Brown was quite tempestuous. She left Brown's organization around 1964, got married to and divorced from another man, recorded a bit for Checker Records, and signed with Motown in 1965. Her voice, her charm, and her looks quickly established her as a company favorite, all much to the chagrin of many of Motown's other female singers. After a couple of moderate hits, "I Can't Believe You Love

135

Me" and "Come On and See Me" in 1966, she was paired with Marvin, a move for which several ex-Motowners take the credit. It was another example of the way in which the company's talent manipulation could pay enormous dividends.

The Gaye-Terrell hits started in April 1967 with "Ain't No Mountain High Enough," written by Ashford and Simpson and produced by Fuqua and Bristol, which has strong devotional lyrics that Marvin attacks with a joyous, shouting, whooping vocal. Tammi is more reserved, and yet she has a vivacious warmth that really seems to inspire Marvin. He sounds as though he's ready to make love to Tammi the minute the song fades out (or that he might be doing it as we listen). Fuqua and Bristol provide one of those classic Motown intros, with bells, vibes, muffled strings, and the sound of drumsticks beat rapidly against the snare drum rim to captivate the ear. The rest of the production isn't as memorable, working simply to support Ashford and Simpson's well-designed rising and falling song structure.

"Your Precious Love" (number two soul, number five pop in September 1967) receives a street-corner doo-wop presentation, with its strolling, finger-popping rhythm, and the Moonglowesque harmonies recreated by Marvin and Fuqua. These elements, combined with Ashford and Simpson's lovey-dovey lyrics, made "Love" a staple at basement parties and a slow-dance classic. Marvin, right at home in this setting, is superb, and yet Tammi is the record's real star, delivering a breathy, husky, sexy reading. At one point Terrell sings the words "I want to show," hesitates, and then comes back with "I want to show my appreciation," as if she wants us to understand just how deep her feelings are. It is one of those beautiful moments when a singer, embellishing a lyric with creative phrasing, communicates deep emotion.

Much more tightly controlled, but just as affecting, is Marvin's romantic, self-penned "If This World Were Mine" (number two soul, number ten pop in December 1967). It opens with bells and chimes and a gently throbbing piano. Then Marvin sings softly as the track builds, piece by piece: guitar, vibes, bass, strings. It is Fuqua and Bristol's most subtle production, as the instruments, particularly Jamerson's bass, are used to counterpoint the vocals. Again Terrell shines, showing great emotion despite a fairly narrow vocal range. She couldn't "wail" like Gladys Knight, but Tammi shared her ability to squeeze the most out of a love song.

"Ain't Nothing Like the Real Thing," "Good Lovin' Ain't Easy to Come By," and "You're All I Need to Get By" were the first of the series written *and* produced by Ashford and Simpson. Where Bristol and Fuqua were extremely competent technicians, Ashford and Simpson had a definite sound and attitude. The same might be said for H-D-H, except that Ashford and Simpson's music was appropriate to songs with the kind of larger-than-life, love-conquers-all stories that could have served as Hollywood movie themes. "Valerie Simpson was one of the most talented musicians and producers to ever work at Motown," Van Dyke recalls. "She would play piano beautifully, write beautifully, and really knew what she was doing in the studio. The songs she and Ashford wrote were the most musical tunes anybody wrote at that company. She was something special."

As part of the Motown system, Fuqua and Bristol cut competing versions of "Ain't Nothing Like the Real Thing" and "You're All I Need to Get By" for judgment by the quality control division. In both cases, Ashford and Simpson's versions got the nod. In fact, after hearing the duo's interpretation of "You're All I Need," Berry—who happened to be attending that day's meeting—simply announced "Ship it" after it was played. As Simpson recalled with pride, "He didn't even let them vote on it, he loved it so much."

"Ain't Nothing" (number one soul in April 1968) is a song with almost no introductory section. Marvin and Tammi roll right into the title, singing the sweet hook in an easy, loving harmony. The music is supple and understated, with violins and flutes chirping happily over a bright drum and tambourine rhythm. The song is structured so that all the instrumentation gracefully heightens the chorus of "Ain't nothing like the real thing, baby." It is the kind of assured pop songwriting and production that Berry had been preaching since he met Smokey ten years before. Terrell's vocal is magnificent, dominating the record while Marvin glides along, seeming to savor the passion Tammy directs toward him.

On "You're All I Need" (number one soul in August 1968) Tammi is great again, but here Marvin matches her note for note. The record begins quietly, building majestically with Marvin, Tammi, Simpson, and Ashford harmonizing on the title over a repeating four-note bass pattern. Gaye opens the song softly; there is a quiver in Tammi's voice as she comes in on the second verse. With each line their singing grows more abandoned as the music swells and falls and swells underneath them. The feeling is almost operatic, and the record is a landmark, as good as anything else created by Motown.

The passion of these records led most outside the company to assume that Gaye and Tammi were lovers. Surely, all that feeling couldn't have been faked. And yes, Tammi was in love with a major Motown singer, but it wasn't Marvin Gaye. It was David Ruffin. In fact, the lean lead singer and the budding young female star shared an apartment on Detroit's Lynwood Avenue. When they weren't on the road, they were often seen driving up to Hitsville in David's mink-lined limousine. To the many people at Motown who disliked Ruffin but adored Tammi, theirs was a horrible mismatch. The conventional wisdom was "she deserved something better." "It didn't make no goddamn difference [to her]," one observer recalls. "She'd be wherever he was . . . Tammi loved David. I mean *loved* him."

David wasn't Tammi's only concern. She suffered from intense migraine headaches that she believed were precipitated by arguments with him and other personal tensions; no one suspected how dangerous they were. Marvin remembered, "I'm not sure she knew how serious it was until she collapsed. In fact, I'm sure she didn't. She felt she was having headaches. She took a lot of pain medicine; she had seen several doctors, and they had said, 'Take a couple of Darvons, whatever, see if it helps.' "

The collapse occurred in the summer of 1967 at Virginia's Hampden–Sydney College. Tammi fell into Marvin's arms at the conclusion of "Your Precious Love." The next three years were a nightmare. She was diagnosed as having a brain tumor, and lost weight steadily, shedding up to forty pounds at one point. She suffered partial loss of muscle coordination and memory, and was operated on eight times in eighteen months. She gamely attempted to record again during this time, but on several records issued under her name it was Valerie Simpson who did most of the vocals. When Tammi died on March 16, 1970, at Graduate Hospital in Philadelphia, it was as if God had finally taken pity on this beautiful tortured angel and let her rest.

Neither Ruffin nor Gaye ever spoke at length about the effect Tammi Terrell's illness and death had on them, though for Marvin, by far the more sensitive of the two, it seemed to signal a profound change in his life, and it would ultimately have a profound effect on his music.

By the end of 1965, Motown's chief executive (Berry Gordy, Jr.) must have received a great vote of confidence from Motown's chief stockholder (Berry Gordy, Jr.). His office was no longer dominated by the dart board Diana Ross had used as a secretary four years before. Now it had wall-sized speakers, a built-in television, a desk microphone to record meetings, and an armchair complete with footrest. The company had grossed eight million dollars in 1965 and was the industry's top-seller of seven-inch singles, with forty-two different singles making the *Billboard* pop chart; and for the third year in a row Jobete was BMI's top publishing company, with twelve songs winning awards from that organization. The company now employed 125 people, most of them black, though most of the key financial positions, such as comptroller, were held by whites. To the Motown, Tamla, and Gordy labels the company had added the Soul, VIP, and country Melody label, while de-emphasizing the financially unsuccessful Jazz Workshop. International Talent Management handled approximately one hundred acts, all of whom were also signed to one of Berry's labels. The company had offices in New York and Los Angeles, employing songwriters, producers, engineers, musicians, singers, and publicists in those entertainment industry capitals.

Instead of using a variety of distributors in different areas, the company now employed one distributor in key markets, lessening paperwork and making these distributors more accountable to, and dependent on, Motown products; this put Berry's company on equal footing with the major labels. In 1965, Motown was also finalizing plans for its albums to be sold by mail order through the Columbia Record Club, which would make their music available to older listeners who didn't frequent record stores. Because of the growing use of eight-track tape cartridges in automobiles, Motown aggressively pursued this market, predicting that cartridges would constitute ten percent of it sales by the end of 1966.

Internationally, different versions of Motown hits were being cut in foreign languages for distribution through the company's worldwide network of licensees. Domestically, Motown was attempting to diversify its image, though with more gusto than selectivity. Signed were the likes of Stepin Fetchit, the actor whose bulging eyes and onstage laziness made him America's prototypical Uncle Tom, and television kiddie comedian Soupy Sales. After much consideration, they turned down a funny young comedian from Peoria named Richard Pryor; his dirty, often controversial material was considered too risqué for the company's image. The great jazz vocalist Billy Eckstine and the beautiful black actress Barbara McNair joined the fold, but then so did washed-up MOR crooner Tony Martin, as well as Paul Petersen, the son on "The Donna Reed Show," and Irene Ryan, "Granny" of "The Beverly Hillbillys."

The signings of Martin and the other television personalities were part of Motown's ongoing effort to be known as more than just a black-owned company. In Berry's, words Motown was a "general market" entity. The desire wasn't misplaced; as the sales of Motown's big acts—the Supremes, Temptations, Four Tops, and Stevie Wonder—all revealed, reaching whites was important to generating large amounts of capital in the record industry. Still, Motown's taste in doing so was never more questionable. For all of its adventurousness in the studio, Berry's institution usually played it safe, and was, alas, never afraid of being corny or pandering to his audiences' most obvious desires. Unfortunately, that tactic often failed, as it would with Sales, Petersen, Ryan, and Martin.

To a large degree this lack of corporate flair reflected Berry's own personal taste. Despite his money, no one ever considered Berry a particularly stylish or fastidious dresser. He favored dark business suits, dark ties that hung straight down against his white shirts, and a short nerdy Afro. Berry was so nondescript (or such a good bluffer) that when he appeared on "To Tell the Truth" in 1965, none of the four celebrity questioners thought he was Berry Gordy. At least he grinned a bit at the end of the program, when they brought out the Supremes; in most pictures, and in his increasingly infrequent public appearences, Berry either wore a scowl or a forced smile that seemed to say his mind was miles away.

Berry had never been the happy-go-lucky type; but at thirty-six he was quite different from the man he'd been just four years before. Success is an inspiration, though not always a sweet one, and it was certainly making him see the world in a new way. Berry now viewed his "one of the boys" relationship with Motown old-timers as a personal strain and, potentially, a stumbling block for Motown. For Berry to expand the company and be the leader that he and others at Motown thought he had to be, a change had to be made.

Stories are told by several people that differ in detail, but not in meaning, about what happened. Backstage at the Apollo Theater one night, Berry was speaking with a major promoter when a Motown artist came up to him and asked him loudly for a substantial amount of money. The word came down from Berry's office that no one was to approach him like that again. No more "Berry, baby"—it was "Mr. Gordy" for everyone. No more just walking into his office—make an appointment and talk to Ralph Seltzer first, the company's internal buffer. Berry, who once did all Motown-related interviews, cut down on his contact with the press. From 1965 on, Barney Ales and other white executives would do Motown's talking in the industry publications.

The days when Berry was easily accessible and knew everybody who worked for him on a first-name basis were gone. In *Corporate Cultures*, Terrence Deal and Allen Kennedy describe managers who behave as Berry did as "bastardly" and "heroic," feeling that "modern managers who try to be humane may at the same time undermine the values upon which

Diana Ross and Berry Gordy embrace at a party in 1985. *(Orchid Public Relations)*

By 1968 Diana Ross was squarely on top, and Cindy Birdsong had replaced Florence Ballard. Mary Wilson (right) stayed in her place.
(Kriegsmann/Ochs Archives)

In classic sixties makeup, Brenda Holloway prepares for a performance in New York. *(Don Paulsen)*

Dapper Eddie Kendricks would at first resist producer Norman Whitfield's efforts to "psychedelicize" the Temptations' music, but as a solo artist he would later benefit from the updated sound. He was Motown's most successful male solo act of the early seventies. *(Don Paulsen)*

Sex had always been a big part of the Supremes' appeal. Here Cindy and Mary flash their legs, though Diana seems reluctant to display hers in profile. *(Michael Ochs Archives)*

Lamont Dozier, Eddie Holland, Brian Holland. *(Michael Ochs Archives)*

Marvin Gaye plays drums prior to a rehearsal as the Four Tops' "Duke" Fakir looks on. *(Don Paulsen)*

The Temptations' brilliant
but troubled lead singer
David Ruffin.
(Kriegsmann/Ochs Archives)

Florence Ballard, following her exile from the Supremes. *(Kriegsmann/Ochs Archives)*

Marvin Gaye signing
photographs in Washington,
D.C., as his father and mother
look on. *(Joe McEwen Archives)*

The mature Stevie Wonder. *(Kwame' Braithwaite)*

Two black entertainment giants of the sixties, Sidney Poitier and Berry Gordy, meet in Central Park in 1984. Poitier was shooting his film *Fast Forward*. *(Juanita Cole)*

The last great product of the production line, the Jackson 5: (left to right) Jermaine, Marlon, Tito, Michael, and Jackie. *(Michael Ochs Archives)*

Levi Stubbs, the Four Tops' lead singer, in 1985. *(Orchid Public Relations)*

the culture of the institution rests. Modern heroes may need to be hard and 'insensitive' to keep a company consistent with its goals and vision —the very elements that made it strong in the first place." So, from that viewpoint of management theory, Berry was making a necessary move. But to the old hands at Motown, it just seemed like Berry had become "an uppity nigger" who was getting bigheaded over success, a success that had been built on teamwork, not dictatorship. Still, few had the courage to criticize him openly.

Also, Berry, once a prolific songwriter, and the teacher of Smokey Robinson, Brian Holland, and so many others, was no longer providing original material. By screening all Motown releases, he still played an important part in the company's creative process. But by not being in the basement "snakepit" on a regular basis, he became distanced from the musicians and producers who were Motown's backbone. He talked to Ales on a daily basis, but not to Van Dyke or to Jamerson. The gap between the music Motown made and the promotion people who sold it grew wide, and it was a gap even a man as driven as Berry would find difficult to bridge.

Berry's personal life was equally turbulent. He had gotten a Mexican divorce from Raynoma in Chihuahua in 1962, and a formal U.S. divorce in 1964. One child had come of their union, a boy named Kennedy, a boy, like many children of the period, named after the late president. Berry would next marry an unassuming, attractive woman from Detroit named Margaret. By 1965, they were married and had a son named Berry IV, continuing that family tradition. His marriage to Margaret was accomplished with great secrecy; most people never knew that Berry ever married again after his divorce from Raynoma. The news media certainly didn't know: from 1965 on, Berry would be romantically linked with several of his protégées.

Probably Berry's least effective attempt at molding a protégée were his efforts on behalf of a tall, striking California-born blonde named Chris Clark. She was a singer, but not a very gifted one. Berry thought differently. During a mid-sixties interview about Motown, Berry surprised the reporter by shifting gears. "Running the corporation is a drag," he said, "but get a load of this girl." He reached through the records piled on his desk and put hers on the turntable. Smiling as it played, Berry commented, "She's white but she's got the sound."

But Clark's disdain for shoes—she hated to wear them—her casual attitude toward dress in general, and her tendency to eat too much, led some at Motown to call her "sloppy" and wonder what Berry saw in her.

And despite singles produced by H-D-H, Marvin Gaye, and Smokey Robinson, and B sides produced by Berry— a sign of his commitment to her career—Clark didn't make a dent on the singles chart. Still, she was rewarded with an album, *Soul Sounds,* and some lugubrious liner notes ("Chris dwells in the limbo of the 'cool' soaring comfortably from the jazz idiom into the bluesy-pop world such as the timid fear to tread.") This album *is* noteworthy for its cover. The styling of her platinum locks, the use of blue eye makeup and a clinging blue sequined dress, and the way her long right arm was posed carefully against her thigh all suggest to an uncanny degree the glamor-gal look of one of Berry's better-known protégées.

Berry had been considerably more successful with his ex-secretary and her two high-school friends. He would sit up front at the Supremes' gigs, his chair turned toward the stage, his mouth occasionally opening the way a child's does when he becomes obsessed with an object. He watched as Flo moved her ample, womanly frame through Cholly Atkins's demure, girlish choreography, using her impish smile to convey a bit of personality across the footlights; Mary, looking radiant, beautiful, and unnaturally happy, danced through the trio's "one-two-three step" half-turns and swaying twist like a perfect wind-up doll; both of them talented counterpoints to Diana, with her eyes as luminous as silver dollars on a poker table, a mouth as wide as her face, projecting an urgent desire to please. They were his girls, and they had to be perfect.

Artist Development director Harvey Fuqua, a man to whom a flashy stage show was as thrilling as a hit record, remembers, "I used to just freak on the Supremes 'cause they were so good; they did everything you told them to do. If you take that out, they take it out. Don't do that anymore, they don't do that anymore. Do a little more of this, they do a little more of that." The progress they'd made from the early tours was amazing, but to Berry they would never be perfect enough, even though the pride he took in their achievements—achievements he always linked to the organization's growth—was immense.

Berry was brutal about little mistakes. Diana bore the brunt of his criticism, for it was she whom Berry had made the group's focal point. Diana was to carry the show, and when she didn't do it with the verve Berry desired, his temper would flare and she'd end up crying under his demanding gaze. Then Berry would soften and soothe her, building her back up and sending her into the clouds with his love. It was the carrot-and-the-stick with Berry and Diana, love and discipline, as he pumped and deflated her ego at his whim. When he needed to be, Berry was a master of mind control. Diana wanted "it"—the love, the acceptance, the stardom—so badly, and he had convinced her that only by living his thoughts, becoming an extension of his dreams, could she live out her own.

"Berry had made her his from the very word go," says Beans Bowles. "On the stage when she came off he would be telling her 'That was great, but you're supposed to do such-and-such a thing.' She always had that pressure." Berry would be standing in the wings by the time she got off or, after receiving a report from someone in Artist Development, he'd talk to her over the phone, questioning, instructing, molding. Like a modern Dr. Frankenstein, Berry had made Diana, and for that reason she would always have a certain control over him that no one else could really fathom. Were they lovers? Neither Berry or Diana have ever admitted it in public; nor will anyone at Motown say so for the record. Yet only a blind man or a fool could ignore the special care Berry put into her career and the worshipful, loving way she spoke of him. They were more than lovers; they were each creations of the other. Diana would never have been the star she was without him. And Diana, by her very makeup—her pop voice, her ambition, and her willingness to be loyal and to learn, to be his sex symbol and his daughter—had made Berry's dream come true.

During 1965 and 1966, Diana became Berry's weapon of subversion, a missile that would penetrate the worlds of show business and social acceptance to which he craved entry. As representative as the H-D-H hits were of Berry's ear for what constituted effective pop music, a series of Supremes albums released to spread the Supremes' appeal show his desire for—and blindness to—the pitfalls of taking integration to the point of pandering.

A Bit of Liverpool (1964) was an homage to the Beatles. But, unlike the Beatles' reverent treatment of Motown songs, it had none of the passion or understanding of the material needed to make it work. *The Supremes Sing Country, Western and Pop* (1965) was a pale shadow of Ray Charles's 1962 pioneering country-soul fusion *Modern Sounds in Country and Western Music.* The album is so bad that it is practically unlistenable today, despite the presence of great songs such as Willie Nelson's "Funny How Time Slips Away." *We Remember Sam Cooke* (1965) has its moments (Flo's vocal on "Good News" for one), but not because it attempts to capture the gospel purity that Cooke gave to even his most secular songs, but because Cooke was the model for Berry's upscale crossover fixation. Since Berry's days writing for Jackie Wilson, he had harbored deep admiration for Cooke's ability to transform himself from gospel star to Copa regular, and this hastily created album reflects Berry's reverence.

But the obvious pride and joy of Berry and the other Motown employees who revered the show business mainstream was *Live at the Copa*, recorded at the club in July 1965 and featuring liner notes by the most mainstream of all black entertainers—Sammy Davis, Jr. The Supremes had built up to that engagement, playing white, monied clubs like Blinstrub's in Boston, the Safari Room in San Jose, the Twin Coaches in Pittsburgh, and the Clay House in Bermuda. The Supremes had become too big for the Motown Revue; in fact, by 1965 the Revue itself was being de-emphasized, as Motown's biggest acts—often with a minor Motown signee as opener—began playing bigger and whiter halls. The Henry Wynnes of the music business—blacks who had promoted or booked Motown acts during the struggling years—were now being passed over, as Motown booked the Supremes, the Four Tops, the Temptations, and others through William Morris, International Creative Management, and other white agencies.

While the Copa dates were sought to build respect for the Supremes among show business's big names, television—a medium in which Motown's grooming would prove itself—was to become the group's bread and butter. Compared to the steps of competing girl groups that often seemed hurriedly staged or underdeveloped, the Supremes' songs were choreographed especially for the tube, each series of steps carefully designed to convey their femininity and grace. The Supremes' first major television gig was Ed Sullivan's Christmas broadcast on December 24, 1964, and during 1965–66 they appeared on network television twenty times: ten times on NBC, including "Hullabaloo," the Orange Bowl Parade, "The Tonight Show," "The Dean Martin Show," and a Sammy Davis, Jr., special; three times on ABC's "Hollywood Palace"; and seven times on the most popular variety show in America, CBS's "The Ed Sullivan Show." Motown developed an excellent relationship with the networks, especially NBC, and as often as possible tied in network appearances with record releases, often debuting singles on television. "I Hear a Symphony" was released November 6, 1966; the Supremes were on Sullivan's show November 10. "My World Is Empty Without You" was released December 29, 1966; they participated in the Orange Bowl Parade New Year's Day. In one of the label's greatest coups, the Supremes debuted "You Can't Hurry Love" on July 24, 1966, and it was in record stores the next morning.

The days when Berry had to approve Diana's purchase of a four-hundred-dollar lynx coat on the installment plan were over. Though Motown kept a firm grip on their finances, by 1965 each of the Supremes was earning $250,000 a year and had moved their families into duplexes in the Buena Vista district. When Cholly Atkins relocated to Detroit, his landlady was Mary Wilson. Florence had an Eldorado Cadillac at one point, later trading that in for a Fleetwood to carry the thousand dollars a month in clothes she was purchasing at the time.

These were great times for the Supremes. In the midst of five number-one records in a row, they rivaled the Beatles as the most commercial group in pop music and were, without challenge, the biggest-selling female act in the history of recorded music. But the paces Motown put them through were frighteningly swift and draining. On stage in Blinstrubs's in Boston, Diana, so skinny now that her sequined dresses seemed too heavy for her body, fainted onstage. For most of the month prior to the Copa engagement Flo had been struck down with pneumonia, and she was able to rehearse only the week prior to the show. Some interpreted her sickness as nerves, seeing in it a certain lack of commitment to the group and to Motown. Flo was not as pliant as Diana or Mary; if she was sick, she was sick. That was her attitude, and not a popular one around Hitsville. Nor was her intimate friendship with Berry's sometimes driver, Thomas Chapman. Supremes—glamorous, cultivated ladies—were not supposed to date chauffeurs. These black marks against Flow were not forgotten.

The drama that was building was unknown to anyone outside Motown; backed by hit records and old-fashioned onstage show-business corn, Motown was busy pushing the Supremes into the great wide heart of mainstream America. In 1965, the girls performed at the opening of the Houston Astrodome, the "Eighth Wonder of the World," along with Judy Garland; in 1966, they were the first pop group to perform at Lincoln Center's Philharmonic Hall; a Supremes' bread was even marketed with Motown's permission. In the highly politicized environment of mid-sixties America the symbolism of three black girls from Detroit sharing the stage with a certified Hollywood star, crashing the home of classical music, and then penetrating supermarket shelves was quite powerful. Just as the Voting Rights Act of 1965 and the marches of Dr. Martin Luther King, Jr., represented the rising tide of black aspirations, the Supremes' every step was seen as a move forward for blacks by the forces of integration. Everything that was good about Motown—the music, the polish, the image, the upward mobility of the company—was epitomized by the

Supremes. The group was at its peak in 1965 and 1966, and so was Motown's production line.

In the eye of this hurricane was Diana Ross, whose ego had now grown as large as the Supremes' record sales. Though most of the Supremes' interviews during this period were marked by an avoidance of any topic remotely objectionable—Maxine Powell was surely pleased—Diana's sense of self-worth came through in a 1966 *Look* magazine interview: "On 'Hullabaloo,' they gave me a cue card with a stupid speech to say," she complained. "How dare they do that? I could be the mistress of ceremonies, but they never ask me. I see all these phonies who never had a number-one hit, runnin' around actin' like big stars. I've got something they don't have, and the kids know. I'm for real."

By mid-1966, Diana was already looking beyond the Supremes. And when Mort Persky of the *Detroit Free Press* went to interview the Supremes for a piece celebrating the group's gala January return to the Roostertail, only Ross was present. It was during this triumphant return home—WXYZ aired the show live and there were lines around the block —that rumors about Diana leaving the group began circulating, probably "leaked" from Motown itself. As always, when it came to the Supremes, Motown's timing and news management was impeccable. What better place to lay the seeds for Diana's solo career than at her homecoming gig?

The show itself, however, at least to *Free Press* reviewer Ken Barnard, was not simply a Diana Ross showcase, but a tribute to the Supremes as a unit. Barnard praised them for singing MOR standards like "Somewhere" and "People." The latter, Barbra Streisand's signature song, was sung by Flo, and revealed the classically trained ballad voice that usually just cooed in the background of Supremes hits. In addition, Flo had fine comic timing. As Cholly Atkins told reporter Jacqueline Trescott, "Florence could keep others in their place with her dry humor. She could knock off a line with a tremendous knack for deadpan."

At the Roostertail, when Diana introduced Flo as "the quiet one," Flo replied with disdain, "That's what you think," and drew laughter from the crowd. Later, Flo would assert that that dialogue, provided by the Artist Development office, was perhaps a subtle message to her. Motown's plans for Flo became clearer in a short time. At a rehearsal at the Twenty Grand with most of the Motown brass in attendance, Flo moved to the front of the stage to sing "People." She had sung only about four bars when Berry Gordy told Flo to hold it. Let Diana do the song, he ordered. As if stabbed in the heart, Flo recoiled and cried. She would never have another solo spot as a Supreme.

As the spotlight tightened, Diana and the hits kept coming, and Flo drifted deeper into the shadows, just a background singer chirping away in the cage of her adolescent dreams. Mary? She just kept her mouth shut until she had to sing. She watched. She said nothing about what was happening. Then she wiggled back and forth, cooing "Ooh, baby, baby" in the background of "Where Did Our Love Go?"

6·CHASING DREAMS

In 1966, Esther Gordy Edwards told *Ebony* magazine, "People try to get us to move away, to take on New York or Hollywood or one of those places. But Berry is crazy about this town [Detroit]. Whenever he has to leave, he always complains. He counts the days until he can get back." It was a statement that played well in Detroit and that fit the "poor boy makes good" sentiment of the black periodical's story. But the truth was that Berry was spending quite a bit of time outside Detroit, particularly in Los Angeles and Las Vegas. Even before the Detroit riot of 1967—a battle of blacks against white policemen and firemen that paralyzed the city and haunts it to this day—Berry was moving toward a decision that would weaken Detroit's spirit as profoundly as the riot had.

Motown was going to leave Detroit—just as thousands of Detroit residents would a decade later—for the Sun Belt, a region of America blessed with golden sun, warm weather, and the promise of new dreams. In Las Vegas, Berry played blackjack and poker, not for the small stakes of the Motown weekends, but for heavy-roller dollars and in the company of the world's biggest gamblers. In Los Angeles he relaxed at Hugh Hefner's mansion with the Playboy bunnies and shot the bull with movie stars and starmakers. But the clearest symbol of the shift from the "snow belt" to the "sun belt" was golf. There is no more tame, upper-class sport than golf, and Berry, Smokey, Marvin, Harvey Fuqua, Barney Ales, and the Temptations all embraced this leisurely, sun-drenched activity, one that was literally and metaphorically miles away from the angry environment of Detroit. It was a statement of how far they'd come, how much they'd won, and just where they were headed.

Las Vegas meant casinos; Motown acts were stepping into the main show rooms, where Sinatra, Sammy Davis, Jr., Eydie Gorme and Steve Lawrence, and the rest of the show-biz establishment held forth for lengthy, lucrative engagements. Los Angeles meant Hollywood, and Hollywood meant films and television, new worlds, new dreams. Berry was a social climber in the grand American tradition and, for all his success, still craved the certification that Las Vegas and Los Angeles could deliver.

In 1967, however, the company's official announcement of its exit from Detroit was still two years away, and the move itself a good four years in the future. Motown was moving into a four-year transition period as important as its first four years, from 1959 to 1963. This time, however, instead of growing, the old Motown family began to wither away, as dissension, overblown egos, lawsuits, and pressure from an industry that began to exploit Motown's own methods, hacked away at its roots. Remarkable music would still emanate from Berry's company—in this period of instability old heads and youngbloods created some enduring masterpieces—but the best of it was too personal, too idiosyncratic to create and establish a "new" Motown Sound.

Even before the 1967 riot took place, rumors that Motown might be leaving were floating around Detroit. But three major purchases by Berry in the late sixties temporarily quieted them. In 1967, he paid almost a million dollars for a posh three-story mansion on Detroit's Boston Boulevard, with marble floors, walls decorated in gold trim, crystal chandeliers, a tunnel linking the main house to a theater, and, not incongruously, a painting of Berry dressed as Napoleon Bonaparte, which had been commissioned by Esther, hanging prominently in the living room.

In a move related to Detroit's soaring crime rate, Motown's administrative offices were shifted from West Grand to an ugly ten-story building on Woodward Avenue, just blocks from Cass Tech and a five-minute ride from the river. It provided better security, since all visitors had to use the main entrance and were photographed before entry. But that this was just a way station for Motown was clear to many from the working conditions in this former municipal authority building. A couch in an office and, maybe, a radiator that worked in the winter were a sign of executive status. There was one small vending machine and the elevators were freight lifts that looked like cages. One English visitor described the place as "horrible," and few argued the point.

The rise of Golden World/Ric-Tic Records hadn't been stifled by

Mickey Stevenson's fines on moonlighting muscians, and so, according to Ric-Tic President LeBaron Taylor, Motown went straight for the throat. For independent labels, as we've seen, nothing could be more important than a good relationship with distributors around the country, and at some point Motown allegedly made it hard for local competitors to receive payment from them. "They'd say, 'LeBaron, I'm sorry. We're making money with you. However, Motown represents ten times as much. Your people are nice and all that. However, this is business.'" Taylor tells this story with obvious admiration, explaining, "All of the independents operated the same way. Berry was just protecting his interest."

Ed Wingate had money and clout in Detroit, but around the country Motown's records made Berry an industry-wide force. So one day in 1968 Taylor went to see Wingate and was told that Golden World, Ric-Tic, the studio—the entire operation—was over. He had sold it all to Berry for a price estimated at a million dollars. George Clinton became a Jobete staff writer, Edwin Starr joined the Motown roster, and Golden World Studio became Motown Studio B.

All of this suggests that Berry was right on top of things in Detroit. But by late 1967 Berry was spending most of his time in Motown's 6255 Sunset Boulevard offices in Los Angeles, talking almost daily by phone with Barney Ales, and several times a week with Ralph Seltzer. At the time he said he still approved the release of every Motown recording. Yet he was surprised when he was told that the team of Brian Holland, Lamont Dozier, and Eddie Holland was no longer making music for Motown. "We had a lack of material and I was unhappy about it," Berry said in a 1971 deposition.

I would call Brian's office and he was not there. Basically, this assistant . . . would answer and I would call his office and I would just simply try to find Brian and he was not in and I might complain to her that they had not given us material and that I was unhappy about it. She would indicate that she would try to find him and bring it to his attention. That sort of thing, and I complained to Ralph Seltzer and I would call Eddie's office about the same thing and he was not there.

When I checked with their offices and then I eventually checked with, I think, Mr. Seltzer, at that time they hadn't recorded anything for like two months. Then I became pretty alarmed. I thought maybe they were recording things and they weren't becoming hits or weren't good enough. When I was informed that they hadn't recorded in the last couple of months' time, then I became a little bit more alarmed.

He should have been. Eddie Holland was never in his office. Neither was Brian Holland. Throughout 1967 and into early 1968, H-D-H and Motown were still making hits: the Supremes' "Love Is Here and Now You're Gone" and "The Happening"; Diana Ross and the Supremes' "Reflections" and "In and Out of Love"; the Four Tops' "Bernadette," "Seven Rooms of Gloom," "You Keep Running Away," and a cover of Left Banke's "Walk Away Renee." It was good music; in fact, it was some of H-D-H's best. But the bulk of the material that was topping the charts at this time had been written and produced in early to mid-1967. Few knew it, but the trio was in the process of walking out the door.

Apparently, Berry's West Coast activities had left him so out of touch that he had ignored how disgruntled Eddie had been over H-D-H's unsuccessful efforts to get a bigger piece of Motown's profits. The days of paying dues at Motown were long gone, and for those who had built Motown with Berry, who had made his vision the beat in millions of teenagers' transistors, who had believed in him as in a father, it was time for some real remuneration, but for many it wouldn't be forthcoming. Beans Bowles, who had played an integral part in running the early Motown Motor Town Revues, was fired for being bad for Motown's image after getting involved in local politics (Smokey Robinson would then hire Beans as musical director for his road band). Jack Gibson, Motown's longtime liaison with black radio stations, was fired by Ales, also for not fitting Motown's image—a move that caused hostility toward Motown from many of its early supporters in black radio (Stax Records gave Gibson a job as promotion director). Cholly Atkins relocated to Las Vegas, where his well-deserved reputation as a wizard of the stage show got him work at casino-hotels and allowed him to work on a free-lance basis with his favorite R&B acts (Gladys Knight and the Pips, the Temptations, the O'Jays). Harvey Fuqua, divorced by 1967 from Gwen Gordy, was free to sign a lucrative production deal with RCA, where he developed the popular band New Birth. (Gwen then married Spinners' lead singer G. C. Cameron, who soon left the Spinners to launch an unsuccessful solo career at Motown.) Mickey Stevenson, a man who had always supervised production as if Motown were his own, and who was as loyal to Berry as any member of his family, asked for stock in the company in 1969. If

Stevenson didn't get it, he felt he'd have to leave and accept an MGM Records offer that included his own label. Berry said no. Stevenson left, and with him went Kim Weston and, not long after, Clarence Paul.

Things were changing inside Motown, often at Berry's instigation, but he did not want to lose H-D-H. At one point during this period, according to H-D-H, Berry did offer them $100,000 a year each against royalties as an inducement to stay. But that was far too little. H-D-H wanted their own thing and, in 1968, they left to find it. After all, Berry had taught them—and everyone else—that that was the only thing to have. Now quite aware of the implications of the situation, Berry made some moves. Young producer-writers Frank Wilson, Deke Richards, R. Dean Taylor, Hal Davis, Marc Gordon, Jeffrey Bowen, Freddie Perren, and Dino Fekaris were moved up to the front line and, in various combinations, were assigned the unenviable task of filling H-D-H's shoes. They formed the nucleus of the new Motown production line, which Berry would oversee in the hands-on manner he had gradually let go of in the past several years. Significantly, most of the new writer-producers were based in Los Angeles, a fact the observant back in Detroit might have noted with some concern.

Motown filed suit first. On August 29, 1968, the company asked for $4 million in damages from H-D-H and asked the court to restrain the team from working for any other recording company. According to Motown, H-D-H had violated their songwriting agreements with Jobete by not producing any songs since late 1967. The suit went to great pains to underline how much the trio had earned at Motown (from 1965 to 1967, Jobete had paid them $2,235,155 in royalties) and point out how valuable a commodity they were.

But Brian, Lamont, and Eddie went after Berry with a vengeance. H-D-H counter-sued Motown with conspiracy, fraud, deceit, over-reaching, and breach of fiduciary relationships in the amount of $22 million. Moreover, they wanted the court to put Motown and all its accounts and copyrights into receivership. If they couldn't get what they wanted by asking, they were going to try to take Motown itself away from Berry.

Today, Eddie's memory of these events is considerably more friendly:

> Well, I don't think it was so much over money. It was probably dealing with a wider creative outlet and at the time, the company was not structured for it. I think, in talking about it, and Berry and I being as close like that, it was difficult for us to discuss it. Then I found myself talking to an attorney and there was a little

friction started between me and the attorney, and the next thing you know, I was on one end of the bridge and he was on the other and somebody was setting fire to the middle. . . . It was one of those prime examples of a little something, a little spark starting and then next thing you know, it's a full blaze.

Eddie's attitude belies the assertions of H-D-H's suit. Among these was the charge that since Brian had joined Berry in 1957 and H-D-H had formed in 1961, they had never been given a contract to study. They claimed that at one point Motown representatives Ralph Seltzer, Harold Noveck, and Sidney Noveck had told them "they had nothing to worry about . . . the company had their best financial interest in mind. . . . They told them that the contracts were only written documents—only a matter of fun," the suit alleged. H-D-H claimed that when their contracts ran out in 1967, Berry refused to renew them in writing but made verbal promises of increased monies to them. So they had decided to walk.

The battle between Berry and H-D-H would go on into the mid-seventies and take many twists and turns. H-D-H would allege that Motown harassed them after they left, blacklisting people who worked with them and using their clout to intimidate business partners. Motown, in turn, attacked the trio's timing, claiming that they had started working on their own projects while still under contract to Motown. When asked what he did during the latter part of 1967, Lamont responded that he "mowed the lawn," and when he played piano, forgot what he played.

Eventually, the cases were settled out of court, with no publicity. But the damage done to Motown was real. H-D-H, after being constrained by Motown lawsuits from recording for two years, released several records on Invictus and Hot Wax Records that rank with their best at Motown: Freda Payne's "Band of Gold," "Bring the Boys Home," and "Cherish What Is Dear to You (While It's Near to You)"; the Honey Cone's "Want Ads" and "One Monkey Don't Stop No Show, Part 1"; and Chairmen of the Board's "Give Me Just a Little More Time" and "Pay to the Piper."

Just as disheartening were some of the revelations found in Berry's depositions for the H-D-H suit. When asked by H-D-H's lawyer, "Who are your main executives who are running the operation here in Detroit when you are not physically present here in Detroit?" Berry replied, "There is Harry Balk, Ralph Seltzer, Barney Ales, and that is about it." Seltzer, vice-president of corporate affairs, Harry Balk, the creative director of the Detroit office, and Ales were all white. So were Michael Roskind, a vice-president who ran the New York office, and the Noveck brothers. These men were now the core of Motown's internal braintrust. The only black executive mentioned prominently by Berry was his sister Esther.

Whites had not totally overrun Motown. An executive who had been at Motown circa 1968 estimates that out of approximately two hundred Motown employees that year, only about ten were white. It wasn't the number that was disturbing, however, it was their placement. The Novecks, the company's key consultants, were white. So were vice-presidents Seltzer, Balk, Roskind, and an aggressive young manager in ITM named Shelly Berger. The sales department, Barney Ales's fiefdom, was largely white; Berry's protégé Miller London was the most prominent black in the department. This was an effective team, but having all those whites in sales did nothing to silence the growing number of blacks who felt that Berry had secretly sold out to white interests.

Which brings us back to the question of who exactly had told Berry that H-D-H were slacking off. When he was asked whether Seltzer or the Novecks had mentioned it to him, or what their role was in advising Berry about the situation, Berry's trial lawyer advised him that he should not answer on the grounds that these were "privileged" conversations. When questions about Seltzer came up, Berry's lawyer, Mr. Warren, interceded: "I do not direct [him to answer] on the basis that it is an attorney-client privilege. Mr. Seltzer, as I understand, is an attorney and he is licensed to practice law in Michigan. His consultations with Mr. Gordy in his capacity as a lawyer and head of the legal department are privileged." About Sidney Noveck, Mr. Warren asserted, "[he] is an accountant regularly retained by Motown and Jobete. As to him, your question invades the statutory privileges granted in the community between an accountant and client and for that reason I direct the witness not to answer." The intention, quite successfully executed in these depositions, was to cloak Berry and his chief advisers in an aura of "executive privilege," which kept them from perjuring themselves on the witness stand, and which kept their corporate meetings secret.

To curtail speculation that Motown was quietly becoming a white-run company, Berry appeared in a three-page story in *Jet* in November 1967 that announced the naming of two blacks to important posts, Ewart Abner as director of ITM and Julius Griffin as director of publicity. The story mentioned that Motown planned to get involved in television, film, and Broadway; that Motown would be getting involved in educational recordings; and that Motown's scholarship for musical excellence (created

conjunction with the United Negro College Fund) and the Loucye
akefield Memorial Business Career Clinic would be growing as well.

According to Berry, his commitment to blacks was stronger than his
sire for profit. "It is true," he said, "that we have been able to substan-
lly increase our activities and our profits each year since we started in
siness some eight years ago, but the important thing to me personally
:hat we are in a stronger position to employ more artists, creative talent,
:cutive, clerical, and secretarial personnel than any other firm headed
a Negro in the annals of the entertainment world.

"After all," he concluded, "we can only grow as fast and as big as
otown employees will allow, and that is precisely the key to our success.
ippy people work for us and that is the way it will always be as long as
m head of Motown." That may have been true even a year earlier, but
wasn't anymore. The list of the disgruntled was as long as Motown's
w unwieldly artists' roster.

A letter written by Motown singer Brenda Holloway to Berry in 1967
eaks volumes about the bureaucracy that Motown had become, and the
ep, undying respect the acts had for Berry despite it all:

Dear Berry:

It's with my regret that I must burden you with my many
problems and unhappiness concerning my future as a recording
artist; and why I have considered leaving Motown, the following
reasons are:

For the past four and one-half years I have had five releases
of some recognition. They are: "Every Little Bit Hurts," "When
I'm Gone," "Operator," "Just Look What You've Done,"
"You've Made Me So Very Happy," and one album entitled
Every Little Bit Hurts.

During my four and one-half years as an artist with Motown,
there have been four other artists who are affiliated with Motown
less than two years, who have had several hits and also one to two
album releases. They have been promoted-publicized and pushed
extremely! Again, I cannot understand why I have been so obviously ignored and pushed aside. My only conclusion is, I'm a *West
Coast Artist.*

On numerous occasions I have asked for my own musicians
in order to play for me when on the road. Such as: a guitar player,
bass player and drummer. I was ignored and dealt with in a

childish manner. I also feel when coming to Detroit to record for producers, they should rehearse with me and find my right key range; and then produce tracks which I'm to record. Previously, a trip to Detroit, to record, I felt to be a disaster because tracks were cut in uncomfortable keys, which unabled me to record successfully and to fulfill my talents as a recording artist.

I feel that the International Talent Management Inc., has not fulfilled all the obligations as managers. Which are as follows:

Television such as: "The Joey Bishop Show," "The Dating Game," "The Johnny Carson Show," "The Dean Martin Show," "The Smothers Brothers," "Carol Burnett," "The Hollywood Palace," and "The Ed Sullivan Show."

So I can't understand why with most of the shows taped in Hollywood, with the exception of the "Johnny Carson Show" and the "Ed Sullivan Show," it seems to be a disadvantage to me living in Hollywood. But a great advantage to the Motown artist living in Detroit. Not having a full opportunity to work in Artist Development in Detroit, I have had to work on my own choreography and arrangements. Also, my own personal grooming. I have had no fully concentrated assistance in the following: Selecting and buying the right costumes for engagements. Suggestions for my makeup and hair styling. Co-ordinating the right song material for certain engagements.

As you very well know there are numerous singers that have not had a hit record or as much experience as myself working on club engagements and concerts, that are constantly touring Europe and other countries. Also singing title songs for films, and working in stage plays and musicals. These people are also performing in Las Vegas and making good salaries and names for themselves. Again I cannot understand why I haven't had any of these opportunities.

To sum up my feelings on my situation I would like to say it has been a great experience being a little part of Motown, and even greater experience having worked for you. You have tried in vain in your own way to help me as far as my financial standings, such as collaborating with my sister Patrice and I in writing songs such as my last release. There should be much more said after being associated with the Motown family and you, for four and one-half years. But I feel I have covered the important areas. Hoping you can be understanding and perspective. I'll close.

Brenda Holloway

P.S. I will always *LOVE* Motown and you!

Holloway was the most beautiful woman ever signed to Motown. Her skin had a striking bronze hue. Her hair was bouncy and straight, with curling ends that highlighted oval, almost Oriental eyes, and full, sensual lips. In any dress, but particularly the tight gold and silver sequined outfits she often performed in, this Atascadero, California, native was a head-turner. In fact, her figure helped her get signed to Motown.

In 1964, Holloway was living in Watts, semi-employed, and dying to sing for Motown Records. She'd sit by her radio singing along to "My Guy" and "Dancing in the Street" with her eyes closed, envisioning herself on "American Bandstand," swaying back and forth for the cameras. Holloway was willing to take the extra steps to make her daydreams real. She heard that a convention of deejays was being held at a Los Angeles hotel and guessed that Berry or someone from Motown would be attending. Squeezing her stately figure into a gold pantsuit and gold shoes, she caught the eye of more than a few deejays. Someone put on a Mary Wells record and the eye-catching Holloway was asked to sing along. Sometime during her performance Berry walked in, enjoyed what he saw and heard, and struck up a conversation. He admired her spunk and her looks. She wondered who this little guy was. Berry, who was so often influenced by first impressions, signed her. For her, this was a crazy dream come true. But it became even more dreamlike when one of her first singles, "Every Little Bit Hurts," became a major hit in the spring of 1964, reaching number thirteen on the pop chart two months before the Supremes' "Where Did Our Love Go?" hit the charts. "Hurts" was the first Motown hit to be recorded on the West Coast. In the summer of 1964, Holloway's sensational body, sexy voice, and budding songwriting talent (her "You've Made Me So Very Happy" would be a two-million-selling single for Blood, Sweat and Tears in 1969) suggested a star on the horizon. Holloway felt that she was on the right road, and the good feeling appeared to be reciprocated by Motown. On her first visit to Motown in Detroit that winter several Motown employees, including Berry himself, affectionately dumped her into the snow.

But somewhere along the way, things went wrong. Since Berry was already turning his attention to California in anticipation of moving his operation there, it's hard to see why Holloway was ignored. It is clear from the many "artist development" functions Holloway performed for herself that, at some point, lower Motown functionaries felt that she wasn't worth the effort involved in long-distance grooming. Berry must have liked her, or he would never have written any songs with her. But, as we now know, Motown's day-to-day machinery was not Berry's primary concern by 1967. His writing credit on a record was no guarantee it would receive a big push, not when the record it was competing with was by the Supremes or the Four Tops.

Holloway wasn't the only pawn on Motown's chess board. Chuck Jackson, the maker of such bombastic early sixties soul-MOR hits as "Any Day Now" on Wand Records, had been wooed to Motown in 1968 with the promise that his strong, masculine baritone would be showcased in the Motown Sound. In 1976, years later, Jackson told *Black Music* magazine that joining Motown was "one of the worst mistakes I ever made in my life—and you can quote me on that. I don't say all the people were bad. I loved Smokey and had a lot of respect for Berry Gordy, but there were also a whole lot of negative elements there. . . . I just got screwed out, that's all."

It wasn't that Jackson made no money at Motown. On the contrary, as an opening act for the Temptations, Four Tops, and later the Jackson 5 (including their memorable first performance at Madison Square Garden), Jackson made good money. But despite being on the company's main label, Motown, Jackson's recording career stagnated. In 1968–69 three of his singles made the bottom end of the *Billboard* black singles chart. Like the Spinners, Jackson was used as a classy, noncompetitive opening act for Motown's stars, and as a gift to deejays around the country for local promotions.

Jackson hadn't realized how far his personal stock had fallen until he asked a booking agent for a gig and quoted his Motown price—the one he'd been getting as a Motown opening act—and was shocked by the agent's surprise. By himself, Jackson wasn't worth that much money anymore. After he began complaining about his situation, Jackson was soon exiled to the VIP label, where none of his subsequent Motown releases made the charts. Jackson left in 1972, his career in disarray.

In contrast, Gladys Knight and the Pips' tenure with Motown ended in triumph, though the group's members felt—with considerable justification—that their potential was never reached there, especially since philosophically Gladys Knight and the Pips and Motown had much in common. Knight, brother Merald "Bubba" Knight, and cousins William Guest and Edward Patten, were everything Motown was telling its acts they had to be when they came aboard in 1965. Their choreography was precise, exciting, and always timed to highlight the lyric. The biggest difference between Knight and the Pips and other Motown acts is that, though they may not have had a great deal of success before Motown, they had had far more experience in show business. Gladys had been on national TV (the "Ted Mack Amateur Hour") at age seven, long before Berry ever dreamed of writing songs, and the Pips had been on the road since the fifties. Onstage, the three male Pips were elegant, sepia Fred Astaires whose sweat never obscured their style. Gladys was the gospel counterpoint, moving left as the guys moved right, her Southern charm flowing sweetly from the stage. "We set a standard for R&B or rock and roll groups," claimed Guest in 1975. "We always had nice suits. Even when we couldn't afford it." This emphasis on showmanship had been cultivated by Maurice King back when they sang with his big band in the late 1950s, and over the years they had polished their look, earning a reputation as the most pleasing live non-Motown stage act in R&B.

What they didn't have was a string of hits, and the record industry power that Motown could provide. For all their grace, Gladys and her comrades had had bad luck with record labels. Since beginning their professional career in 1956, they had recorded for four different companies, including two that were owned by blacks, had had a hit with a remake of Johnny Otis's "Every Beat of My Heart," but had seen very little money for their efforts. They had the stuff to be major stars, but without quality music they couldn't headline the Apollo, much less the Copa or Las Vegas. The male members of the Pips contacted King about joining Motown, feeling that they could blow the highly touted Temptations off any stage. With a couple of those "Motown Sound" hits behind them, Guest, Patten, and Bubba felt that they'd be Motown's biggest stars in no time.

Gladys was more cautious. "I had a lot of doubt about what Motown could do for us. I thought we would have to come after the stars who were already there," she later noted. "When we were approached by Motown with a contract, we took a vote on whether we should accept. The guys voted to sign. I voted no. I was outvoted."

So off to Detroit they went in 1965 for an unsatisfying eight-year stay, where they never completely felt that they were part of the Motown family. Their opinion wasn't always given the weight it deserved; for example, after meeting the Jackson 5 at Chicago's Regal Theater, they

WHERE DID OUR LOVE GO?

asked a Motown representative to come down and check out the Jackson's show. No one came. Later, they praised the Jacksons to Motown again —and again the company took no action. In the company's subsequent Jackson 5 hype, Gladys's early advocacy of the group was ignored in favor of the story that they had been discovered by Diana Ross.

Still, Gladys and the Pips became consistent hitmakers when backed by the Motown music machine. Earl Van Dyke says that Gladys and the musicians had a special relationship. "We struck a groove right away," he recalls, " 'cause we knew how Gladys sang . . . Gladys had a drive just like we had and the more you drive Gladys, the more she sings."

In contrast to the beige sounds of Ross and Levi Stubbs, Gladys performed best when her church roots were given free rein; the Pips weren't placed on the Soul label by mistake. The key record, of course, was "I Heard It Through the Grapevine," a great, churning, tambourine-driven call-and-response song into which producer Norman Whitfield let Knight and company have considerable creative input because of his respect for the group. According to Knight, Whitfield allowed them to craft the song's brilliant vocal arrangement:

> When we got that song, it was nowhere near the song it ended up being. Norman Whitfield approached us with it and said, "I got a great song that I think will work for you guys. See what you think about it, take it home." We lived with that song at home, on the road, we ate, slept, everything with it for two months. We brought it back for Norman one day the way we had done it. . . . He went into the studio that minute, put Smokey out so we could go upstairs and record! . . . We didn't have anything to do with the writing, but the structure is so important in production. We tore it apart, we did all the little things.

"Grapevine" sold 2.5 million copies, going to number one R&B and number two pop in 1967. As a result, the rest of the Pips' Motown hits were built around Knight's great gospel shouts, whether uptempo Whit-field productions ("Friendship Train," "The Nitty Gritty") or the soap opera soul of Clay McMurray's productions ("If I Were Your Woman," "Make Me the Woman That You Go Home To"). By 1972, Gladys Knight and the Pips were major stars, but they were nagged by the continuing feeling that they really weren't major stars inside the company's walls. Whitfield still gave the same songs to them that he gave the Temptations or Edwin Starr, and Gladys, despite being hailed by many critics as the successor to Aretha Franklin as the "Queen of Soul," was still not treated as if she were in Diana Ross's league, even if Gladys could sing her under the table.

During much of 1973, New York's Buddah Records, which had recently signed a distribution deal with the Isley Brothers' T-Neck Records, wooed Gladys Knight and the Pips, telling its members that they would no longer be cogs in a machine. Despite this attractive offer, though, Buddah's president Art Kass feels that if Berry Gordy had made a firm personal plea at Motown, they would have stayed. Like so many other acts who joined after the company had already been established, Gladys Knight and the Pips' respect for Gordy had kept them at Motown in the face of what they may have felt was unfair treatment by underlings. But even after the massive hit "Neither One of Us (Wants to Be the First to Say Goodbye)" in 1973, Berry didn't reach out to them, and they signed with Buddah later that year—going on to enjoy precisely the mass acceptance they'd sought at Motown.

The misadventures of Chuck Jackson and Gladys Knight at Motown were typical of the experience of acts signed by the company after 1965. They were lured to Motown by the sound, and the power that sound gave to Berry's enterprise. When it didn't work out, their disappointment was natural. But for Berry's babies, the acts he'd raised from schoolyard to supper club, the changes at Motown had even deeper psychological effects.

Martha Reeves's tenure at Motown had, by any objective measurements, been quite successful. Of the twelve Martha and the Vandellas singles released between 1963 and 1967, ten made the pop Top Thirty, and five of them made the soul Top Five. Despite backing by eight different Vandellas combinations, Martha's husky vocals had been enough to provide uptempo groove songs like "Nowhere to Run," "Jimmy Mack" (the last mating of Martha and H-D-H), and "Honey Chile" with the fuel they had needed.

Yet, inside Martha's head, there was pain. For a moment she'd been at the top of the world; now, she was just one of many second bananas. Martha's demands for better treatment did nothing but cause hostility at Motown. As she said in 1974, "Berry took his personal time to tell me, 'You can't run my record company' and I said, 'No. And you can't either,' and then he really got mad at me. . . . I retaliated where other people would be quiet. I speak." She told writer Gerri Hirshey that, during the late sixties, "I think I was the first person at Motown to ask where the money was going."

By 1968, Martha's isolation from the Motown hierarchy was profound. As her recording sessions dwindled and she found herself being put on hold by employees to whom she was merely a name on a greatest-hits collection, the vulnerability that lay beneath her worldly exterior sent her into depressions and, in 1969, the first of a series of nervous breakdowns. She would suffer two more in the next three years, all part of the downward arc of her career.

In 1972, she was, after the prerequisite legal wrangling, released by Motown. It would be nice to say that, like Gladys Knight, Martha Reeves found success after escaping from Diana Ross's shadow, but that was not to be. Over the next several years she made records for three major labels, including the critically acclaimed album *Martha Reeves*, produced by Richard Perry, which took eighteen months to complete—but none of them sold. The voice was still there—in fact, Martha seemed to have increased her range with time—but she now spends most of her time performing as an oldies attraction throughout the United States and Europe.

No one at Motown, however, suffered as greatly as Florence Ballard, a lady whose life grew more difficult with each step the Supremes took forward. Diana was distant, involved more with Berry, and with stardom, than with maintaining harmony within the group. Mary was still a friend, but she found it convenient to overlook how the show was being structured totally around Diana, or how many people at Motown were on Florence's case. They claimed that she was gaining weight and drinking too much, and that her relationship with Berry's driver Thomas Chapman was hurting her concentration. Too often she was performing below standard. Word had leaked out that she had left high school too early (a fact Motown releases had originally lied about). Not surprisingly, Flo did not feel wanted.

Then, in the spring of 1967, a meeting was held at Berry's Detroit mansion to discuss the Supremes' future. Berry spoke openly about making Diana a solo star—a chance the others grudgingly agreed to. Florence made it clear to all that she'd cause no further trouble and that, above all, she wanted to remain a Supreme.

But it wasn't long before the reality of what was happening began to affect her. Twice that spring she missed performances because of "illness," forcing Diana and Mary to perform as a duo. Then on April 30, 1967, when the Supremes headlined a show with the Buffalo Springfield, the Fifth Dimension, and Johnny Rivers, a most telling event occurred. Flo was ill again, this time with the flu, but the Supremes weren't going on as a duo. Cindy Birdsong, a former member of Patti LaBelle and the Blue Belles, and a lady who bore a remarkable physical resemblance to Florence, stepped onstage in place of the missing Supreme, a fact few attending seemed to mind; even the *Los Angeles Times* called Birdsong "a strong sub . . . blending effectively."

Cindy Birdsong was no last-minute understudy; she had been in training for many weeks. Diana had befriended Cindy during the Supremes' chitlin-circuit days, when they had performed occasionally on the same bill. Diana used to show her different ways to use eyeliner, blusher, and so on, for which Cindy was extremely grateful. When the decision was finally made to phase out Florence, it was Diana's idea to recruit Cindy. A Motown representative called her mother, some hasty negotiations were held, and Birdsong was soon studying the Supremes' harmonies and choreography, being sent around the country with the Supremes, "just in case" she was needed.

That next week, at the Copacabana, Florence was back, in what *Variety* called an act "polished to a high gloss." But on "The Tonight Show," just a few days later, Johnny Carson asked Diana about the group's rigorous schedule, and Diana mentioned for the first time that there was a replacement on call for Florence and Mary, but not for herself. An innocent enough response, and it was surely of only passing interest to Carson's viewers. But, in retrospect, its timing seems quite convenient for Motown, since it spotlighted Diana's uniqueness and suggested how expendable the other Supremes had become.

In mid-June, the Supremes broke down yet another social barrier, making their debut at Los Angeles's counterpart to the Copa, the Coconut Grove. Again, the *Variety* reviewer was laudatory, praising them as a trio of "obvious talent"; indeed, none of the reviewers who saw the show during this period complained of any fall-off in the Supremes' showmanship. From June 29 to July 13, the Supremes were booked into the Flamingo for a second time. On the surface, this may have looked like just another step in Berry's ongoing legitimization of the Supremes, his attempt to convince the dubious in Vegas of the group's star quality. Berry, though, had bigger plans.

Onstage the group was a smash. The hokey jokes, the feline spit and polish, the show-biz standards, the H-D-H hits—all worked for this well-primed audience; the Supremes were so popular that the engagement was extended to July 20. But by that third week, these ladies were no longer the Supremes. The Flamingo's marquee now read, DIANA ROSS AND THE SUPREMES. All across America, copies of "Reflections," credited to this familiar yet newly rechristened group, hit the stores and radio stations, causing a buzz throughout the record industry and among Supremes fans worldwide. In one stroke Berry had established a separate identity for Diana, while not abandoning the still valuable Supremes name.

And that wasn't all Berry had done. For a couple of nights that third week, Cindy Birdsong was positioned prominently backstage, watching the show and waiting, though even she still wasn't completely sure why. And then, she knew. One night, Florence was next to Diana and Mary. The next night, Cindy stood in her place.

At the time, Motown told everyone that the Supremes' hectic schedule had been too much for poor Florence, and that she needed a rest (later, Motown lawyers would say that it was for "poor behavior"). The move was, of course, only temporary. After being kept from going onstage she was whisked from Las Vegas to Detroit's Ford Hospital, for "treatment."

A meeting on July 26, 1967, between Florence, Motown vice-president Mike Roskind, and Motown adviser George Schiffer, was held at Detroit's Northland Inn. As usual in her dealings with Motown, Flo had no legal counsel present. Flo was told that she was no longer a Supreme, though they did offer her a contract extension, which she refused. Instead, Flo agreed to a payment of $2,500 a year for six years—a grand total of $15,000 for her contributions to the Supremes. In return, she was restricted from ever identifying herself as an ex-Supreme or receiving any further royalties from the company. Flo left the meeting in tears.

She and boyfriend Thomas Chapman realized that she needed help, and they hired Leonard Baun as her attorney and business manager. As at Motown, Flo left all of her legal dealings in the hands of others. In September, after much foot-dragging, Motown gave Flo $75,000, her share of the Supremes' joint bank account. For the next four months, Baun negotiated with Ralph Seltzer and Harold Noveck for a fairer, more detailed release. Finally, on February 22, 1968, Flo and Motown reached a settlement. Again, she couldn't publicize her tenure as a Supreme or receive further royalties. Even more damaging was a section of the agreement that forbade Flo from instituting civil action against Motown, Ross, Wilson, Birdsong, or anyone else associated with Motown. On the plus side, Motown issued three checks to Flo: $20,195.06 for her work with the Supremes, $5,000 from Diana Ross and the Supremes, and $134,804.94 from Motown Record Company. This money, plus an additional $140,000 in assets, were entrusted to Baun. A week later she married Chapman, who named himself her business manager, though most of Flo's money still passed through Baun. The Supremes were represented on the chart with "Forever Came Today" in the spring of 1968, but Flo didn't mind, because in March 1968 she signed a two-year pact with ABC Records in New York.

The signing lifted her out of a deep depression, a period during which she had just sat around her home, refusing to even listen to music. Flo's world had collapsed around her; the dream she'd harbored since childhood had now been packaged as someone else's fantasy. She was bitter. However, no matter how hard interviewers tried, they couldn't pry a bad word about Motown from her lips, nor any juicy detail of her exit from the Supremes. Her strategy was to talk about the future and to use that Motown charm school training to ward off questions about the past. She wanted to focus on the future. She wanted to talk about *her* record.

At that time, ABC was not a major distributor of black music, and, despite the legal restraint on publicizing Flo's past as a Supreme, her Motown pedigree was clearly what attracted the company. This point was emphasized by ABC's assignment of ex-Motown staffer George Kerr to produce and write for Florence. "It Doesn't Matter How I Say It," the A side of her first single, was a spirited, if clumsy, reworking of the Temptations' "The Way You Do the Things You Do," while the B side was a superior cover of Little Anthony and the Imperials' "Goin' Out of My Head," which showcased the big ballad voice Supremes fans remembered from "People."

Flo Ballard's solo debut was mentioned in an ad for several new ABC releases in *Billboard*'s May 11, 1968, issue. Chapman hired Al Abrams, an ex-Motown publicity man, to hype Ballard, and he hired the Joe Glaser Agency to arrange nightclub dates. Both were only marginally effective. Flo's unwillingness to discuss her exit from the Supremes and her inability to use her Supremes background in press releases frustrated Abrams's efforts, and any sympathetic press her first single would have received from the Detroit press was stifled by a newspaper strike that closed both the *Detroit News* and the *Detroit Free Press*. She did get to appear on some teen dance shows on the East Coast, and on a few occasions she opened for Wilson Pickett. In May 1968, she appeared at Yorktown High School in Arlington, Virginia, an indication of the quality of the venues she was forced to play. "It Doesn't Matter How You Say It" flopped.

That summer she was back in New York, cutting with the once-important Motown staff producer-writer Robert Bateman, whose career had been mediocre at best since leaving Detroit for New York. He cut four tracks with Florence, including one by ex-Motown arranger Van McCoy (later a key figure in the rise of disco) called "Love Ain't Love."

The song has a driving, strident beat that really pushed her; *Detroit Free Press* writer Barbara Holiday would later remark about this record: "The Ballard voice? You begin to understand why a trio might split—with two lead singers and only one being featured." "Love Ain't Love" even briefly made Detroit's WCHB's playlist, after Chapman took boxes of 45s to local radio stations and stimulated sales. However, other local stations didn't play it and, without support in her own backyard, the record failed to generate national interest.

Florence slowly became convinced that she wasn't getting a fair shake at ABC, and suspected that Motown was behind it. Flo said in 1975 that ABC's president Larry Newton told her it wasn't good to switch record labels, and that he was an occasional golf partner of Berry Gordy's, which Flo interpreted as a message that her recording career, no matter how many records were released, would go nowhere. That George Kerr declined to work with her again heightened her suspicions. Though twelve tracks had been cut, Flo's album *You Don't Have To* was shelved.

"Things looked good when I first started out as a single," Flo remarked later. "I had signed with a new company and was pleased with the initial releases, and even had a few engagements lined up. Then all of a sudden it seemed as if I was blackballed. My records weren't played and there were no bookings. People would have come to see me out of curiousity alone that first year."

In the fall and winter of 1968, she clung to the fringes of the entertainment industry, appearing in a Chicago parade with Godfrey Cambridge and opening for Bill Cosby at Chicago's Auditorium Theater in September. She had twin daughters, Nicole and Michelle, that winter, and she sang at one of the inaugural balls for President Nixon on January 20, 1969. It was a well-paying and prestigious gig, more like what she had been used to with the Supremes. Though ABC dropped the option on her two-year contract, Flo felt that maybe, using the Motown settlement, she could build a career as a cabaret performer.

Those plans were crushed when, shortly after Flo's return to Detroit, Baun told her that she was dead broke; according to Baun, every dime she'd gotten from Motown was gone. Stunned, Flo went to Baun's office to collect her papers. He later admitted that he still had the five thousand dollars from the Supremes and many of her other documents. On April 2, 1969, Flo officially fired Baun. The summer was consumed by the search for a new lawyer (it was difficult finding a local lawyer who'd handle the case) and then getting someone, anyone, to investigate Baun. The FBI, the Michigan attorney general's office, the American Bar Association, the IRS, and several congressmen and state representatives were appealed to for justice. It wasn't until September that she was able to obtain representation, from the black law firm of Patmon, Young, and Kirk.

She filed an $8.5 million suit against Motown, asserting that the company had withheld monies from her attorney. However, the general release Baun had advised her to sign upon leaving Motown was ruled binding by the circuit court and the Michigan Supreme Court unless Flo could pay back Motown the $160,000 it had originally awarded her. She then sued Baun for co-mingling his money with hers. Baun was disbarred as a result of the investigation; it was discovered that he had a history of bilking clients. Flo would eventually squeeze $50,000 out of Baun, but not until a long battle had been fought and won.

It was a tribute to how skillfully Motown had handled the announcements of the Supremes' name change and Ballard's exit that, in the years immediately after these moves were made, few except hardcore Supremes fans questioned what had happened. When Diana and Mary told the *Detroit Free Press* a month after the Flamingo engagement that Flo simply got tired of the road and wanted to stay home ("We all understand," Mary said. "It's hard work traveling around all the time"), it was taken at face value. That Flo's absence didn't seem to bother many fans is apparent to anyone who listens to *Live at London's Talk of the Town.* A journalist who attended the show later commented that Mary, Cindy, and Diana "enjoyed scenes of adulation . . . never before encountered by any female entertainers."

On record, things weren't quite as sanguine. With the exit of H-D-H, Motown went to extraordinary lengths to keep Diana's name (and the group's) hot. The team of Berry Gordy, Frank Wilson, Hank Crosby, Deke Richards, and R. Dean Taylor combined to produce and write "Love Child" (number two R&B, number one pop, 1968) and "I'm Livin' in Shame" (number eight R&B, number ten pop, 1969), two Whitfield-influenced "social commentary" records. The first was a genuinely moving song about illegitimate children; the second was a typical Motown follow-up. Then Berry teamed them with the Temptations for an album, *Diana Ross and the Supremes Join the Temptations,* spawning the single "I'm Gonna Make You Love Me" (number two pop, 1968). Smokey even took a shot and came up with "The Composer," which sounded more like an H-D-H "classical period" production than one of Smokey's own quirky compositions (number twenty-one pop, 1969).

All of these records were substantial hits, but the excitement that once greeted each Supremes single was gone, with the fans and the industry waiting for Motown to drop the other shoe and announce the start of Diana's solo career. Meanwhile, the groundwork for Ross's departure from the group was being laid on television, pushing her face alone into America's living rooms. From January 1968 to December 1969, Diana Ross and the Supremes appeared on network television twenty-five times. The first appearance of the cycle was on NBC's "Tarzan" adventure show, with Diana, Mary, and Cindy playing three nuns working in the jungle (guess who got the most lines?). That experience was the prelude to two Christmas season specials, "TCB (Taking Care of Business)" in 1968, and "Getting It Together: Diana Ross and the Supremes and the Temptations" in 1969. These were Motown's first television productions—the fruits of Berry's West Coast orientation and relationship with NBC—and were each built around Diana's surprising versatility. For all the nastiness that surrounded Flo's dismissal, Diana herself had metamorphosed into a very special talent. The years of charm school, her diligence, and her own unbridled ambition had coalesced into a charming, glamorous, artificial yet fascinating larger-than-life public persona that worked on record, in concert, and on television. And Berry hoped that it would soon work on the big screen.

So, with big dreams in the hearts of Diana and Berry, Diana exited the Supremes at the Frontier Hotel in Las Vegas, January 14, 1970, before Nevada Senator Howard W. Cannon, Dick Clark, basketball star Bill Russell, Joe Louis, Steve Allen, and lots more stars, as well as the whole Motown family. Jean Terrell, a tall, statuesque singer (and sister of boxer Ernie Terrell), was given the unenviable task of replacing Diana, while Mary seemed content to remain in the background. These new Supremes would go on to make a couple of fine records, notably "Stoned Love" and "Nathan Jones," both good, updated girl-group records. Yet they would be very much second-class citizens, haunted by a shadow that their records, no matter how good, could never elude.

The recording career of Diana Ross would be quite erratic in the years after her Supremes farewell—"Someday We'll Be Together"— in 1969. There would be great moments ("Love Hangover"); there would also be a remarkable number of nondescript records. But then, Diana was going to be above all that. Berry wanted to make her the black Barbra Streisand and, to some degree, that's what he did.

It was a gamble, but one Berry and Diana took with gusto. The night of her exit from the Supremes, Diana retired to the blackjack table, where she played into the morning surrounded by agents, managers, and men in alligator shoes. Using twenty-five-dollar chips, she drew blackjack twice in a row on two-hundred-dollar bets, winning eight hundred dollars in about two minutes. "An agent or manager shakes his head appreciatively at the show of nerve and luck," wrote Barry Farrell in *Life* magazine. " 'She may weigh 90 pounds but she's got a will of iron,' one said." And she used it to make her dream come true.

"It took a lot of research and I really consider myself somewhat of a perfectionist. I don't like to speculate and I don't take chances with my guys. My thing was to try and revolutionize the sound—cause it was a challenge to me, too—but without speculating." With these words Norman Whitfield described the impetus behind musical changes that would, in fact, do more than revolutionize the Motown Sound; it would make all of the company's previous music obsolete and help alter the very nature of black pop music.

An imposing man with his round bushy Afro, finely sculptured beard, and mean, arrogant countenance, Norman was no longer a minor member of the Motown family. In the wake of H-D-H's departure and Smokey's ongoing creative somnambulance, Norman was now *the man* Motown was looking to to salvage its once prolific production line. To do so he was forced to utilize a new team of Funk Brothers. Benny Benjamin's substance abuse had finally taken its toll. By the time of Gladys Knights' "Heard It Through the Grapevine," Benny had grown so weak that he could no longer be counted on to keep a steady beat. Uriel Jones was brought in to play the main rhythm on "Grapevine," while Benny merely added coloration on cymbals. In 1969 he finally had to be hospitalized and, on a Sunday, while his protégé Stevie Wonder was cutting the little-remembered "You Can't Judge a Book by Its Cover"—a title so appropriate to the relationship between Benny's behavior and his talent —someone came into the studio to say, "Hey, man, we're not gonna do it today. Benny just died." Two drummers, Jones and local jazzman Richard "Pistol" Allen, had to be brought in to replace Benny.

The performance of Benny's musical counterpart James Jamerson was deteriorating as well. Though still involved in the label's important recordings, Jamerson was no longer the main cat. Bob Babbitt, a young white bassist who had learned his craft as Golden World Records' house player, was soon sharing duties with Jamerson. Two new guitarists, Dennis Coffey, a white player with a rock background, and Melvin Ragin (nicknamed "Wah-Wah Watson" for his use of a foot pedal that produced a "wah-wah" sound similar to the effect achieved by Jimi Hendrix, as well as for his Sherlock Holmes-style hat), added freshness to the music. In addition, Whitfield was cutting much of his new music in Los Angeles studios, giving him access to more sophisticated technology than was available back in Detroit.

To all this Whitfield brought a vision of what Motown's new sound would be. Whitfield was quite aware of the impact Sly Stone was having in the marketplace. Stone, an ex-San Francisco deejay steeped in gospel and pop-rock—he produced Bobby "The Swim" Freeman, the Beau Brummels, and the Great Society (which introduced Grace Slick, later of the Jefferson Airplane to recording)—injected R&B's rhythmic precision and stuttering horn arrangements with pop melodies and lyrics in tune with the hippie love-and-peace philosophy. The result was a music that cut across racial boundary lines as H-D-H's Motown music once had done, but with a hip, counterculture "vibration" right in stride with the psychedelic times.

Sly Stone's work made Whitfield take stock and realize that record production was "a science, the science of sound," and that sonically music was moving into a larger, more expansive period that would make both the Motown Sound and the Stax soul sound anachronisms. James Jamerson observed that Norman had never just wanted danceable grooves, but "monstrous funk" that used two or three basic chords to separate the different grooves on any particular record. In 1968, according to drummer Uriel Jones, Whitfield "came into the studio one day and said, 'I wanna do something different. I wanna do something fresh.'" The result was "Cloud Nine," and the new long-play production-line soul, precursor of the seventies disco explosion. With the Temptations providing the voices and Barrett Strong most of the words, Whitfield revolutionized Motown, first with "Cloud Nine" (1968), then "Psychedelic Shack" (1970), "Ball of Confusion" (1970), and the haunting "Papa Was a Rollin' Stone" (1972).

All of these records were based on riffs that were to a large degree improvised by Motown musicians under Whitfield's guidance. The pioneering "Cloud Nine," according to Jones:

> began as a beat on the cymbal. [Norman] would come and tell you this is what he wanted on the cymbal. He'd have you sit and play that two or three minutes by itself, and he'd tell you to add a certain beat on the foot. Actually, what he's doing is just listening to see what he wants to add to it. Then he turns the whole band down on this tune. He may hear a little something else that he

wants and then tell you to change this to this. Norman had in mind what he wanted, but the tune really materialized once we started playing it. We'd be playing and a musician would come up with a lick and he'd say, "Keep that in. That's good. I want that." A lot of times we'd just sit and play and just rap on the tune until somebody just opens up and does something, and then we'd use that. We'd have as many as twelve or thirteen guys in there just grooving on the rhythm.

"Cloud Nine" was quite explicitly about getting high, and the music's kinetic drive seemed to approximate the drug rush. Strong's words don't condemn drug abuse, though later Motown would unconvincingly claim that "Cloud Nine" didn't celebrate it, either. "When that came out the establishment was a little bit stunned," said Otis Williams. "They were used to us singing 'Ol' Man River' and 'Ain't Too Proud to Beg,' but suddenly we were into a heavier kind of song." The importance of what Whitfield and Strong accomplished wasn't lost on Isaac Hayes, Barry White, Curtis Mayfield, or the Philadelphia-based production team of Kenny Gamble and Leon Huff; these men, who were to be the cutting edge of black music in the early 1970s, all owed a debt to "Cloud Nine" for opening up black music and preparing the black audience for more progressive directions.

Just as profoundly, Whitfield's music—along with the records of these men—would affect the very nature of the marketing of black music, of the black pop single, and of black radio programing. Motown had been talking about beefing up its album sales since 1965 and had wooed veteran executives, such as ex-*Billboard* and Columbia Records staffer Tom Noonan in 1968, to aid in this effort. Yet the problem was that, for the most part, Motown albums consisted of one or two hit singles, and then a lot of filler. In contrast, to enjoy Whitfield's Cinemascope soul, one really had to purchase the album—with all eleven minutes and forty-five seconds of "Papa Was a Rollin' Stone." For the first time Motown was offering on 33 rpm something that couldn't be bought on one of their 45-rpm records.

Black radio, which since its inception in the 1940s had featured fast-talking, jivey deejays, segueing from hit to hit, was challenged both by the length of Whitfield's ambitious works (even the "short" version of the majestic "Papa" was over six minutes) and its subject matter (a jive "street" father). The longer cuts and more sophisticated lyrics of Whitfield–Strong, along with Hayes, Mayfield, and others, forced black radio to evolve into a slicker, more adventurous counterpart to rock's "underground" FM stations. Urbane, laid-back announcers slowly began replacing the old-school black deejays.

For Whitfield, the sound was the thing. Be it with white soul-rockers Rare Earth ("I Just Want to Celebrate") or with the husky, often-neglected voice of Edwin Starr ("War," "Stop the War Now," "Funky Music Sho Nuff Turns Me On"), Whitfield–Strong created furiously rhythmic tracks that propelled words that alternated between pseudo-hipness and a fashionable social consciousness (after "Cloud Nine" 's objective treatment of drugs, Whitfield and Strong's lyrics came down squarely on one side of an issue or the other).

Now Whitfield wanted more than hits. As much as he admired the music of Sly and Hendrix, he was also moved by their striking visual presence. It was one thing for the Temps—now looking fashionably funky in suede vests, granny glasses, and multi-colored pants—to do "Funky Music Sho Nuff Turns Me On" (a sight that bothered Cholly Atkins to no end), but quite another for the Whitfield-sponsored group the Undisputed Truth to do it. The trio of Brenda Evans, Billy Calvin, and Joe Harris were young, eager, and ready to wear white facial makeup, blond Afros, and silvery metallic outfits—what Whitfield called "the cosmic thing"—for a hit.

With a confidence born of success, the once silent Whitfield promised the Undisputed Truth a hit within their first three singles. According to Whitfield, he "just turned on the hit machine" and gave them "Smiling Faces Sometimes," a dark, paranoid record that showed that Norman had his finger on the public pulse (at the time, many liberals took it as a commentary on the Nixon administration). "Faces" went to number three, and Norman felt that musically and visually, this group could fulfill his vision.

Meanwhile, Whitfield's relationship with the Temptations had cooled considerably; they resented the fact that, to Whitfield, no song was sacred. Motown acts had always recorded the songs of other acts—it was part of the system to try different acts on a single song, and, of course, each version would increase Jobete's royalties—but, damn, Norman wanted each group to record "War" or "Funky Music" as a single. For his part, Norman felt that the group recording under the Temptations name was no longer the one he'd loved and crafted songs for all these years.

Whitfield had a point. David Ruffin had split after the recording of "Cloud Nine," and many around the group weren't unhappy to see him go. The man was a great performer and singer—but any pretense that

David was a team player had disappeared as his prominence had increased. He wanted a separate limo. He wanted more money. He wanted it to be David Ruffin and the Temptations. And then he wanted out. It still isn't completely clear whether David just quit one day or if Motown fired him. Either way, David was gone—though during the period following his exit David showed up at several Temptations' shows, seemingly unsure if he'd made the right move. He was right to worry.

David not only left the Temptations, he attempted to escape Motown as well, signing with C. B. Atkins for management and Associated Booking for live engagements. The twenty-seven-year-old singer claimed that Motown had held him in "economic peonage," that he wasn't sure how much he had made in 1967 because Motown had handled all his financial affairs, and that his contract "was one-sided . . . appropriate only for a relationship between a guardian and a child or mental incompetent." David's new management team offered him for club engagements and submitted his name for a role in Roger Vadim's shlock masterpiece *Barbarella* (starring Jane Fonda). His name was also proposed by Atkins and Associated for a part in a film biography of Cassius Clay. However, in October 1966, David had signed a binding one-year contract with Motown and a four-year contract with ITM. The label sued and, clearly in its rights, won the case. David did get his solo career, but on Motown. It started quite auspiciously with "My Whole World Ended (the Moment You Left Me)," a strong, yearning love song produced by Harvey Fuqua and Johnny Bristol, perfect for Ruffin's emotive style. But after two Top Twenty soul singles in 1969, he wouldn't have another hit single until 1975, with the overproduced "Walk Away From Love." At some point, perhaps as a delayed reaction to the lawsuit, David Ruffin wasn't a priority at Motown anymore. (In the 1970s he would spend some time in jail for tax evasion, reportedly paint houses in Cincinnati, and, in 1983, he'd participate in the Temptations' *Reunion* tour, by which time his once dramatic voice had withered away to a hoarse whisper.)

Eddie Kendricks was next to go. Like Ruffin, Kendricks sought solo stardom, but his exit was accomplished with Motown's cooperation. His last Temptations performance, "Just My Imagination," was sweet and dreamy, wonderfully appropriate for the wistful story about a lovestruck young man imagining life with an unattainable lady. It was perhaps Whitfield–Strong's best single lyric and possibly their finest song. Paul Riser's string and horn arrangement was sublime, and the rhythm track was as supple as Kendrick's feathery falsetto.

With the aid of Whitfield disciple producer-writer Frank Wilson, the slender tenor would soon enjoy a string of dance floor, proto-disco hits (e.g., "Boogie Down," "Keep on Truckin' "). His departure, however, did have the unfortunate result of leaving Paul Williams without an anchor, one he desperately needed, as his life was slowly unraveling. Paul had fallen deeper and deeper into a depression intensified by drugs and alcohol. He was an unhappy man, though no one could really explain why. What was clear was that, from about 1967 on, he went downhill. Once the Temptations' best dancer, Paul was missing beats; his once steady baritone wavered; he forgot lyrics. Richard Street, an original Distant, an ex-Monitor, and a staff member of Artist Development, began traveling with the Temptations to sing Williams's parts from an offstage microphone, and eventually to learn his steps and replace him.

This was one Motown personnel switch that created no animosity or bitterness. Berry was generous, in fact, making Paul Williams a Motown consultant and placing him on salary "while he sat around on corners waiting for something to happen to his life," as Kendricks told the *Detroit Free Press*. He had an interest in a barbershop and still helped the Temps with their steps. "But all that was only good enough to make him feel bad every time he looked up on the wall and saw all that gold." Kendricks last saw Williams alive in mid-August 1973. Just before parting, Williams grabbed his arm and said, "Remember, man, you're only as good as your last show." A week later, on August 17, 1973, he shot himself in the head while parked in a car, wearing only swimming trunks, just two blocks from the Hitsville studio.

Though musically and spiritually the Temptations were weakened by these departures, one man benefited from the changes. Dennis Edwards had toiled with the Contours before being brought into the Temptations. For a while, people had compared him unfavorably to David Ruffin, but with time Edwards came to be recognized as a great singer in his own right. He lacked Ruffin's subtlety and range; however, Edwards could "blow" with the unbridled emotion of all the great soul singers, and with time would gain control. In the group's post-Whitfield years, it would be Edwards's wailing low tenor that made the Temptations worth hearing.

From late 1969 to 1971, Marvin Gaye seemed to be living in a daze. He didn't perform live, he stopped working with Motown's staff producers, and he spent a lot of time getting high and disagreeing with his wife Anna. In the wake of Tammi Terrell's illness, Marvin was torn between his life as a sex symbol and singing star and his father's religious teachings. A deep, unexplainable emptiness settled into his soul. He and Berry were at odds over just about everything except the purchase of Berry's Boston Road mansion, which Anna had engineered. While Berry was doing business in Los Angeles, Marvin was brooding in the Motor City, looking for a direction.

Then in 1970, Marvin, then thirty-one, got an idea, one that would obsess him and give him a goal, something to motivate his flagging spirits. He was going to join the Detroit Lions. "Had I not become an entertainer I'm sure I'd have been a pro athlete," he told sportswriter Jack Saylor, with the deep conviction Marvin could bring to even the most outrageous statements. "I love baseball and basketball and I played golf in the mid-sixties, but football is the only thing I've had a real feeling for. I've watched the pros over the years and it has become a part of me. I learned to love it and have confidence I could play."

Marvin had been a pseudo jock for years, since the days when he used to play sandlot football in Washington, even though he was forbidden to play by his father. His fascination with sports was rivaled only by his interest in music and women, which, considering Marvin's passion for both, was saying a lot. People who knew him at Motown weren't surprised by Marvin's desire. But then, nothing about that cat shocked them. Marvin was Marvin.

His belief that he might have a chance to make the Lions originated at a postgame party in Detroit where Marvin, who was friendly with star running back Mel Farr and cornerback Lem Barney, asked coach Joe Schmidt for a tryout. Schmidt agreed. The next thing Schmidt knew, Marvin was working with weights, bulking up from 160 to 207 pounds (this forced him to purchase ten thousand dollars' worth of new clothes for his new body), and asking when to report to rookie camp. "It's like me saying I'm going to sing at the Copacabana," said his buddy Farr. "He's never trained for it, but being a football player is a real obsession with him." The Lions, the team that let author George Plimpton play quarterback for his book *Paper Lion,* said no, even refusing to let Marvin attend rookie camp for a day. Following this disappointment, Marvin got involved with boxing, working out regularly at the King Solomon Gym with many of Detroit's professional prize fighters.

Fortunately, Marvin was also making some music during this period, music that had little to do with being a jock (though Lem Barney and Mel Farr would eventually play a role in it) or, for that matter, with the carefully crafted singles he'd recorded previously for Motown. "Baby, I'm for Real" (1969), written for the Originals, much like "Your Precious Love," which Marvin had written and recorded with Tammi Terrell, harked back to his doo-wop roots in its use of the voices in Freddy Gorman's group. Yet there was a supple, jazzy feeling supplied by a recurring saxophone motif and an eerie, intangibly spiritual tone to the lyrics—he could have been writing about God as easily as about a woman —that made "Baby" not an act of nostalgia but a prelude to greatness.

Marvin was moving toward a more individual style that mirrored his interest in jazz and his roots in doo-wop and gospel. He was in a profound period of transition, one that would come to a head with a little help from his friends. Those friends turned out to be Jobete staff writer Al Cleveland and Four Tops member Renaldo "Obie" Benson. Cleveland, co-writer with Smokey of "I Second That Emotion," was hanging out at Benson's house one afternoon while the Four Top fooled around on acoustic guitar. Benson began fingering a meditative melody while discussing the social upheavals of the late sixties with Cleveland. Together they formed the melody into a song. Three weeks later, Cleveland, sitting in his car and looking out at Lake Michigan, came up with the hook line that would make the song a classic. Benson and Cleveland felt the completed song would be perfect for Marvin's supple voice and contemplative personality.

At first, Marvin Gaye didn't want to record "What's Going On." "We begged him for about a month to do the tune," Cleveland recalls. "He hadn't had a record out in a year and a half, and he wasn't doing too good financially. As a result he was not into a good frame of mind." Marvin kept the tape while Cleveland, planning to relocate permanently to the West Coast to be close to Motown's new headquarters, traveled out to Los Angeles. While he was away, Marvin cut "What's Going On," and the record's timely message of social protest, plus Marvin's inspired vocal performance, made it the most powerful record of 1971.

However, a problem arose as a result of the record's amazingly swift acceptance. There was no album ready. When Cleveland and Benson rushed back to Detroit they found Marvin, with the aid of arranger David Van DePitte, hastily organizing recording sessions. "We'd talked about the concept for the album when we wrote the song, but Marvin had started it without us," says Cleveland, still somewhat miffed after all these years.

The album's sessions linger in Johnny Griffith's mind. He remembers, "One day Marvin came in an hour and a half late with a bucket full of fried chicken. He said, 'We're gonna do something different this time.' But it wasn't a surprise to us. Seven or eight years before he used to say, 'If I ever get a chance I'm gonna get into something different.' "

"I do something and then I listen to it and say, 'Wow, this will sound good on this,' " Marvin said of the record's creation. "And I listen to that and say, 'Wait, here I can put behind that, this' and then when I do that, I say, 'Wow, a couple of bells, ding ding, here,' and that's the way you do it. You build. Like an artist paints a picture. He starts slowly, he has [to] paint each thing at a time." So many years later, *What's Going On* still has that painterly quality, its music hanging like a work of art in the air whenever it is played.

What's Going On, though started reluctantly by Marvin Gaye, would become his masterpiece, the first great Motown "concept" album and arguably a recording on par with the Beatles' *Sgt. Pepper's Lonely Hearts Club Band* or Sly and the Family Stone's *Stand*. "In fact, if one were to say that James Brown could be the Fletcher Henderson and Count Basie of rhythm and blues, then Marvin Gaye is obviously its Ellington and Miles Davis," wrote jazz critic Stanley Crouch. In *The Village Voice* Crouch remarked, "Through overdubbing, Gaye imparted lyric, rhythmic, and emotional counterpoint to his material. The result was a swirling stream-of-consciousness that enabled him to protest, show allegiance, love, hate, dismiss, and desire in one proverbial swoop. . . . The upshot of his genius was the ease and power with which he could pivot from a superficially simple but virtuosic use of rests and accents to a multilinear layered density."

The lyrics of *What's Going On*'s nine songs received the most attention, as the press reacted positively to the range of social issues covered —from poverty and crime in "Inner City Blues (Make Me Wanna Holler)," Vietnam in "What's Going On," pollution on "Mercy Mercy Me (The Ecology)"—and to the deep spiritual feeling that infused the entire album. But over time it is the album's music that has made it endure. Every song is imbued with pieces of gospel, R&B, Hollywood soundtrack flourishes, and third-world rhythms, and Gaye's voice is saxophonelike in its phrasing, communicating ecstasy and pain, coolness and compassion, tying together the threads of the music.

Marvin's singing and sensibility were at the album's core, but like all artistic efforts of a large scale, the album wasn't done alone. The angelic strings and horns arranged by David Van DePitte; Renaldo Benson and Al Cleveland's songs "Wholly Holy," "Save the Children," and the title cut; James Nyx's aid to Marvin in composing "Inner City Blues," "God Is Love," and "What's Happening Brother"—all were vital to its brilliance. So were James Jamerson, Johnny Griffith, Robert White, Joe Messina, and Jack Ashford—all of whom were credited, for the first time, on the back of a Motown album; their jazz sensibility could be felt in the music's intricate, shifting rhythms and quiet intensity. Marvin's sense of team spirit extended even to his would-be Detroit Lions teammates Mel Farr and Lem Barney; it is their partying voices that can be heard at the beginning of "What's Going On."

Motown wasn't thrilled with the album, and resisted releasing it. Berry, a man whose sense of what made for pop music had once been unerring, doubted its appeal. Yet, in large part because they needed a new album on Marvin to follow the single's success, *What's Going On* hit the street in 1971. With Marvin staring beatifically into space through rain-drops on the cover, the album became the biggest-selling album in Motown history up to that date, and continued the expansion of black music's scope that Whitfield had instigated.

A very interested observer of Marvin's saga, and ultimately its chief beneficiary, was a young man yearning to come of age. In February 1971, "What's Going On" went to number one on the soul chart and number two on the pop, and the album reached number one in both markets. On May 13, 1971, Steveland Morris turned twenty-one years old, and was anxiously awaiting public reaction to *Where I'm Coming From*. With his wife of less than a year, ex-Motown secretary Syreeta Wright, writing some lyrics, Stevie had attempted a statement of his own. After talking with Berry, he'd gotten permission to produce the entire album himself.

It wasn't really a major risk; Stevie had written or co-written eight of his seventeen hit singles, including the excellent pop-soul "Signed, Sealed, Delivered, I'm Yours." Just the year before, he had provided the music for the Miracles' first number one pop and soul record in years, "Tears of a Clown."

Giving Stevie his way might also prove to be an important bargaining chip when "Little Stevie" turned twenty-one and brought his contract up for renewal. Berry was correct in believing that Stevie could deliver a hit; "If You Really Love Me" (number four soul, number eight pop in 1971), was a song with a cooking Motown groove and an unusual spoken break that reflected Stevie's growing musical adventurousness. But both men were, at least initially, kept from achieving their larger goals. *Where I'm Coming From* is an awkward, quite forgettable exercise. In retrospect, Stevie admitted it was premature and too hastily conceived.

For Berry, the disappointment came in stages. First, when he turned twenty-one, Stevie received about a million dollars that Motown owed him in back royalties. Then, displaying a trait that would become something of a personal trademark, Stevie took his time getting back to Motown about the contract. Finally, after almost six months of waiting, he told Motown, "I'm not gonna do what you say anymore. Void my contract." A true Taurus—he named his production company Taurus and his publishing company Black Bull—Stevie had made up his mind, and that's all there was to it.

In 1971, Stevie, his wife, and his money moved to New York City. As he explained to Constance Eisner:

> I wanted to do an album with the money I had accumulated. But this time it wasn't so much a question of where I was coming from but where I was going to. I had to find out what my direction and my destiny was. And there was no way that I could just go on from where I had stopped at Motown. It was a completely different thing that was in my head. I don't think you can gradually leave a kind of music. You can't mix one concept with another. It has to be an abrupt change where you say, "Okay, this is what I want to do from now on and all the other stuff belongs to the past."

Away from the Motown colony in Detroit and also, not coincidentally, away from Los Angeles, where Motown was putting down its own new roots, Stevie's attitudes toward the world, toward music, and toward business would undergo an evolution, one that was accelerated by his new environment and by the freedom money bought for reflection and extravagance. His most important financial contact came when folk singer Richie Havens introduced him to a wavy-haired, scruffy-looking attorney named Jonathan Vigoda. Vigoda handled Havens's affairs and had done work for Jimi Hendrix as well. A detractor described him as "a cat laying on the floor of his office, spitting pumpkin seeds out the side of his mouth in fatigues all day long." But another Wonder associate asserts that Vigoda's laid-back demeanor and Woodstock connections disguised a "wise man" as stubborn and demanding as Stevie. Vigoda was given the assignment of fielding the many recording offers flooding in. Clive Davis the charismatic CBS boss, was hovering around, wooing Stevie for his growing operation. Atlantic Records' co-founder Ahmet Ertegun was talking to Vigoda; so was Elektra. They all brought thick checkbooks—a good thing, since Stevie and his new attorney were asking for an unprecedented amount of money. And, yes, Motown was still calling and talking to Vigoda, though most in the industry thought the door had been shut to them when Stevie relocated.

While the offers came in, Stevie began exploring the parameters of his new creative freedom in a frenzied, feverish manner, and the new vehicle was the synthesizer. He'd used a rather primitive model, the RMI, to strengthen the bass line on "If You Really Love Me," and had used the clavinet, what writers called "a funky harpsichord," in his live shows. But it was an album called *Zero Time*, by a group called Tonto's Expanding Head Band, that made Stevie a synthesizer junkie.

The synthesizer is an electronic device that, through the use of transistors and microchips, can produce tones that simulate the sounds of conventional instruments, and also unique sounds all its own. In addition, the synthesizer has the ability to control the rhythm, volume, and harmonies it creates. On *Zero Time* the Expanding Head Band, really two musician-technicians named Malcolm Cecil and Robert Margouleff, used Tonto (an acronym for The Original New Timbral Orchestra), a huge circular mass of synthesizers, to create what *Keyboard* magazine hailed as "arguably the first purely electronic album to take the synthesizer to the limits of its liberating capabilities while still making music that laymen could enjoy." It was *Zero Time*'s balance of advanced technology and musicality that led Stevie to seek out Cecil and Margouleff.

"Stevie showed up with the Tonto LP under his arm," remembers Malcolm Cecil. "He said, 'I don't believe all this was done on one instrument. Show me the instrument.' He was always talking about seeing. So we dragged his hands all over the instrument, and he thought he'd never be able to play it. But we told him we'd get it together for him." And they certainly did, for over the next year Stevie, Margouleff, and Cecil would record material that would be the backbone of his next four albums, *Music of My Mind* (1972), *Talking Book* (1972), *Innervisions* (1973), and *Fullfillingness' First Finale* (1974).

At Stevie's request, the mammoth synthesizer was moved from midtown Manhattan's Media Sound to Jimi Hendrix's Electric Lady Studios in Greenwich Village. The trio was supposed to work on one album together but, in the words of an ex-Wonder employee, they "went nuts. Nuts, nuts, nuts." Working evenings, often starting after midnight and working into the daylight and even the next afternoon, going on and on, much as Hendrix himself had while creating the *Electric Ladyland* album in that same studio, they spent almost $250,000 in recording fees. In that first year alone, they completed thirty-five tracks, with Stevie supplying the ideas and Margouleff and Cecil the technology to realize them. Aside from the songs that appeared on those four albums, Cecil has estimated there were some forty other songs completed and mixed, and some two hundred and forty others "in various stages of development." Stevie had waited his whole professional life for this kind of freedom, and with the synthesizer, he had a control no pop musician before had exercised over his recordings.

Stevie was so prolific that he almost ran into trouble with the American Federation of Musicians. A crew of young musicians, all enthralled watching Stevie's magical music blossom, contributed to the sessions. The hours were so erratic that the considerable paperwork involved in recording sessions, a part of the business Stevie disdained, fell way behind. Forms weren't being filed, and so paychecks and pension papers were either late or missing. Gene Kee, the Motown staff arranger who had arranged "Alfie" for Stevie, finally had to fly in from Detroit to clean up the administrative mess.

Despite the haphazard, chaotic atmosphere surrounding the sessions, a condition that would bedevil Stevie's sessions for the rest of his career, the music that flowed through the Electric Lady speakers would establish Stevie as one of the most innovative musicians of the 1970s. The first album released from these sessions, *Music of My Mind*, in 1972, established a "formula" that the subsequent, superior works would follow.

This is not to say that Stevie hasn't expanded his repertoire since *Music*. The brassy, big band horns of "Sir Duke," the kinetic jazz fusion of "Contusion"—written by future pop star Mike Sembello—and the orchestral ambition of *Journey Through the Secret Life of Plants*, all show Stevie's continuing growth. Yet there are thematic threads in *Music*, musically and lyrically, which Stevie has continued refining, and from which he has not deviated greatly since that period. Stevie has a wider, more sophisticated series of formulas than any other musician of the rock era; Michael Jackson, Paul McCartney, Prince, and a few others do a number of things well—some as well as or better than Stevie—but none do as *many* as well as he.

The first song on *Music of My Mind*, "Love Having You Around," opens with Stevie talking in a jive, high-pitched voice, saying "baby" repeatedly before singing in a slurred Slyesque voice about riding a camel. Despite Stevie's serious fatback drumming, everything else on this song has a very playful, jokey quality, from the guitar riffs (or is it synthesizer?) to Art Baron's trombone solo. The mischievous side of Stevie that once bedeviled Motown staffers shines through here, a part of Stevie's personality apparent later in the spoken intro to "Don't You Worry 'Bout a Thing," the playful "Do I Do," and the slurred street-corner vocals of "Boogie on Reggae Woman," "Master Blaster (Jammin')," and "Maybe Your Baby." All these songs, including "Having You Around," have the loose, flowing feel of improvised jams, even though Stevie played most or all of the instruments.

The next cut on the album, "Superwoman (Where Were You When I Needed You)," segues into "I Love Every Little Thing About You"; this was a technique he'd employ often (e.g., "Looking for Another Pure Love" segues into "I Believe" on *Talking Book*, and "Summer Soft" into "Ordinary Rain" on *Songs in the Key of Life*). Both of these songs have an airy, floating quality built around glowing electric piano chords. It is an atmosphere Stevie would find conducive to a series of romantic mid-tempo compositions, the best known of which is "You Are the Sunshine of My Life," though many would argue that "Golden Lady," "Send One Your Love," and "Rocket Love" are just as good and not as gooey. All these songs owe much to "My Cherie Amour," though their ethereal delicacy are products of Stevie's synthesizer fixation.

"Happier Than the Morning Sun" and "Girl Blue" have unusual synthesized musical backgrounds: "Happier" uses a clavinet to create a harpsichord sound that compliments Stevie's classically influenced choral backing harmonies; "Girl" has an eerie, disjointed musical backing track that on the verses runs counter to the melody. Stevie's voice on "Girl Blue" has a distant, disembodied quality he'd repeat on "Village Ghetto-land" and "Big Brother."

The prototype for beautiful ballads such as "Heaven Is Ten Zillion Light Years Away," "You and I," "Lately," and "Ribbon in the Sky," "Seems So Long" is a rambling melody that builds on an effective melodramatic crescendo. Unfortunately, in 1972, Stevie's understanding of how to produce a ballad wasn't as advanced as his songwriting. Throughout "Seems" he uses production touches (such as the reverberation of drumsticks against cymbals) that detract from the song's romantic melody. This is one piano ballad where the piano sound is obscured, a mistake he'd never make again—as the graceful "You and I" and "Ribbon" demonstrate.

Similarly, *Music*'s only social commentary song, "Evil," isn't up to the standards of those that would follow. Its lyric, about how evil wreaks havoc on the world, is too vague and unfocused to be a powerful statement. Still, "Evil" is a significant harbinger of the humanitarian concerns that would, by the mid-eighties, make Wonder as important politically as he was musically. "You Haven't Done Nothing," "Pastime Paradise," the epic "Living for the City," "Cash in Your Face," the Vietnam veteran tribute "Front Line," and "Happy Birthday," a song that catalyzed the successful movement to make Martin Luther King's birthday, January 15, a national holiday, reflect deep political and social convictions that influenced Stevie as much as the old Motown rhythm section. Using his prominence as a black star to help other black Americans became a healthy obsession for him, and in the future when he gave sanctimonious or rambling, self-important speeches, Stevie would be forgiven because it came from the soul. He was always putting his money and time behind his musical good intentions.

And it was those very convictions that finally led him back to Motown, back to the black-owned company that raised him, to release *Music* and all the great records that followed. It was yet another case where Motown's "blackness" gave it an advantage in dealing with artists. But this time—over a decade after its founding—Motown would finally pay through the nose. Motown ended up giving Stevie a contract several zillion light years away from any previous agreement. With Vigoda leading a battery of lawyers in negotiating with Ewart Abner, Motown's first appointed black president, Stevie was given a contract guaranteeing total creative control and more money than any Motown act had ever received (it proved to be a prelude to the unprecedented, seven-year, thirteen-million-dollar pact he'd sign in 1974. Abner, Motown president during both of these contract negotiations, would, by 1977, join Stevie's Black Bull operation and, along with Vigoda, become Stevie's chief business adviser.)

Stevie's *Music* and contract, like Gaye's *What's Going On* and stubbornness, was dragging a reluctant Motown into the 1970s. Old hands at the company, however, would still point to the Jackson 5 and say that the old system worked, failing to see the ways in which the rise of this Gary, Indiana, family indicated quite clearly that the old ways at "Motown U" were dead.

The Jackson 5 success story, as presented by Motown, is well known: a five-member family group is spotted by Diana Ross, at a benefit for Gary, Indiana's black Mayor Richard Hatcher. Ross excites Berry with her enthusiasm. Marlon, Jackie, Tito, Jermaine, and Michael, following extensive grooming and musical preparation, go to number one with their first four singles ("I Want You Back" in 1969 and "ABC," "The Love You Save," and "I'll be There" in 1970), confirming that the production line was still moving.

The hits were real—in fact "I Want You Back" and "The Love You Save" were as durable as the best of H-D-H—but the rest of the story warrants closer examination. Ex-guitarist Papa Joe Jackson had, with the

183

blessing and tender advice of wife Katherine, pushed his sons into show business after they'd displayed flashes of talent around the house. Led by little Michael's lively lead vocals and James Brown-clone moves, the Jackson family (a neighbor gave them the "Jackson 5" handle) became chitlin-circuit regulars, piling into vans on weekends and holidays to perform as far away as New York, Philadelphia, and Phoenix, thus building a reputation in black music circles well before signing with Motown. They cut two obscure singles on a small Gary label, Steeltown, and attracted the attention of many established artists. Sam Moore of Sam and Dave loved them, but felt the gutsy soul style of his label (Stax) wouldn't suit them. Gladys Knight told her ITM manager Taylor Cox about them on two occasions, but to no avail. Finally, it was the VIP label's Bobby Taylor, the black leader of an integrated band called the Vancouvers (their hit "Does Your Mama Know About Me?" was about an interracial love affair), who, after watching the Jacksons electrify an audience at Chicago's High Chaparral Club in 1968, got them a Motown audition.

James Jamerson remembered laughing at their name, because it reminded him of an old slang expression ("the Jackson jive") and Louis Jordan's back-up band (the Tiffany Five). But after members of the Motown staff finished watching them, they found the Jacksons to be quite serious indeed. Though musically crude—cousin and keyboardist Ronnie Ransom was then the band's best player—the Jackson boys did have an undeniable vitality, something a black and white sixteen-millimeter film of them auditioning at Motown displayed quite vividly to executives who had missed the audition. It was a quality that went well with Berry's Hollywood dreams.

Ross herself didn't meet the group until a party at Berry's Detroit mansion, where the Jacksons performed for staffers. Later, at a staff meeting, the decision was made to use Ross to market the group, since it was felt that her sponsorship would give the group entrée to Ed Sullivan and other network shows, where their pint-sized charisma would surely excel. Not since Stevie's early days had Motown had a genuine kiddie act, but the impact of the Five Stairsteps, a black family group with the pop hit "O-o-h Child," and of the Monkees (via their NBC television show), revealed that a large, prepubescent audience existed. The Jacksons were about to be embraced by Motown, but unlike the Supremes, Stevie Wonder, Marvin Gaye, and others, the Jackson 5 already had a well-defined visual style and committed management (their parents). The Jackson 5's contract didn't vary radically from the standard (some were now calling it "substandard") Motown agreement. The group received a 2.7-percent royalty rate, better than previous deals, but hardly generous in an era when royalty rates were often 8 percent.

Soon after the Detroit party the boys and Papa Joe were whisked away to Los Angeles for grooming and recording. Artist Development as it had existed in Detroit was now a memory. As the company moved west the once busy Artist Development building was abandoned; Atkins, Fuqua, and King had all left. Instead of the old pros and the system Motown once employed in Detroit, Berry, sisters Gwen and Anna, Ross, and two recent additions to the company, Suzanne DePasse and her cousin Tony Jones, came together in Los Angeles to polish the Jacksons in a one-time-only deal.

Though Ross received much credit, not all of it unjustified, for Michael Jackson's poise, the key Motown advisor was DePasse, a beautiful, aggressive product of Harlem's black bourgeoisie who had talked her way into the booking agent's job at New York's hip Cheetah disco in 1968. Berry met her there one evening and was drawn to her energy and ambition, qualities all shared by his previous female protégées. When the Jackson 5 became a Motown priority he assigned her the job of road manager/adviser.

DePasse was quick-witted, loyal, and resourceful. But this was not like the old days, when veteran show-biz figures coached inexperienced youngsters; the Jacksons had been active in show business longer than DePasse had. Moreover, the Jacksons ran their own rehearsals, with DePasse acting more as a guide than an instructor. She told them to cut the James Brownisms, selected their trendy Day-Glo stage garb, and wrote cute banter for the boys. The Jacksons respected DePasse, but there was nothing of the student/mentor relationship of Artist Development's production line years. Moreover, after the Jackson 5's acceptance, DePasse would become a Motown vice-president, an administrator with her hands into too many different pies to perform the day-to-day artist development duties essential to molding acts. The breakdown in Artist Development would be so complete that by 1984 Eldra DeBarge, lead singer of Motown's promising family group DeBarge, would say in response to a *Los Angeles Times* question about tour preparation, "Coaching? What coaching? I haven't been fortunate enough to have people around to show me things. I wish I did. Basically, I'm out there by myself."

To launch the Jackson 5 properly, Berry knew he needed top material. However, he just couldn't push buttons anymore. H-D-H were gone.

185

Norman Whitfield was preoccupied. Smokey was slowing his activities, in preparation for a three-year retirement in 1972. Ashford and Simpson weren't right for the Jackson 5 (and besides, they were concentrating on building Valerie's solo career). Bobby Taylor desperately wanted to produce the group, but Berry felt the project was too important to rely on Taylor alone.

So, as he had with the last few Ross-led Supremes singles, Berry got actively involved in developing material. He took a song three Jobete staffers, Deke Richards, Fonce Mizel, and Freddie Perren, had written for Gladys Knight and the Pips, had them change the words, lower the key, and recut the track. "He listened to it," remembers Perren, "turned to us, and said, 'You guys are getting ready to blow a hit,' and proceeded to tell us what was wrong, from the arrangement to the lyrics." The resulting record was an explosive burst of youthful enthusiasm backed by immaculate, dynamic production and a clever lyric to which Berry had clearly contributed his expertise. Once again Berry had demonstrated his mastery of the increasingly anachronistic three-minute single.

By labeling the "I Want You Back" team of Richards, Mizell, Perren, and himself "the Corporation," Berry was apparently trying to keep the other members from rising to prominence. Moreover, his active involvement, so critical to their success, was another short-term arrangement at Motown, a move necessary to fill a gap. Back in Detroit, hiding the record's producers under "the Corporation" tag might have worked. Many music fans in the mid-sixties never knew the first names of H-D-H, or thought maybe they were white. But Motown was now in Los Angeles, subject to the same talent raids as any other company in a town where entertainment industry secrets were always for sale. The offers flooded in and Perren, who would prove himself the most talented of the original three Corporation members, was wooed away from Motown to write Jackson 5-style tunes with another ex-Jobete staffer, Dino Fekaris, for the Sylvers and Tavares, and later standards for Peaches and Herb ("Reunited") and Gloria Gaynor ("I Will Survive").

Thus the foundation the Jackson 5 was built upon, on and off record, was not applicable, in the long run, to young acts that would join Motown in the seventies. Another difference in the Jackson 5–Motown relationship that eventually would have profound consequences for the company was the group's view of Berry. For many of Motown's Detroit acts and employees, Berry was a symbol of successful black manhood in a world where black males in power positions were rare. But in Papa Joe the Jackson clan had a headstrong leader who demanded respect, took no crap from his sons, and liked his will to prevail whenever possible. This attitude, an independence most new acts would attempt to exercise, was clearly at odds with Motown's Berry-knows-best philosophy. So a wary, in this case somewhat adversarial, relationship evolved between Joe and Berry. Joe was overjoyed with his sons' achievement but, according to Jackson associates from the period, felt Motown went out of their way to play up Diana and Berry, while minimizing the role of his wife and himself. So with the same diligence that had led the Jacksons to trek across the nation by van, Joe began appraising just how much his sons were worth on the open market.

To Motown, of course, the Jackson 5 were worth plenty of dollars and tremendous publicity. Not since the Supremes had Motown had such a delicious product to peddle: wholesome, cute, a safe middle-American antidote to black militancy, the Jacksons were made for network television. It was the Jackson 5, and particularly Michael, playing Frank Sinatra in one skit and singing "ABC" in another, who were really the highlights of Ross's ABC special, in 1970. In fact, after that initial exposure with Ross, it would be the Jackson 5—via their own television special ("Goin' Back to Indiana") and a cartoon series—who would give Motown its most profound television success.

Launching Ross and the Jackson 5 had, temporarily, brought Berry back to music, but throughout this period Berry had become increasingly obsessed with a film idea he'd harbored for years, the screen version of Billie Holiday's autobiography, *Lady Sings the Blues*. "Lady Day" had died the year Motown was founded, an eerie coincidence, since the film Berry would make about her would cause Motown to take a fateful turn. For if the Jackson 5's rise signaled the end of the production line, the making of *Lady* threw dirt on the grave.

Berry was chasing a dream. His very special gift for pop songwriting was abandoned in an attempt to recreate the flavor of the jazz clubs he had haunted as a teen. Wish fulfillment? Nostalgia? Boredom with music? No more bridges to cross? These factors all may have played a part in leading Berry away from his strength and into a world where, for all his millions, he was still a very little fish in a big, mean pond. Meanwhile, the record division would battle, unsuccessfully, an industry trend that had already changed the shape of black music.

By 1972, the year the entire operation was finally settled in Los Angeles, Motown's status as the leading maker and manufacturer of black music was being challenged, not by Stax or Chess or Atlantic, but by huge corporate-controlled labels based in New York and Los Angeles. Stax signed with CBS for distribution, as did Kenny Gamble and Leon Huff's Philadelphia International. That same year James Brown left King for Polydor, the U.S. arm of the international conglomerate Phonodisc. The Isley Brothers would join CBS under their T-Neck label. Ashford and Simpson, frustrated by Motown's lackluster efforts to develop Valerie as an artist, went as a duo to Warner Bros. The Four Tops signed with ABC, and other top black performers would follow the trend.

CBS went so far as to get a research team from the Harvard University Business School to prepare "A Study of the Soul Music Environment," a twenty-four-page blueprint for dominating black music, known in the industry as the Harvard Report. In a section on competitors in the market, the report said of Motown, Atlantic, and Stax: "They are entrenched and control half the total market. They have the most established soul artists, with management and professional staffs with the most experience and understanding of the subtleties."

By the mid-seventies, Stax would be destroyed in a costly legal battle with CBS, while Atlantic would merge with Elektra and Warner Bros. to form WEA, a distribution combination almost as powerful as CBS. Artistically, Atlantic would de-emphasize black music for white rockers like Led Zepplin, Crosby, Stills and Nash, Bad Company, Yes, and Emerson, Lake and Palmer. These changes in the marketplace led CBS, which in 1970 had two progressive acts with a substantial black following, Sly and the Family Stone and Santana, to expand so aggressively that, by 1980, they would have 125 black-oriented acts, one-third of their total roster.

Meanwhile, Motown's record division floundered. Of the middle-level acts, only Eddie Kendricks and a young band from Tuskeegee, Alabama, the Commodores, showed any sales consistency, while Thelma Houston, the Sisters Love, David Ruffin, Syreeta Wright, G. C. Cameron, and even Diana Ross had records that were hit-or-miss affairs.

Part of the problem could be traced to the exit of Barney Ales. From the very beginning, Ales had been squeezing distributors for overdue dollars and pushing his salesmen; he was the business backbone of Motown. Then, in 1972, he left the executive suite, staying behind in Detroit as the company settled in the West. Barney had grown rich at Motown, but, citing a need for new challenges and resistance from his family, he stayed in Detroit. At first he managed David Ruffin and Rare Earth, and subsequently opened his own label, Prodigal—a comment perhaps on his departure from Motown (or Motown's departure from Detroit).

At this point, Ewart Abner was elevated to Motown's presidency. Abner's blackness was a definite plus for Motown's image. Still, during this time, when Motown's roots were being attacked by internal and industry-wide changes, this shift hurt deeply. For if Berry had provided Motown Records with inspiration, Barney's ability to get the money had been its guts. Without either of these men active in the company, Motown became just another record company—despite the continuing presence of Stevie Wonder, Marvin Gaye, the Jackson 5, and Norman Whitfield. By the time Barney rejoined Motown as president in 1975 the Motown mystique was gone, and he couldn't bring it back alone.

Ironically, following Motown's lead, a generation of top black musicians migrated West; singers, writers, and players from Chicago, Memphis, New Orleans. Philadelphia, and Detroit followed the sun, stripping the top layer of black talent from these local scenes. A top session musician can live well in Los Angeles—amid swimming pools, great weather, and a relaxed atmosphere—and perhaps this unconsciously changed the nonmusical attitudes of these players. Motown began tapping into the same talent pool as everyone else in Los Angeles, and they got the same sound as everyone else in town. So by 1973, the year Motown was listed by *Black Enterprise* magazine as the biggest black-owned company in America, grossing $40 million and employing 135 people, the elements that had given Motown its magic were either disengaged (Berry), gone (H-D-H, Barney Ales, the Funk Brothers, Artist Development) or quiescent (Smokey). Motown would do a lot of new and different things in the coming years; they just wouldn't do them as well as they used to.

7·JUST ANOTHER RECORD COMPANY

In the 1980s, Detroit, Michigan, once a city of long cars and high hopes, is a place where prosperity, optimism, and jobs have disappeared or moved away. Unemployment and crime haunt this city like a death in the family. The darkest story in town is, of course, the sorry state of the American auto industry. Cars were Detroit's lifeblood, its rolling machines of upward mobility. Now the auto industry's leaders talk about "efficiency" when they lay off workers and "productivity" as the city's welfare rolls swell with their discarded ex-employees. There is a hole in Detroit's soul because of this human misery, and there is nothing on the horizon ready to fill it.

For anyone who loves pop music and finds in it a force that, even at its most trivial, fills life's melancholy moments with careless joy, cataloguing the remnants of Motown's marvelous machine scattered idly around Detroit is as morbidly fascinating as watching out-of-work auto workers gather at the unemployment office. At Bert's, a friendly, warm bar just across the street from Hart Plaza and the Detroit River, Thomas "Beans" Bowles often sits in, searching on his sax for the sounds that had seemed so elementary at the Twenty Grand years ago. Over in the dark green, smoky Motor Bar of the once elegant Book Cadillac Hotel, ex-Motown drummer Pistol Allen occasionally drops in some Motownesque licks as he backs a jazz combo, while customers sip gin and tonics and shout requests for jazz standards. And down in the basement of Detroit's Wayne County Courthouse resides a mountain of Motown-related lawsuits, filling reams of paper and rolls of microfilm that constitute a highly unofficial history of Motown Records.

The company's abandoned Woodward Avenue office building is just a few blocks from the recently renovated Fox Theater, home of those fondly remembered Christmas shows. Unlike the now sporadically active Fox, the Motown building sits empty, a symbol for many locals of the city's fruitful musical past and barren present. Back over on West Grand Boulevard there is Hitsville, U.S.A., today a grossly underutilized museum, open every Friday for only three hours. Esther Edwards administers the company's participation in various local charities from the same second-floor offices that were once Motown's nerve center. Esther can be seen frequently at events in support of black mayor Coleman Young and other local politicans, showing the cynical that the Gordys still care about their hometown.

Over drinks at Bert's, at the Salamander in the Pontchartrain Hotel, or in living rooms around Detroit and its suburbs, there is a mix of bitterness, sadness, and glee when the post-Detroit history of Motown is discussed. In the Motor City, Berry Gordy is seen as an old friend who got bad advice, didn't lose his money, but somehow forgot how he'd made it. "Motown has no sound now," says one Detroiter whose views echo so many others. "It's just another record company. And it can't be playing that Tinsel-town game right or they would have made more movies. All they do out there is live off the past."

On a certain level that seems like a mean and inaccurate statement. Just look at *Black Enterprise* magazine's list of the top one hundred black businesses: since the list's introduction in 1973, Motown has been the largest black business in America for ten out of eleven years. In that period Motown backed one successful Broadway musical, was involved in the making of several motion pictures and television specials, and still released some influential and lucrative recordings. Not bad.

Yet, for all this activity, the criticisms have a certain ring of truth, as a look at Motown's last decade and a half reveals. After establishing the Jackson 5, Berry Gordy turned to filmmaking, seeking out vehicles for Diana Ross and his movie-mogul ambitions. Motown had done well with its television specials, producing six during the early 1970s, utilizing the Supremes/Temptations combination, the solo Ross, and the Jackson 5. Motown's investment in the Broadway musical *Pippin* sprung Ben Vereen to national prominence and landed Motown its first cast album.

But it was *Lady Sings the Blues*, a shmaltzy, historically distorted biography of Billie Holiday's tragic life, that epitomized Motown West. The screenplay, partially written by Berry's protégées and Motown executives Suzanne DePasse and Christine Clark (once recording artist Chris Clark), transformed Holiday's story into a parable of Motown's rise: a strong black man, played charmingly by Billy Dee Williams (the "black Clark Gable," an actor then managed by Motown, and later by ex-ITM staffer Shelly Berger), battles to harness a female singer's headstrong energy and ambition. Ross was quite convincing as Holiday; her character's journey from unsophisticated girl to jaded diva was hardly foreign to her. Ross garnered an Oscar nomination as best actress, and might have won if not for a gaudy Berry Gordy-instigated movie-trade advertising blitz that alienated the Hollywood establishment.

That was a disappointment, but Berry took it in stride. After all, he'd gone up against the big boys and won. Throughout the film's production he'd battled distributor Paramount Pictures over the budget, finally buying back creative control for two million dollars when Paramount threatened to shut down production because of soaring costs. On the set he acted as Ross's de facto director, to the consternation of director Sidney J. Furie. In a market then glutted with blood-drenched black action flicks and white male leading men, *Lady Sings the Blues'* appeal to blacks and white women made Ross a star and Berry a potential force in the film industry.

Announcements emanated from Motown about projects in development. The *Los Angeles Times* reported that Motown had twelve features and three plays in the works, including vehicles not just for Ross, but for Smokey Robinson, Marvin Gaye, Stevie Wonder, Michael Jackson, and Thelma Houston as well. It mentioned cinema and theater pros like William Huyck and Gloria Katz, co-writers of *American Graffiti* with George Lucas, playwright Joseph Russell of the prize-winning *The River Niger,* and the famed British director Ken Russell.

In reality, however, Motown would be involved in only five more features from 1975 to 1984—*Mahogany* in 1975, *The Bingo Long Traveling All-Stars and Motor Kings* in 1976, and *Almost Summer, Thank God It's Friday,* and *The Wiz,* all in 1978—and one made-for-television film that was shown in a few theaters (*Scott Joplin: King of Ragtime,* in 1978). None of these projects would feature any of the established names announced originally, nor would they involve any Motown acts other than Ross (and Michael Jackson in *The Wiz* only) in prominent roles. Six films by a new independent production company over such a span isn't embarrassing. Yet when one considers Motown's impact in music, and the auspicious start they had had with *Lady,* one can see that Motown really hasn't grown in Hollywood.

In fact, two of these projects profoundly weakened Motown's Hollywood reputation. During the filming of *Mahogany* in 1974, Berry's overbearing presence on the set became too much for Oscar-winning director Tony Richardson. By mutual agreement, Richardson left and Berry took over directorial control of this fairy tale of a black girl (Diana Ross) from Chicago's South Side who renounces international modeling for the love of an activist politician played by Billy Dee Williams. Audiences found it hard to imagine Ross giving up glamour for any man, especially considering the disjointed, frantic performance she gave, something that can possibly be blamed on Berry's lack of experience behind the camera. The theme of the film was: "Success is nothing without someone you love to share it with you," a line Berry created on the set, and that sounds like a Supremes lyric. *Mahogany* broke box-office records its first week in New York, but then cooled off considerably, killed by poor word of mouth.

The second blow to Motown's cinematic credibility was the *The Wiz*. That the gifted dramatic director Sidney Lumet failed miserably in transferring this all-black Broadway musical to the screen wasn't Motown's fault. But Berry had let Diana talk him into letting her play Dorothy, a part originated on Broadway by Stephanie Mills, a singer half her age. The premise of Frank L. Baum's original book, *The Wizard of Oz*, and of every version since, is that Dorothy moves from childhood to near-maturity due to her adventures in Oz. Hiring the very adult Ross meant altering the story and wrecking its basic appeal. The thirty-million-dollar production needed to take in sixty million dollars at the box office to break even—and it didn't come close. The failure of *The Wiz* put the finishing touch on the already ebbing tide of black films in the seventies. In its wake, Hollywood asserted that the vogue for blacks on screen, with the exception of Richard Pryor, was over. On a more personal level, Ross's efforts to portray Josephine Baker on screen—a project she's talked about since the shooting of *Mahogany*— have been frustrated, largely as a result of her role in *The Wiz*.

As if to prove correct the criticisms of Detroiters, Motown's most successful non-record venture of the last ten years was the May 1983 broadcast of "Motown 25: Yesterday, Today, and Tomorrow" on NBC, a program that—ironically—contrasted Motown's robust musical past with its mediocre present. Forty-seven million Americans tuned in to enjoy the voices of the past and watch Michael Jackson, Marvin Gaye, and Diana Ross, all of whom had left Motown, return to the family for just one night.

The Jacksons' exit to Epic had been engineered by Papa Joe Jackson to get his sons the dollars Motown wouldn't pay, the creative control it wouldn't allow, and the crossover sales to whites it could no longer guarantee. His son Jermaine, married to Berry's daughter Hazel, stayed with Motown, but under the company's guidance Jermaine never fully blossomed as a creative talent, and, foregoing touring, he lost touch with the record-buying audience, while his brothers, especially little Michael, matured into major sales forces. Michael, who at the time of the special was watching his *Thriller* album set all-time sales records, demanded that he be allowed to perform his new single, "Billie Jean"—or he wouldn't perform at all. His now legendary performance of that song—an intense moment in American popular culture, comparable to the Beatles' appearance on the Ed Sullivan show in 1964—wasn't just the special's highlight, but significantly provided the evening's only non-Motown music.

Where Michael was show-biz flash, Marvin Gaye's solo turn projected his sensitive, self-conscious side. Picking out bits of jazz, gospel, and blues at the piano and speaking in a gentle, sensual voice, Marvin ran through a stream-of-consciousness history of black music that paralleled the fusion of styles on his post-*What's Going On* albums. Throughout the seventies, on songs such as "Let's Get It On," "Trouble Man," "Got to Give It Up, Pt. 1," and "After the Dance," Marvin developed an ability to balance sensuality and spirituality, commercially and experimentation, into a sound as idiosyncratic as it was beautiful. In his brief onstage appearance, all these strains of his artistry came through crystal clear.

At the time of the special, Marvin should have been on an emotional high, as he was coming out of a time of pain. After a bitter divorce from Anna Gordy—an estrangment that resulted in the angry album *Here, My Dear* in 1978, an analysis on vinyl of his marriage that served as part of the divorce settlement—had dug him into a deep emotional and financial hole, there had been drugs of every description, a short-lived second marriage to a woman seventeen years his junior (just as he had been seventeen years younger than Anna), and finally bankruptcy, which had led him to unfinished recordings, suicide attempts, and a European exile, first to England and finally to Belgium.

There, with the aid of old mentor Harvey Fuqua, Marvin recorded one great song—"Sexual Healing"—which was released on Columbia after that company purchased Marvin's contract from Motown for two million dollars, and the IRS agreed to allow Gaye to pay two million dollars in back taxes in "reasonable" installments. The deal bought Marvin back to America, but money and the acclaim for "Sexual Healing" couldn't fend off Marvin's personal demons. While on tour to capitalize on "Sexual Healing" in 1983, following the Motown special, he suffered bouts with stage fright, sore throats, and paranoia based on mysterious death threats. Drugs and the seedy world that surround them seemed to be pulling him down and no one, certainly not his old Motown comrades, was able to help. On the special he'd sung "What's Going On," lingering over the phrase "Father, father/ There's no need to escalate" in an angel's voice. On April 1, 1984, while deep in an ongoing depression, he argued violently with his father at his Los Angeles home, striking him repeatedly at one point. His father, a minister who'd grown taciturn and sad with time, responded by shooting Marvin dead. Reverend Gaye was eventually released on the grounds that at the time of the shooting he was mentally unstable, a judgment that many felt could have been made about his son as well.

If, at the Motown special, Michael Jackson was dynamic and Marvin Gaye beatific, Diana Ross was remarkable both in and out of character. Backstage she kept a regal distance from the other old Motowners, and then flouted the rules of show-business decorum by sneaking on stage during Adam Ant's pathetic version of "Where Did Our Love Go?" She was, of course, awarded a diva's grand entrance in the program's concluding segment, in keeping with her posture as Motown's grandest creation.

Yet so much had changed over the last ten years. To the amazement of almost everyone, she'd married a white man, Robert Silberstein, and not Berry Gordy. Yet, during Diana's six years of marriage to Silberstein, Berry was a regular companion, be it on the beach, at the tennis courts, or in business meetings. For a time, they were Los Angeles's strangest trio. When the marriage ended, Silberstein would complain to *People* magazine that his wife "was totally dominated by a man who never read a book in his life." After *The Wiz,* Ross moved to New York and began the process of seeking her own identity, a process that ultimately led her to foresake Motown for a multimillion-dollar deal with RCA in the United States and EMI worldwide. It would have appeared that this ex-Motown star had moved forward, away from her past.

However, her East Coast lifestyle and fresh label affiliations didn't wipe away the fact that Motown and Berry had molded her. Onstage with Mary Wilson and Cindy Birdsong during the Supremes reunion segment, Ross was wild-eyed and way off-key, as if the weight of the years was pressing upon her larynx. Mary, in an unexpected act of self-confidence (or was it defiance?), usurped the lead on "Someday We'll Be Together." Then she went even further, urging Berry to come down from his box seat to the stage. Diana then shocked the live audience (it was edited out of the television tape) by shoving Mary several feet, after which *she* invited Berry down.

It was an amazing moment of public revelation for someone who had worked so hard at controlling her image, and no one who was there will forget it. And it had to make even the most insensitive think about the Supreme who wasn't there. Not once during the special was Florence Ballard's name uttered. She had died eight years earlier, alone and on welfare in a Detroit housing project depressingly similar to the one she'd grown up in. The money she'd finally received from the Motown settlement hadn't lasted. Her marriage with Thomas Chapman had disintegrated. Then one day after shopping she fell down and never woke up. The coroner called it cardiac arrest.

In December 1981 a musical called *Dreamgirls* captivated Broadway. It made the Florence Ballard character a tragic figure, portrayed Berry as a cunning, manipulative businessman, and depicted Diana as a puppet who only displayed backbone when she desired a shot at movie stardom. Mary Wilson said it was truly the Supremes' story. Diana wouldn't go see it. Though the story wasn't completely true to the Supremes' rise, it struck a deep chord in the popular imagination and serves as a powerfully cynical testament to Flo's life and the control one man can exercise over many.

As Mr. Berry Gordy, Jr., himself approached the stage of the Motown special, the viewer could survey the gathering crowd of Motowners, past and present, collecting to greet him. Norman Whitfield stood near stage left. Once an innovator, Whitfield was, in 1983, as cold as a Minneapolis ice skating rink in the eyes of the music industry. In 1976 he had left Motown, scoring the soundtrack to *Car Wash* and starting a band called Rose Royce in the process—a band that was as much a Whitfield vehicle as the late-sixties Temptations and the Undisputed Truth had been. He quickly followed that triumph with the founding of the Warner Bros.– distributed Whitfield Records, and was on top of the world.

Then, suddenly, after all of those years, Whitfield lost his magic touch. Once a skilled observer of musical trends, Whitfield became locked into the musical dogma of his past hits; in the late seventies, for instance, he still relied on the wah-wah guitar sound, long after it had become a cliché. By 1983, Whitfield Records was closed, and his only presence in contemporary music was in the praise he received from Lionel Richie, ex-Commodore lead singer and Motown's most important solo act of the eighties, who cited Whitfield's advice as essential to his maturation as a songwriter.

The creative stagnation of Holland-Dozier-Holland, now standing at the back of the stage among the artists they had helped propel to stardom, had come much earlier. After an auspicious early seventies start with their

JUST ANOTHER RECORD COMPANY

own Hot Wax and Invictus labels, the H-D-H team broke up. Lamont Dozier went his own way, signing with ABC Records as a solo artist in 1973. Dozier had a hit single, "Fish Ain't Bitin'," which displayed his continuing command of the dictates of pop songwriting, but was flawed by his thin, odd-sounding voice. Over the next decade Dozier would record a number of albums, with ever-decreasing commercial impact.

The Holland brothers went into semi-retirement, occasionally taking on assignments—even from Motown. Unfortunately, their sound was even more dated than Whitfield's, and their attempts to update it unsuccessful. In 1980, now back on friendly terms with Motown and Jobete, the Hollands did a special promotional recording of their catalogue, *Past, Present & Future*, combining rearrangements of past hits and new material. It was a timely effort, for in the eighties H-D-H material and the whole Jobete catalogue would be tapped into by acts from every part of the pop music spectrum. Without a trace of bitterness, Eddie said that H-D-H had made more money in royalties from Jobete in 1983 than when they worked for Motown.

Martha Reeves, Mary Wells, and Junior Walker couldn't have made the same comment. They were treated like mere sidebars to the Motown story on the special, consigned to brief snatches of their greatest hits ("Heat Wave," "My Guy," "Shotgun") during a medley segment. After the show, Walker would release a little-noted new album on Motown, but for the most part this trio's only ongoing Motown profit came from small royalty payments for album reissues and participation in shoddily organized Motown Revues held around the country.

The Temptations and the Four Tops, after bouncing around, had both returned to Motown. In 1972 the Tops had, after the prerequisite lawsuit, left Motown for ABC and some fine records, such as the dramatic "Keeper of the Castle" and the funny "Catfish." In 1981, the Tops had a major hit with the self-consciously old-fashioned "When She Was My Girl." But, just in time for the Motown special, Levi Stubbs, Renaldo Benson, Lawrence Payton, and Abdul Fakir, celebrating thirty years together, felt it was time to come back to the site of their most consistent success.

The Tops faced the Temptations in a vocal group duel, though the Temptations were quite literally not their old selves. Only Melvin Franklin and Otis Williams remained from the Primes. David Ruffin and Eddie Kendricks had returned the year before for a Temptations reunion tour that was nostalgic onstage and acrimonious offstage. As soon as it ended, Ruffin and Kendricks had split again—Ruffin to musical obscurity and a stint in a Detroit jail for tax evasion, and Kendricks to Atlanta, where he cut a poorly promoted album on a small label. Even Dennis Edwards, whose playful vocal duel with Stubbs during the special was so exhilarating, would leave the Temptations for a solo career by year's end.

Some viewers asked, "Where was Gladys Knight and the Pips?" When asked that question by Harry Weinger after the taping, Knight at first answered, "Well, we were working." But after a long pause replied:

> We have felt for so long that one of the things that was really unfair about Motown was that the artists were really the backbone of the company and they got so mistreated over there. The least they could have done was said, "We're going to do this tribute to Motown people, period. Including Mr. Gordy as the number-one person." I don't think you heard it. I might have missed it, but on the show they didn't say, "And we thank all these acts here tonight, because in actuality if it weren't for them, there wouldn't be any Motown. Or Mr. Gordy, for that matter." So we felt it was a little hypocritical to go and be a part of that.

Stevie Wonder, still on Motown, was there, too, though his set on the special was lackluster in comparison to those of Michael Jackson and Marvin Gaye. Stevie was the one star who not only had remained with Motown throughout its many changes, but had maintained the high standards of musicality and commerciality upon which the company had once prided itself. But Motown had paid a price for getting Stevie the freedom he needed; Berry and company had to endure the kind of flights of creative temperament the production line had once circumvented. Stevie now had so much control over his career that no one at Motown could predict or demand when he'd turn in his albums. The waiting periods took not months, but—quite literally—years. At the time of the special Motown had been waiting on an album for two years. When Stevie finally delivered a new release in 1984, it was *The Woman in Red,* a movie soundtrack, and not Stevie's much anticipated, long-in-development studio album, *In Circle Square.* The bottom line was that Stevie Wonder, once Motown's baby, not only controlled his career, his artistic decisions (whether an album was ready or not) profoundly affected Motown's financial health. Little Stevie hadn't just grown up. His musical clout now made him man of the house.

But perhaps the deepest revelation of the Motown special, one that said so much about the company and its escape from history, was a supposedly light-hearted focus on "What was the Motown Sound?" The answer was given in a series of brief comments from Motown employees. One employee cites the drum and bass sound. Hal Davis says "finger-popping" tempo, tambourine, and heavy bass. Smokey says, "It is the bottom; got the foot working [on the bass drum], hear the bass real good." H-D-H are seen in the studio, with Brian saying, "A lot of treble, high end to it," followed embarrassingly by canned laughter, as if the comment were a joke in a sit-com. Berry Gordy continues in this comedic vein, offering the old "a combination of rats, roaches, love, and guts" reply he'd been offering to that question for over two decades. Echoing "the chairman," Motown public relations director Bob Jones claims that "chitlins, grits, and the ghetto" make up the Motown Sound. Finally, we go back to Berry Gordy for the punch line: "the point is that I don't know what the Motown Sound is exactly."

And yet what of Robert White, Earl Van Dyke, Benny Benjamin, Uriel Jones, Pistol Allen, and the "heavy bass" sound of James Jamerson? In a few old clips, the name Earl Van Dyke Revue could be seen in onstage lights, but otherwise the musicians who actually made the music were ignored in the special, and, in fact, most hadn't even been invited. Neither H-D-H nor Whitfield were mentioned by name, but they were at least invited to attend the show. Most of the old cats were out in Detroit, but Jamerson was living in Los Angeles and in desperate need of just such an affirmation of his worth. He had fallen far by 1984. Unlike most of his old musical compatriots, Jamerson had relocated permanently to the West Coast, where, theoretically, he was to have been guaranteed work with Motown.

But time caught up to him, too. Just as there were new sounds, there were new musicians. One was his son, James Jamerson, Jr., whom his father had trained. Suddenly the calls for James Jamerson weren't for father, but for son. And the elder Jamerson's hands had lost their sense of time—that intangible element of musicianship. Work came less and less frequently, his marriage faltered, and he spent too much of the eighties in and out of sanatoriums. "Everybody, as time went on, got sort of strange," he said of the Motown "family" the month before the special, "especially after Motown moved out to California. If they see you they're glad to see you. They just change their phone numbers so much. I don't believe in changing mine. I don't believe some of them know I'm still alive." Four months after the special aired, Jamerson died of complications from a heart attack in Los Angeles.

Finally, after shaking hands with Whitfield and Harvey Fuqua, hugging Smokey warmly, being embraced by Michael Jackson and grabbed by Diana Ross, Berry Gordy stood at center stage. What a testament to his achievement all this was! Berry Gordy was being honored for his role in American history on national television, an honor that few black Americans—with the exceptions of Dr. Martin Luther King, Jr., and a handful of sports and entertainment heroes—have enjoyed. Like all successful American businessmen, Berry had manipulated, stepped on, and pushed people in order to grow. Control was his watchword, and in his pursuit of it, his judgments had altered the lives of many. Was it worth it?

Undoubtedly, Berry thinks so. For while many people hate him, there are a great many who love and respect him. As it did the night of the special, and as it does every time a Motown record is played, the music speaks eloquently about the wages of Berry's efforts. The compositions of Smokey Robinson, Holland-Dozier-Holland, Norman Whitfield and Barrett Strong, Nick Ashford and Valerie Simpson, Marvin Gaye, and the rest of the Jobete writing family have been inspired, molded, and polished by the standards he set.

And so have so many others. The pre-Los Angeles music of Motown is, to this day, part of the heartbeat of popular music. In the summer of 1985, twenty years after the production line first rumbled forth, Katrina and the Waves' "Walking on Sunshine," a delightful appropriation of "the Motown Sound," established the band as one of the year's success stories. It was also the latest hit of the 1980s to unashamedly hark back to the sound Jamerson, Benjamin, Van Dyke, et al., created. Phil Collins went to number one with a faithful cover of "You Can't Hurry Love" in 1982. Bananarama had a major British hit in 1983 with "He Was Really Sayin' Somethin'," a 1965 Velvelettes record written by Norman Whitfield. Hall and Oates's "Maneater," with its Jamersonseque bass line, topped the *Billboard* chart in 1982, while Wham did the same in 1984 with "Wake Me Up (Before You Go Go)," a buoyant Motown imitation with the bouncy spirit of "Going to a Go Go," "Uptight," and several other Motor City classics.

A slew of England's best young talent find inspiration in Motown's musical richness. Boy George echoed Smokey Robinson's vulnerability on "Do You Really Want to Hurt Me," and Culture Club tapped into Motown's percolating rhythms on "Miss Me Blind" and its other similar-sounding hits. Alison Moyet was so impressed with Motown she recruited Lamont Dozier to write her first solo single, "Invisible." Elvis Costello's wry lyrics and taut melodies owe much to Robinson and Holland-Dozier-

Holland. Paul Young, quite consciously, modeled himself after singers such as Levi Stubbs, the Temptations, and Marvin Gaye (one of his first hits, "Wherever I Lay My Hat," was a Gaye B side written by Gaye, Norman Whitfield, and Barrett Strong). Sade cited Marvin Gaye's *What's Going On* as crucial to suggesting the fusion of jazz, Third-World rhythms, and pop she so effectively employs.

These English musicians, all of them children when the first Motown Revue toured their country, have become spiritual children of Motown. This legacy, as much as Motown's current acts and ubiquitous catalogue, testifies to the impact of "the Motown sound."

Equally important as a Motown legacy is its symbolic power to black America. To that repressed American minority, Motown is the ultimate myth of black capitalism, one that says to car dealers and bankers and grocery store owners that "Yes, it can happen. The odds can be beaten." In the record business, Motown has provided the benchmark for black musical entrepreneurs as diverse as Earth, Wind and Fire's Maurice White, Parliament's George Clinton, Philadelphia International's Kenny Gamble and Leon Huff, Solar Records president Dick Griffey, and Prince, each of whom has tried, in varying ways, to develop self-contained musical "families" to ensure financial and musical independence. None, however, has managed to control the range of their activities and be as successful in the pop marketplace as Berry Gordy. It may be that no black musical entrepreneur ever will.

The co-option of black music, and for that matter, all American musics, by major corporate record companies is now complete. CBS (primarily through Columbia and Epic), WEA (via Warner Bros., Elektra, and Atlantic), PolyGram, RCA, MCA, and Capitol-EMI, together control over eighty-five percent of the American music market. In the face of these giants' ability to advance artists millions of dollars and run powerful promotion and distribution networks, independent labels are decreasing in number. Indies find themselves faced with either making smaller profits and watching their best acts eventually be seduced by the majors, or making a distribution deal with the majors that erodes autonomy.

In 1984, after the Motown Special and despite having Lionel Richie, Stevie Wonder, and funkster Rick James on the roster, Berry took the latter option, signing with MCA for distribution, a move that brought Berry into financial harmony with the industry trends Motown had been founded to buck. Motown was the last of the major indies, and its agreement with MCA was a historic industry event. Berry had come full circle; once again he was using a bigger company to distribute his music, but he no longer had to wait for his check.

Today, Berry is the Howard Hughes of black America. From his mansion in Bel Air he invests in thoroughbred horses, plays tennis, and entertains graciously. When he travels, he is flanked by bodyguards, and usually uses a pseudonym. On occasion, Berry has even sought refuge in disguise. Since his father's death at ninety in 1978 (mother Bertha passed away in 1975), Berry has been the nominal head of the Gordy clan, though time and money have put a certain distance between Berry and the Gordys' fourth generation (after all, it's not always easy to contact a multimillion-dollar uncle when you need a bit of advice). Not surprisingly, many of the young Gordys work in the family business. Roxanna and Rodney Gordy, children of Robert Gordy, for example, both work for Jobete Music. Currently, the most prominent Gordy offspring is Berry's son Kennedy, aka Rockwell, who has a thin voice but has displayed some of his father's flair as a songwriter. His 1984 Top Ten single, "Somebody's Watching Me," though aided considerably by Michael Jackson's guest vocal, was a witty, well-observed song about modern paranoia that immediately made Rockwell a minor pop star.

What a long journey it has been for the Gordys. From Georgia plantations, to the assembly lines of Detroit, to the laid-back life in Los Angeles, with its swimming pools and movie stars. But there is just one problem. Once you reach the California shore, the end of our country, it is easy to be impressed by just how far you've come; but before long it becomes clear you've got to either keep moving on or else slowly— peacefully—bake in that golden sun. Since its move to Los Angeles, Motown has had moments of glory, but the magic of the production line has been lost, discarded, or buried.

DISCOGRAPHY

This discography lists the Top Forty pop and/or R&B hits of the most important Motown acts from 1962 to 1971, the years of the label's greatest success. Some records that weren't major hits at the time of their release but had significant cover versions recorded later (e.g., Bonnie Pointer had a major hit in 1979 with the Elgins' "Heaven Must Have Sent You") are included as well. *Billboard*, on whose charts this discography is based, did not publish an R&B listing in 1964, which explains the gap there. The original album is listed for all songs, even if it appeared later on any of Motown's innumerable repackaging projects; many of these albums have been reissued with their original cover art by the company. Motown encouraged and, in some cases, ordered their acts to record other Jobete copyrights. Listed here are only Motown covers of other label recordings of special commercial importance or artistic merit (e.g., Gladys Knight and the Pips and Marvin Gaye both cut "I Heard It Through the Grapevine").

SONG	YEAR	WRITER
▶ The Contours		
"Do You Love Me"	1962	Berry Gordy
"Shake Sherry"	1963	B. Gordy
"Can You Do It"	1964	Thelma Gordy Richard Street
"Can You Jerk Like Me"	1965	William Stevenson
"The Day When She Needed Me"	1965	Smokey Robinson
"First I Look at the Purse"	1965	Bobby Rogers S. Robinson
"Just a Little Misunderstanding"	—	Luvel Broadnax Clarence Paul Stevie Wonder
"It's So Hard Being a Loser"	—	Sam McMullen William Weatherspoon James Dean
▶ Elgins		
"Darling Baby"	1966	Holland-Dozier-Holland
"Heaven Must Have Sent You"	1966	H-D-H
▶ The Four Tops		
"Baby I Need Your Loving"	1964	Holland-Dozier-Holland
"I Can't Help Myself (Sugar Pie, Honey Bunch)"	1965	H-D-H
"Ask the Lonely"	1965	William Stevenson Ivy Hunter
"It's the Same Old Song"	1965	H-D-H
"Something About You"	1965	H-D-H
"Reach Out I'll Be There"	1966	H-D-H
"Shake Me, Wake Me (When It's Over)"	1966	H-D-H
"Loving You Is Sweeter Than Ever"	1966	Stevie Wonder I. Hunter
"Standing in the Shadows of Love"	1967	H-D-H
"Bernadette"	1967	H-D-H

PRODUCER	POP CHART	R & B CHART	ALBUM	COVER VERSION
Berry Gordy	3	1	*Do You Love Me*	The Dave Clark Five
B. Gordy	43	21	*Do You Love Me*	—
Smokey Robinson	41	—	no album	—
William Stevenson	47	15	no album	—
S. Robinson	—	37	no album	
S. Robinson	57	12	no album	J. Geils Band
Clarence Paul W. Stevenson	85	18	no album	—
William Weatherspoon James Dean	79	35	no album	—
Brian Holland Lamont Dozier	72	4	*Darling Baby*	—
B. Holland L. Dozier	50	9	*Darling Baby*	Bonnie Pointer
Lamont Dozier Brian Holland	11	—	*Four Tops*	Johnny Rivers O.C. Smith
L. Dozier B. Holland	5	2	*Second Album*	Kate Taylor
William Stevenson Ivy Hunter	24	9	*Four Tops*	—
L. Dozier B. Holland	1	1	*Second Album*	Bonnie Pointer Donnie Elbert
L. Dozier B. Holland	19	9	*Second Album*	Dave Edmunds
L. Dozier B. Holland	1	1	*Reach Out*	Gloria Gaynor Merrilee Rush Michael Narada Walden
L. Dozier B. Holland	18	5	*On Top*	Barbara Streisand
I. Hunter	45	12	*On Top*	—
L. Dozier B. Holland	6	2	*Reach Out*	Deborah Washington Rod Stewart
L. Dozier B. Holland	4	3	*Reach Out*	

SONG	YEAR	WRITER
"Seven Rooms of Gloom"	1967	H-D-H
"You Keep Running Away"	1967	H-D-H
"Walk Away Renee"	1968	Michael Brown Bob Calilli
"If I Were a Carpenter"	1968	Tim Hardin
"Still Water Love"	1970	Frank Wilson Smokey Robinson

Marvin Gaye

SONG	YEAR	WRITER
"Stubborn Kinda Fellow"	1962	William Stevenson Marvin Gaye George Gordy
"Hitch Hike"	1964	M. Gaye Clarence Paul W. Stevenson
"Pride and Joy"	1963	Norman Whitfield M. Gaye W. Stevenson
"Can I Get a Witness"	1963	Holland-Dozier-Holland
"You're a Wonderful One"	1964	H-D-H
"What's the Matter With You, Baby" (with Mary Wells)	1964	C. Paul W. Stevenson Barney Ales
"Once Upon a Time" (with Mary Wells)	1964	C. Paul W. Stevenson B. Ales
"Try It Baby"	1964	Berry Gordy
"Baby, Don't You Do It"	1964	H-D-H
"How Sweet It Is to Be Loved by You"	1965	H-D-H
"I'll Be Doggone"	1965	Smokey Robinson Warren Moore Marvin Tarplin
"Pretty Little Baby"	1965	C. Paul M. Gaye Dave Hamilton
"Ain't That Peculiar"	1965	S. Robinson W. Moore M. Tarplin

PRODUCER	POP CHART	R & B CHART	ALBUM	COVER VERSION
L. Dozier B. Holland	14	10	*Reach Out*	—
L. Dozier B. Holland	19	7	*Greatest Hits*	—
L. Dozier B. Holland	15	14	*Reach Out*	Left Banke (original)
L. Dozier B. Holland	20	17	*Reach Out*	Bobby Darin Tim Hardin (original)
Frank Wilson	11	4	*Still Waters Run Deep*	O'Bryan
William Stevenson	46	8	*That Stubborn Kinda Fella*	—
W. Stevenson	30	12	*That Stubborn Kinda Fella*	The Rolling Stones
W. Stevenson	10	2	*That Stubborn Kinda Fella*	Georgie Fame
Brian Holland Lamont Dozier	22	15	*Greatest Hits*	Lee Michaels
B. Holland L. Dozier	17	—	*How Sweet It Is*	—
W. Stevenson	17	—	*Together*	—
Clarence Paul	19	—	*Together*	—
Berry Gordy	15	—	*How Sweet It Is*	—
B. Holland L. Dozier	27	—	*How Sweet It Is*	The Band
B. Holland L. Dozier	6	4	*How Sweet It Is*	James Taylor Jr. Walker and the All Stars
Smokey Robinson	8	1	*The Moods of Marvin Gaye*	Bob Weir
C. Paul	25	16	*Marvin Gaye Anthology*	—
S. Robinson	8	1	*The Moods of Marvin Gaye*	Stevie Woods Diamond Reo Fanny

SONG	YEAR	WRITER
"One More Heartache"	1966	W. Robinson W. Moore Ronald White M. Tarplin Robert Rogers
"Take This Heart of Mine"	1966	M. Tarplin W. Robinson
"Little Darling I Need You"	1966	H-D-H
"It Takes Two" (with Kim Weston)	1967	Sylvia Moy W. Stevenson
"Ain't No Mountain High Enough" (with Tammi Terrell)	1967	Valerie Simpson Nickolas Ashford
"Your Unchanging Love"	1967	H-D-H
"Your Precious Love" (with Tammi Terrell)	1968	V. Simpson N. Ashford
"If I Could Build My Whole World Around You" (with Tammi Terrell)	1968	Harvey Fuqua Vernon Bullock Johnny Bristol
"You"	1968	Jeffrey Bowen Ivy Hunter Jack Goga
"Ain't Nothing Like the Real Thing" (with Tammi Terrell)	1968	V. Simpson N. Ashford
"You're All I Need to Get By" (with Tammi Terrell)	1968	V. Simpson N. Ashford
"Chained"	1968	Frank Wilson
"Keep on Lovin' Me Honey" (with Tammi Terrell)	1968	V. Simpson N. Ashford
"I Heard It Through the Grapevine"	1968	Barrett Strong N. Whitfield
"Good Lovin' Ain't Easy to Come By" (with Tammi Terrell)	1969	V. Simpson N. Ashford
"Too Busy Thinking About My Baby"	1969	N. Whitfield Jamie Bradford
"That's the Way Love Is"	1969	Barrett Strong N. Whitfield
"What You Gave Me" (with Tammi Terrell)	1969	V. Simpson N. Ashford

PRODUCER	POP CHART	R & B CHART	ALBUM	COVER VERSION
S. Robinson	8	1	*The Moods of Marvin Gaye*	—
Warren Moore S. Robinson	44	4	*The Moods of Marvin Gaye*	—
L. Dozier B. Holland	47	10	*The Moods of Marvin Gaye*	The Doobie Brothers
W. Stevenson	14	4	*Take Two*	—
Johnny Bristol Harvey Fuqua	17	3	*United*	Diana Ross
L. Dozier B. Holland	33	7	*The Moods of Marvin Gaye*	—
H. Fuqua J. Bristol	5	2	*United*	Al Jarreau and Randy Crawford
H. Fuqua J. Bristol	10	2	*United*	—
Ivy Hunter	34	7	*In the Groove*	—
V. Simpson N. Ashford	8	1	*You're All I Need*	Donny and Marie Osmond Aretha Franklin
V. Simpson N. Ashford	7	1	*You're All I Need*	Aretha Franklin Tony Orlando & Dawn Johnny Mathis & Deniece Williams
Frank Wilson	32	8	*In the Groove*	Paul Peterson
V. Simpson N. Ashford	24	11	*You're All I Need*	—
N. Whitfield	1	1	*In the Groove*	Gladys Knight and the Pips (original) King Curtis Creedence Clearwater Revival
V. Simpson N. Ashford	30	11	*Easy*	—
N. Whitfield	4	1	*MPG*	—
N. Whitfield	7	2	*MPG*	—
V. Simpson N. Ashford	49	6	*Easy*	—

SONG	YEAR	WRITER
"The End of Our Road"	1970	Roger Penzabene B. Strong N. Whitfield
"How Can I Forget"	1970	B. Strong N. Whitfield
"The Onion Song" (with Tammi Terrell)	1970	V. Simpson N. Ashford
"What's Going On"	1971	Alfred Cleveland Renaldo Benson M. Gaye
"Mercy Mercy Me (the Ecology)"	1971	M. Gaye
"Inner City Blues (Make Me Wanna Holler)"	1971	James Nyx M. Gaye

▶ Brenda Holloway

SONG	YEAR	WRITER
"Every Little Bit Hurts"	1964	Ed Cobb
"When I'm Gone"	1965	Smokey Robinson
"Just Look What You've Done"	1967	Frank Wilson
"You've Made Me so Very Happy"	1967	F. Wilson Berry Gordy Patrice Holloway Brenda Holloway

▶ Isley Brothers

SONG	YEAR	WRITER
"This Old Heart of Mine (Is Weak for You)"	1965	Holland-Dozier-Holland
"Take Me in Your Arms (Rock Me)"	1968	H-D-H

▶ Jackson 5

SONG	YEAR	WRITER
"I Want You Back"	1969	The Corporation
"ABC"	1970	The Corporation
"The Love You Save"	1970	The Corporation
"I'll Be There"	1970	Willie Hutch Berry Gordy Hal Davis/Bob West
"Mama's Pearl"	1971	W. Hutch B. Gordy H. Davis/B. West
"Never Can Say Goodbye"	1971	Clifton Davis
"Maybe Tomorrow"	1971	The Corporation
"Sugar Daddy"	1971	The Corporation

PRODUCER	POP CHART	R & B CHART	ALBUM	COVER VERSION
N. Whitfield	40	7	*MPG*	Gladys Knight & The Pips (original)
N. Whitfield	41	18	MPG	—
V. Simpson N. Ashford	50	18	*Easy*	—
M. Gaye	2	1	*What's Going On*	Grover Washington, Jr. Weather Report
M. Gaye	4	1	*What's Going On*	Grover Washington, Jr.
M. Gaye	9	1	*What's Going On*	Gil Scott-Heron
Marc Gordon Hal Davis	13	—	*Every Little Bit Hurts*	Spencer Davis Group
Smokey Robinson	25	12	no album	—
Frank Wilson	68	21	no album	—
Berry Gordy	39	—	no album	Blood, Sweat & Tears
Lamont Dozier Brian Holland	12	6	*This Old Heart of Mine*	Rod Stewart
L. Dozier B. Holland	—	22	*Doin' Their Thing*	Kim Weston (original) The Doobie Brothers
The Corporation	1	1	*Diana Ross Presents Jackson 5*	Graham Parker
The Corporation	1	1	*ABC*	—
The Corporation	1	1	*ABC*	—
Hal Davis	1	1	*Third Album*	—
H. Davis	2	2	*Third Album*	—
H. Davis	2	1	*Maybe Tomorrow*	Isaac Hayes Gloria Gaynor
H. Davis	20	3	*Maybe Tomorrow*	—
H. Davis	10	3	*Greatest Hits*	—

SONG	YEAR	WRITER
Michael Jackson		
"Got To Be There"	1971	Eliiot Willensky

Gladys Knight and the Pips

SONG	YEAR	WRITER
"Everybody Needs Love"	1967	Eddie Holland Norman Whitfield
"I Heard It Through the Grapevine"	1967	N. Whitfield Barrett Strong
"The End of Our Road	1968	Roger Penzabene B. Strong N. Whitfield
"It Should Have Been Me"	1968	William Stevenson N. Whitfield
"I Wish It Would Rain"	1968	B. Strong N. Whitfield
"Didn't You Know"	1969	Valerie Simpson Nickolas Ashford
"The Nitty Gritty"	1969	Lincoln Chase
"Friendship Train"	1969	B. Strong N. Whitfield
"You Need Love Like I Do (Don't You)"	1970	B. Strong N. Whitfield
"If I Were Your Woman"	1970	Clay McMurray Pam Sawyer Gloria Jones Leon Ware
"I Don't Want To Do Wrong"	1971	Johnny Bristol William Guest Catherine Schaffner Gladys Knight Merald Knight
"Neither One of Us (Wants to Be the First to Say Goodbye)"	1973	Jim Weatherly

Shorty Long

SONG	YEAR	WRITER
"Devil With a Blue Dress On"	1964	Shorty Long William Stevenson
"Function at the Junction"	1966	Eddie Holland S. Long
"Here Comes the Judge"	1968	Billie Jean Brown S. Long Suzanne de Passe

PRODUCER	POP CHART	R & B CHART	ALBUM	COVER VERSION
The Corporation Hal Davis	4	4	*Got To Be There*	Chaka Khan
Norman Whitfield	39	3	*Everybody Needs Love*	—
N. Whitfield	2	1	*Everybody Needs Love*	Marvin Gaye CCR
N. Whitfield	15	5	*Feelin' Bluesy*	Marvin Gaye
N. Whitfield	40	9	*Feelin' Bluesy*	Kim Weston (original)
N. Whitfield	41	15	*Silk 'n' Soul*	The Temptations (original)
Valerie Simpson Nickolas Ashford	63	11	*Nitty Gritty*	—
N. Whitfield	19	2	*Nitty Gritty*	Shirley Ellis (original)
N. Whitfield	17	2	*Greatest Hits*	—
N. Whitfield	25	3	*Greatest Hits*	—
Clay McMurray	9	1	*If I Were Your Woman*	—
Johnny Bristol	17	2	no album	—
Joe Porter	1	1	*Neither One of Us*	—
William Stevenson	—	—	*Here Comes the Judge*	Mitch Ryder & The Detroit Wheels Bruce Springsteen and The E Street Band
Shorty Long	8	4	*Here Comes the Judge*	—
Brian Holland Lamont Dozier	97	42	*Here Comes The Judge*	—

SONG	YEAR	WRITER
Martha and the Vandellas		
"Come and Get These Memories"	1963	Holland-Dozier-Holland
"Heat Wave"	1963	H-D-H
"Quicksand"	1963	H-D-H
"Live Wire"	1964	H-D-H
"Dancing in the Street"	1964	William Stevenson Marvin Gaye
"Wild One"	1964	W. Stevenson Ivy Hunter
"Nowhere to Run"	1965	H-D-H
"You've Been In Love Too Long"	1965	Clarence Paul W. Stevenson I. Hunter
"My Baby Loves Me"	1966	Sylvia Moy I. Hunter W. Stevenson
"I'm Ready for Love"	1966	H-D-H
"Jimmy Mack"	1967	H-D-H
"Honey Chile"	1967	Richard Morris S. Moy
"Love Bug Leave My Heart Alone"	1967	R. Morris S. Moy
The Marvelettes		
"Please Mr. Postman"	1961	William Garrett Georgia Dobbins Robert Bateman Brian Holland
"Twistin' Postman"	1962	B. Holland R. Bateman William Stevenson

PRODUCER	POP CHART	R & B CHART	ALBUM	COVER VERSION
Lamont Dozier Brian Holland	29	6	*Come and Get These Memories*	—
L. Dozier B. Holland	4	1	*Heat Wave*	The Who The Jam Linda Ronstadt
L. Dozier B. Holland	8	—	*Dance Party*	—
L. Dozier B. Holland	42	—	*Greatest Hits*	
William Stevenson	2	—	*Dance Party*	The Kinks Mamas and the Papas Laura Nyro with Labelle Mick Jagger & David Bowie Grateful Dead Van Halen
W. Stevenson Ivy Hunter	34	—	*Dance Party*	
L. Dozier B. Holland	8	5	*Greatest Hits*	Grand Funk Railroad Laura Nyro with Labelle
I. Hunter W. Stevenson Clarence Paul	36	22	*Greatest Hits*	Bonnie Raitt
W. Stevenson	22	3	*Greatest Hits*	—
L. Dozier B. Holland	9	2	*Watch Out!*	—
L. Dozier B. Holland	10	1	*Watch Out!*	Laura Nyro with Labelle
Richard Morris	11	5	*Ridin' High*	—
R. Morris	25	14	*Ridin' High*	—
Brianbert	1	1	*Please Mr. Postman*	The Carpenters The Beatles
Brianbert William Stevenson	34	13	*Please Mr. Postman*	—

SONG	YEAR	WRITER
"Playboy"	1962	B. Holland W. Stevenson Gladys Horton R. Bateman
"Beechwood 4-5789"	1962	Marvin Gaye George Gordy W. Stevenson
"Someday, Someway"	1962	Freddie Gorman Lamont Dozier B. Holland
"Strange I Know"	1962	Lamont Dozier F. Gorman B. Holland
"Locking Up My Heart"	1963	Eddie Holland L. Dozier B. Holland
"Forever"	1963	H-D-H
"Too Many Fish in the Sea"	1964	E. Holland Norman Whitfield
"I'll Keep Holding On"	1965	Ivy Hunter W. Stevenson
"Danger, Heartbreak Dead Ahead"	1965	W. Stevenson Clarence Paul Ivy Hunter
"Don't Mess With Bill"	1966	Smokey Robinson
"You're the One"	1966	S. Robinson
"The Hunter Gets Captured by the Game"	1967	S. Robinson
"When You're Young and in Love"	1967	Van McCoy
"My Baby Must Be a Magician"	1968	S. Robinson
"Here I Am Baby"	1968	S. Robinson
"Destination: Anywhere"	1968	Valerie Simpson Nickolas Ashford

The Miracles

SONG	YEAR	WRITER
"Shop Around"	1961	Smokey Robinson Berry Gordy
"What's So Good About Good-Bye"	1962	S. Robinson
"I'll Try Something New"	1962	S. Robinson
"You've Really Got a Hold on Me"	1963	S. Robinson
"A Love She Can Count On"	1963	S. Robinson
"Mickey's Monkey"	1963	Holland-Dozier-Holland
"I Gotta Dance to Keep From Crying"	1964	H-D-H

PRODUCER	POP CHART	R & B CHART	ALBUM	COVER VERSION
Brianbert	7	4	*Playboy*	—
W. Stevenson	17	7	*Playboy*	The Carpenters
Brian Holland	—	9	*Playboy*	Robert Gorden Marshall Crenshaw
B. Holland	49	10	*Marvelous Marvelettes*	—
B. Holland Lamont Dozier	44	25	*Greatest Hits*	—
B. Holland	78	24	*Greatest Hits*	—
Norman Whitfield	25	15	*Greatest Hits*	Mitch Ryder and the Detroit Wheels
Ivy Hunter W. Stevenson	34	11	no album	—
Clarence Paul Ivy Hunter	61	11	*Greatest Hits*	Kim Weston Bonnie Raitt
Smokey Robinson	7	3	*Greatest Hits*	June Pointer
S. Robinson	48	20	*Sophisticated Soul*	—
S. Robinson	13	2	*The Marvelettes*	Blondie
William Weatherspoon James Dean	23	9	*The Marvelettes*	Ruby and the Romantics (original) Choice Four Ralph Carter
S. Robinson	17	8	*Sophisticated Soul*	—
S. Robinson	44	14	*Sophisticated Soul*	Barbara McNair
Valerie Simpson Nickolas Ashford	63	28	no album	—
Smokey Robinson Berry Gordy	2	1	*Hi! We're the Miracles*	Captain & Tennille
B. Gordy	35	16	*I'll Try Something New*	—
S. Robinson B. Gordy	39	11	*I'll Try Something New*	The Supremes A Taste of Honey
S. Robinson	8	1	*The Fabulous Miracles*	The Beatles
S. Robinson	31	21	*The Fabulous Miracles*	—
Holland-Dozier-Holland	8	3	*Doin' Mickey's Monkey*	The Rascals
H-D-H	35	—	*Doin' Mickey's Monkey*	—

SONG	YEAR	WRITER
"I Like It Like That"	1964	S. Robinson Marvin Tarplin
"That's What Love Is Made Of"	1964	Warren Moore Robert Rogers S. Robinson
"Ooo Baby, Baby"	1965	W. Moore S. Robinson
"The Tracks of My Tears"	1965	S. Robinson W. Moore M. Tarplin
"My Girl Has Gone"	1965	S. Robinson M. Tarplin W. Moore
"Going to a Go-Go"	1966	S. Robinson M. Tarplin W. Moore
"Choosey Beggar"	1966	S. Robinson W. Moore
"Whole Lot of Shakin' in My Heart (Since I Met You)"	1966	H-D-H
"Come 'Round Here (I'm the One You Need)"	1966	H-D-H
"The Love I Saw in You Was Just a Mirage"	1967	S. Robinson M. Tarplin
"More Love"	1967	S. Robinson
"I Second That Emotion"	1967	S. Robinson Al Cleveland
"If You Can Want"	1968	S. Robinson
"Yester Love"	1968	S. Robinson A. Cleveland
"Special Occasion"	1968	S. Robinson A. Cleveland
"Baby, Baby Don't Cry"	1969	A. Cleveland Terry Johnson S. Robinson
"Doggone Right"	1969	S. Robinson A. Cleveland M. Tarplin
"Abraham, Martin and John"	1969	Dick Holler
"Here I Go Again"	1969	William Robinson Terry Johnson A. Cleveland W. Moore
"Point It Out"	1970	S. Robinson A. Cleveland M. Tarplin

PRODUCER	POP CHART	R & B CHART	ALBUM	COVER VERSION
S. Robinson	27		*From The Beginning*	—
S. Robinson	35		*From The Beginning*	—
S. Robinson	16	4	*Going to a Go-Go*	Linda Ronstadt The Five Stairsteps
S. Robinson	16	2	*Going to a Go-Go*	Johnny Rivers Linda Ronstadt Aretha Franklin
S. Robinson	14	3	*Going to a Go-Go*	—
W. Moore S. Robinson	11	2	*Going to a Go-Go*	The Rolling Stones
S. Robinson	—	35	*Going to a Go-Go*	—
B. Holland L. Dozier	46	20	*Away We A Go-Go*	—
B. Holland L. Dozier	17	4	*Away We A Go-Go*	—
S. Robinson W. Moore	20	10	*The Tears of a Clown*	—
S. Robinson	23	5	*The Tears of a Clown*	Kim Carnes
S. Robinson A. Cleveland	4	1	*The Miracles Greatest Hits with Smokey Robinson*	—
S. Robinson	11	3	*Special Occasion*	—
S. Robinson	31	9	*Special Occasion*	—
S. Robinson A. Cleveland	26	4	*Special Occasion*	—
S. Robinson W. Moore Terry Johnson	8	3	*Time Out*	—
S. Robinson	32	7	*Time Out*	—
S. Robinson	33	16	*Time Out*	Dion (original)
W. Moore T. Johnson	37	15	*Time Out*	—
S. Robinson A. Cleveland	37	4	*Four In Blue*	—

SONG	YEAR	WRITER
"Who's Gonna Take the Blame"	1970	Nickolas Ashford Valerie Simpson
"The Tears of a Clown"	1970	Henry Cosby S. Robinson Stevie Wonder
"I Don't Blame You at All"	1971	S. Robinson
"Crazy about the La La La"	1971	S. Robinson
"Satisfaction"	1971	S. Robinson

▶ Originals

SONG	YEAR	WRITER
"Baby, I'm for Real"	1969	Marvin Gaye
"The Bells"	1970	Anna Gaye M. Gaye Elgie Stover Johnny Bristol
"We Can Make It Baby"	1970	James Nyx M. Gaye
"God Bless Whoever Sent You"	1971	Pam Sawyer Clay McMurray

▶ Rare Earth

SONG	YEAR	WRITER
"Get Ready"	1970	Barrett Strong Norman Whitfield
"(I Know) I'm Losing You"	1970	N. Whitfield
"Born to Wander"	1970	Tom Baird
"I Just Want to Celebrate"	1971	Dino Fekaris Nick Zesses
"Hey, Big Brother"	1971	D. Fakaris N. Zesses

▶ Diana Ross

SONG	YEAR	WRITER
"Reach Out and Touch (Somebody's Hand)"	1970	Valerie Simpson
"Ain't No Mountain High Enough"	1970	V. Simpson Nickolas Ashford
"Remember Me"	1971	V. Simpson N. Ashford
"Reach Out, I'll Be There"	1971	V. Simpson N. Ashford
"Surrender"	1971	V. Simpson N. Ashford

PRODUCER	POP CHART	R & B CHART	ALBUM	COVER VERSION
Nickolas Ashford Valerie Simpson	46	9	*Four In Blue*	—
Henry Cosby S. Robinson	1	1	*Tears of A Clown*	The English Beat
S. Robinson	18	7	*What Love Has Joined Together*	—
S. Robinson	56	20	*What Love Has Joined Together*	—
S. Robinson T. Johnson	49	20	*What Love Has Joined Together*	—
Marvin Gaye	14	1	*Baby, I'm for Real*	—
M. Gaye	12	4	*Portrait of the Originals*	—
M. Gaye	74	20	*Naturally Together*	—
Clay McMurray	53	14	*Naturally Together*	—
Rare Earth	4	20	*Get Ready*	The Temptations (original)
Norman Whitfield	7	20	*Ecology*	Rod Stewart The Temptations (original)
Tom Baird	17	48	*Ecology*	—
T. Baird Rare Earth	7	30	*One World*	—
T. Baird Rare Earth	19	48	*In Concert*	—
Valerie Simpson	20	7	*Diana Ross*	—
V. Simpson Nickolas Ashford	1	1	*Diana Ross*	Marvin Gaye and Tammi Terrell (original)
V. Simpson N. Ashford	16	10	*Surrender*	—
V. Simpson	29	10	*Surrender*	—
V. Simpson N. Ashford	38	16	*Surrender*	—

SONG	YEAR	WRITER
▶ David Ruffin		
"My Whole World Ended (The Moment You Left Me)"	1969	Harvey Fuqua Pam Sawyer James Roach Johnny Bristol
"I've Lost Everything I've Ever Loved"	1969	Tom Kemp J. Bristol
"I'm So Glad I Fell For You"	1969	A. Posey G. Session
▶ Jimmy Ruffin		
"What Becomes of the Brokenhearted"	1966	J. Dean Paul Riser W. Weatherspoon
"I've Passed This Way Before"	1966	William Weatherspoon James Dean
"Gonna Give Her All the Love I've Got"	1967	Norman Whitfield Barrett Strong
"Don't You Miss Me a Little Bit Baby"	1967	Roger Penzabene B. Strong N. Whitfield
"Stand by Me" (David Ruffin)	1970	Ben E. King Elmo Glick
▶ Spinners		
"I'll Always Love You"	1965	Ivy Hunter William Stevenson
"Truly Yours"	1966	I. Hunter W. Stevenson
"It's a Shame"	1970	Syreeta Wright Lee Garrett Stevie Wonder
"We'll Have It Made"	1971	S. Wright S. Wonder
▶ Edwin Starr		
"Twenty-five Miles"	1968	Johnny Bristol Harvey Fuqua Edwin Starr
"I'm Still a Strugglin' Man"	1969	Don McNeil J. Bristol
"War"	1970	Norman Whitfield Barrett Strong

PRODUCER	POP CHART	R & B CHART	ALBUM	COVER VERSION
Harvey Fuqua Johnny Bristol	9	2	*My Whole World Ended*	Carl Graves
J. Bristol	58	11	*My Whole World Ended*	—
Berry Gordy	53	18	*Feelin' Good*	—
W. Weatherspoon J. Dean	7	6	*Jimmy Ruffin Sings Top Ten*	Martha Velez
William Weatherspoon James Dean	17	10	*Jimmy Ruffin Sings Top Ten*	—
Norman Whitfield	29	14	*Jimmy Ruffin Sings Top Ten*	—
N. Whitfield	68	27	*Ruff 'n' Ready*	—
Frank Wilson	—	24	*I Am My Brother's Keeper*	Ben E. King (original)
Ivy Hunter William Stevenson	35	8	*The Original Spinners*	—
I. Hunter W. Stevenson	—	16	*The Original Spinners*	—
Stevie Wonder	14	4	*Second Time Around*	—
S. Wonder	89	20	*Best of the Spinners*	—
H. Fuqua, J. Bristol	6	6	*Twenty-Five Miles*	—
J. Bristol	80	27	*Twenty-Five Miles*	—
Norman Whitfield	1	3	*War and Peace*	The Temptations Frankie Goes to Hollywood

SONG	YEAR	WRITER
"Stop the War Now"	1970	N. Whitfield B. Strong
"Funky Music Sho Nuff Turns Me On"	1971	N. Whitfield B. Strong

▶ The Supremes

SONG	YEAR	WRITER
"Let Me Go the Right Way"	1962	Berry Gordy
"When the Lovelight Starts Shining Through Your Eyes"	1964	Holland-Dozier-Holland
"Where Did Our Love Go"	1964	H-D-H
"Baby Love"	1964	H-D-H
"Come See About Me"	1964	H-D-H
"Stop! In the Name Of Love"	1965	H-D-H
"Back In My Arms Again"	1965	H-D-H
"Nothing But Heartache"	1965	H-D-H
"I Hear a Symphony"	1965	H-D-H
"My World Is Empty Without You"	1966	H-D-H
"Love Is Like an Itching In My Heart"	1966	H-D-H
"You Can't Hurry Love"	1966	H-D-H
"You Keep Me Hanging On"	1966	H-D-H
"Love is Here and Now You're Gone"	1966	H-D-H
"The Happening"	1967	H-D-H
"Reflections"	1967	H-D-H
"In and Out of Love"	1967	H-D-H
"Forever Came Today"	1968	H-D-H
"Some Things You Never Get Used To"	1968	Nickolas Ashford Valerie Simpson

PRODUCER	POP CHART	R & B CHART	ALBUM	COVER VERSION
N. Whitfield	26	5	*Involved*	—
N. Whitfield	64	6	*Involved*	The Temptations, Undisputed Truth
Berry Gordy	90	26	*Meet The Supremes*	—
Brian Holland Lamont Dozier	23	—	*Where Did Our Love Go*	—
B. Holland L. Dozier	1	—	*Where Did Our Love Go*	Soft Cell J. Geils Band
B. Holland L. Dozier	1	—	*Where Did Our Love Go*	—
B. Holland L. Dozier	1	3	*Where Did Our Love Go*	Jr. Walker and the All Stars Nella Dodds
B. Holland L. Dozier	1	2	*More Hits*	The Hollies
B. Holland L. Dozier	1	1	*More Hits*	—
B. Holland L. Dozier	11	6	*More Hits*	—
B. Holland L. Dozier	1	2	*I Hear a Symphony*	—
B. Holland L. Dozier	5	10	*I Hear a Symphony*	José Feliciano
B. Holland L. Dozier	9	7	*The Supremes a Go-Go*	—
B. Holland L. Dozier	1	1	*The Supremes a Go-Go*	Phil Collins
B. Holland L. Dozier	1	1	*Supremes Sing Holland-Dozier-Holland*	Vanilla Fudge
B. Holland L. Dozier	1	1	*Supremes Sing Holland-Dozier-Holland*	—
B. Holland L. Dozier	1	12	*The Supremes' Greatest Hits*	—
B. Holland L. Dozier	2	4	*Reflections*	—
B. Holland L. Dozier	9	16	*Reflections*	—
B. Holland L. Dozier	28	17	*Reflections*	Jackson 5
Nickolas Ashford Valerie Simpson	30	43	*Love Child*	—

SONG	YEAR	WRITER
"Love Child"	1968	Pam Sawyer R. Dean Taylor Frank Wilson Deke Richards
"I'm Gonna Make You Love Me" (with the Temptations)	1969	Ken Gamble Jerry Ross Jerry Williams
"I'm Livin' in Shame"	1969	P. Sawyer R. Dean Taylor F. Wilson B. Gordy
"I'll Try Something New" (with the Temptations)	1969	S. Robinson
"The Composer"	1969	S. Robinson
"No Matter What Sign You Are"	1969	B. Gordy H. Cosby
"Someday We'll Be Together"	1969	Jackie Beavers Johnny Bristol Harvey Fuqua
"Up The Ladder To The Roof"	1970	Vincent DaMirco
"Everybody's Got the Right to Love"	1970	F. Wilson
"Stoned Love"	1970	F. Wilson Yoshirma Samont
"River Deep—Mountain High"	1970	Phil Spector Jeff Barry Ellie Greenwich
"Nathan Jones"	1971	Leonard Caston Kenny Wakefield

The Temptations

SONG	YEAR	WRITER
"Dream Come True"	1962	B. Gordy
"The Way You Do the Things You Do"	1964	Robert Rogers Smokey Robinson
"I'll Be In Trouble"	1964	S. Robinson
"Girl (Why You Wanna Make Me Blue)"	1964	Norman Whitfield Eddie Holland
"My Girl"	1965	S. Robinson Ronald White
"It's Growing"	1965	S. Robinson Warren Moore
"Since I Lost My Baby"	1965	S. Robinson W. Moore

PRODUCER	POP CHART	R & B CHART	ALBUM	COVER VERSION
Berry Gordy Frank Wilson Henry Cosby Deke Richards	1	2	*Love Child*	—
F. Wilson N. Ashford	2	2		Dee Dee Warwick Madeline Bell
B. Gordy F. Wilson H. Cosby D. Richards	10	8	*Let the Sun Shine In*	—
F. Wilson D. Richards	25	8	*Diana Ross and The Supremes and The Temptations*	The Miracles (original)
S. Robinson	27		*Let the Sun Shine In*	—
B. Gordy H. Cosby	31	17	*Let the Sun Shine In*	—
Johnny Bristol	1	1	*Right On*	—
F. Wilson	10	5	*Right On*	—
F. Wilson	21	11	*Right On*	—
F. Wilson	7	1	*New Ways But Love Stays*	—
N. Ashford V. Simpson	14	7	*The Magnificent Seven*	Ike and Tina Turner (original) Deep Purple
F. Wilson	16	8	*Touch*	—
B. Gordy	—	22	*Meet the Temptations*	—
Smokey Robinson	11	—	*The Temptations Sing Smokey*	Rita Coolidge Hall & Oates
S. Robinson	33	—	*The Temptations Sing Smokey*	—
Norman Whitfield	26	—	*Temptin' Temptations*	—
S. Robinson Ronald White	1	1	*The Temptations Sing Smokey*	Lillo Thomas Bobby Vee
S. Robinson	18	3	*The Temptations Sing Smokey*	Otis Redding
S. Robinson	17	4	*Temptin' Temptations*	Luther Vandross

SONG	YEAR	WRITER
"You've Got to Earn It"	1965	S. Robinson
"My Baby"	1965	S. Robinson W. Moore Robert Rogers
"Don't Look Back"	1965	S. Robinson Ronald White
"Get Ready"	1966	S. Robinson
"Ain't Too Proud to Beg"	1966	N. Whitfield Eddie Holland
"Beauty Is Only Skin Deep"	1966	N. Whitfield E. Holland
"(I Know) I'm Losing You"	1966	N. Whitfield E. Holland Cornelius Grant
"All I Need"	1967	Frank Wilson E. Holland R. Dean Taylor
"You're My Everything"	1967	N. Whitfield C. Grant Roger Penzabene
"Loneliness Made Me (Realize) It's You That I Need"	1967	N. Whitfield E. Holland
"I Wish It Would Rain"	1968	N. Whitfield Barrett Strong R. Penzabene
"I Could Never Love Another (After Loving You)"	1968	N. Whitfield B. Strong R. Penzabene
"Please Return Your Love to Me"	1968	N. Whitfield B. Strong Bruce Neely
"Cloud Nine"	1968	N. Whitfield B. Strong
"I'm Gonna Make You Love Me" (with the Supremes)	1969	Ken Gamble Jerry Ross Jerry Williams
"I Can't Get Next To You"	1969	B. Strong N. Whitfield
"Runaway Child, Running Wild"	1969	N. Whitfield B. Strong
"I'll Try Something New" (with the Supremes)	1969	S. Robinson
"Don't Let the Joneses Get You Down"	1969	N. Whitfield B. Strong
"Psychedelic Shack"	1970	N. Whitfield B. Strong

PRODUCER	POP CHART	R & B CHART	ALBUM	COVER VERSION
S. Robinson	—	22	*Temptin' Temptations*	—
S. Robinson	13	4	*Temptin' Temptations*	—
S. Robinson	83	15	*Temptin' Temptations*	Peter Tosh & Mick Jagger
S. Robinson	29	1	*Gettin' Ready*	Rare Earth
N. Whitfield	13	1	*Gettin' Ready*	The Rolling Stones
N. Whitfield	3	1	*Gettin' Ready*	—
N. Whitfield	8	1	*With a Lot O' Soul*	Rod Stewart Rare Earth
Frank Wilson	8	2	*With a Lot O' Soul*	—
N. Whitfield	6	3	*With a Lot O' Soul*	—
N. Whitfield	14	3	*With a Lot O' Soul*	—
N. Whitfield	4	1	*I Wish It Would Rain*	Bobby Womack Gladys Knight and the Pips
N. Whitfield	13	1	*I Wish It Would Rain*	—
N. Whitfield	26	4	*I Wish It Would Rain*	—
N. Whitfield	6	2	*Cloud Nine*	Mongo Santamaria
Frank Williams Nickolas Ashford	2	11	*The Supremes Doin' the Temptations*	Dee Dee Warwick Madeline Bell
N. Whitfield	1	1	*Puzzle People*	Al Green
N. Whitfield	6	1	*Cloud Nine*	—
F. Wilson Deke Richards	25	8	*Diana Ross and The Supremes and The Temptations*	The Miracles (original)
N. Whitfield	20	2	*Puzzle People*	—
N. Whitfield	7	2	*Psychedelic Shack*	—

SONG	YEAR	WRITER
"Ball of Confusion (That's What the World Is Today)"	1970	N. Whitfield B. Strong
"Just My Imagination Running Away With Me"	1971	N. Whitfield B. Strong
"It's Summer"	1971	N. Whitfield B. Strong
"Superstar (Remember How You Got Where You Are)"	1971	N. Whitfield B. Strong

▶ # Undisputed Truth

SONG	YEAR	WRITER
"Smiling Faces Sometimes"	1971	Barrett Strong Norman Whitfield
"You Make Your Own Heaven and Hell Right Here on Earth"	1971	B. Strong N. Whitfield

▶ # Junior Walker and the All Stars

SONG	YEAR	WRITER
"Shotgun"	1965	Autry DeWalt
"Do the Boomerang"	1965	Henry Cosby
"Shake & Fingerpop"	1965	Willie Woods Lawrence Horn A. DeWalt
"Cleo's Mood"	1966	W. Woods
"(I'm a) Road Runner"	1966	Holland-Dozier-Holland
"How Sweet It Is (to Be Loved by You)"	1966	H-D-H
"Pucker Up Buttercup"	1967	Danny Coggins H. Fuqua Johnny Bristol
"Come See About Me"	1967	H-D-H
"Hip City, Part 2"	1968	Eddie Willis A. DeWalt
"What Does It Take (to Win Your Love)"	1969	Vernon Bullock J. Bristol H. Fuqua
"Home Cookin' "	1969	H. Cosby Melvin Moy Eddie Willis
"These Eyes"	1969	Burton Cummings Randy Bachman
"Gotta Hold on to This Feeling"	1970	Joe Hinton J. Bristol Pam Sawyer

PRODUCER	POP CHART	R & B CHART	ALBUM	COVER VERSION
N. Whitfield	3	2	*Greatest Hits Vol. 2*	Tina Turner Love and Rockets
N. Whitfield	1	1	*The Sky's the Limit*	Lillo Thomas The Rolling Stones
N. Whitfield	51	29	*The Sky's the Limit*	—
N. Whitfield	18	8	*Solid Rock*	
Norman Whitfield	3	2	*Undisputed Truth*	—
N. Whitfield	72	24	*Face to Face With the Truth*	—
Berry Gordy	4	1	*Shotgun*	Vanilla Fudge
William Stevenson	36	10	*Shotgun*	—
Berry Gordy Lawrence Horn	29	7	*Shotgun*	—
Harvey Fuqua	50	14	*Shotgun*	Tommy James and the Shondells
Lamont Dozier Brian Holland	20	4	*Shotgun*	Humble Pie
L. Dozier B. Holland	8	3	*Road Runner*	Marvin Gaye
H. Fuqua, Johnny Bristol	3	11	*Road Runner*	—
L. Dozier B. Holland	24	8	*Home Cookin'*	The Supremes (original)
L. Horn	31	7	*Home Cookin'*	—
H. Fuqua J. Bristol	4	1	*Home Cookin'*	—
Henry Cosby	42	19	*Home Cookin'*	—
J. Bristol	16	3	*These Eyes*	The Guess Who (original)
J. Bristol	21	2	*These Eyes*	—

SONG	YEAR	WRITER
"Do You See My Love (for You Growing)"	1970	J. Bristol Jackie Beavers
"Take Me Girl, I'm Ready"	1971	P. Sawyer Leon Ware J. Bristol

Velvelettes

SONG	YEAR	WRITER
"Needle in a Haystack"	1964	Norman Whitfield William Stevenson
"He Was Really Sayin' Something"	1965	N. Whitfield W. Stevenson Eddie Holland

Mary Wells

SONG	YEAR	WRITER
"The One Who Really Loves You"	1962	Smokey Robinson
"You Beat Me to the Punch"	1962	Ronald White S. Robinson
"Two Lovers"	1962	S. Robinson
"Laughing Boy"	1963	S. Robinson
"Your Old Stand By"	1963	S. Robinson
"What's Easy for Two Is Hard for One"	1963	S. Robinson
"You Lost the Sweetest Boy"	1963	H-D-H
"My Guy"	1964	S. Robinson
"What's the Matter with You" (with Marvin Gaye)	1964	William Stevenson Clarence Paul
"Once Upon a Time" (with Marvin Gaye)	1964	Dave Hamilton C. Paul

Kim Weston

SONG	YEAR	WRITER
"Love Me All the Way"	1963	William Stevenson
"Take Me in Your Arms"	1965	Holland-Dozier-Holland
"Helpless"	1966	H-D-H
"It Takes Two" (with Marvin Gaye)	1967	Sylvia Moy W. Stevenson

Stevie Wonder

SONG	YEAR	WRITER
"Fingertips-pt. 2"	1963	Clarence Paul Henry Cosby
"Workout Stevie, Workout"	1963	C. Paul H. Cosby

PRODUCER	POP CHART	R & B CHART	ALBUM	COVER VERSION
J. Bristol	32	3	*A Gassss*	—
J. Bristol	50	18	*Rainbow Funk*	Eric Mercury
Norman Whitfield	45	—	no album	—
N. Whitfield	—	21	no album	Bananarama
Smokey Robinson	8	2	*One Who Really Loves You*	—
S. Robinson	9	1	*One Who Really Loves You*	Gene Chandler
S. Robinson	7	1	*Two Lovers*	—
S. Robinson	15	6	*Two Lovers*	—
S. Robinson	40	8	*Greatest Hits*	Jeannie Tracee
H-D-H S. Robinson	29	8	*Greatest Hits*	—
Brian Holland Lamont Dozier	22	10	*Greatest Hits*	—
S. Robinson	1	—	*My Guy*	Sister Sledge The Boones Petula Clark
William Stevenson	17	—	*Together* (with Marvin Gaye)	—
Clarence Paul	19	—	*Together*	—
William Stevenson	88	24	no album	—
Lamont Dozier Brian Holland	50	4	no album	The Doobie Brothers
L. Dozier B. Holland	56	13	no album	Jackie Moore
Henry Cosby W. Stevenson	14	4	*Take Two* (with M. Gaye)	—
Berry Gordy	1	1	*Little Stevie The 12-Year-Old Genius*	—
Clarence Paul	33	?	no album	—

SONG	YEAR	WRITER
"Hey, Harmonica Man"	1964	Marty Cooper Lou Josie
"High Heel Sneakers"	1965	Robert Higginbotham
"Uptight (Everything Alright)"	1966	Stevie Wonder H. Cosby Sylvia Moy
"Nothing's Too Good for My Baby"	1966	S. Moy H. Cosby William Stevenson
"With a Child's Heart"	1966	S. Moy H. Cosby S. Wonder
"Blowin' in the Wind"	1966	Bob Dylan
"A Place in the Sun"	1966	Bryan Wells Ron Miller
"Travelin' Man"	1967	B. Wells R. Miller
"Hey Love"	1967	Morris Broadnax S. Wonder C. Paul
"I Was Made to Love Her"	1967	Lula Hardaway S. Wonder S. Moy H. Cosby
"I'm Wondering"	1967	S. Moy S. Wonder H. Cosby
"Shoo-Be-Doo-Be-Doo-Da-Day"	1968	S. Moy S. Wonder H. Cosby
"You Met Your Match"	1968	L. Hardaway D. Hunter S. Wonder
"For Once in My Life"	1968	Orlando Murden R. Miller
"I Don't Know Why I Love You"	1969	Paul Riser L. Hardaway D. Hunter S. Wonder
"My Cherie Amour"	1969	S. Moy S. Wonder H. Cosby
"Yester-Me, Yester-You, Yesterday"	1969	B. Wells R. Miller

PRODUCER	POP CHART	R & B CHART	ALBUM	COVER VERSION
Marc Gordon Hal Davis	29	—	*Stevie at the Beach*	—
Robert L. Gordy	59	30	*Motown Review in Paris*	—
Henry Cosby	3	1	*Uptight*	Ramsey Lewis Jazz Crusaders Nancy Wilson
H. Cosby William Stevenson	20	4	*Uptight*	—
H. Cosby C. Paul	—	8	*Uptight*	—
Clarence Paul	9	1	*Uptight*	Bob Dylan (original) Peter, Paul and Mary
C. Paul	9	3	*Down to Earth*	—
C. Paul	32	31	*Down to Earth*	—
C. Paul	90	9	*Down to Earth*	—
H. Cosby	2	1	*I Was Made To Love Her*	King Curtis
H. Cosby	12	4	no album	—
H. Cosby	9	1	*For Once In My Life*	—
Don Hunter S. Wonder	35	2	*For Once In My Life*	—
H. Cosby	2	2	*For Once In My Life*	Frank Sinatra Jackie Wilson Tony Bennett
D. Hunter S. Wonder	39	16	*My Cherie Amour*	—
H. Cosby	4	4	*My Cherie Amour*	Soul Train Gang
Harvey Fuqua Johnny Bristol	7	5	*My Cherie Amour*	—

SONG	YEAR	WRITER
"Never Had a Dream Come True"	1970	S. Wonder S. Moy H. Cosby
"Signed, Sealed, Delivered, I'm Yours"	1970	L. Hardaway Syreeta Wright Lee Garrett S. Wonder
"Heaven Help Us All"	1970	R. Miller
"We Can Work It Out"	1971	John Lennon Paul McCartney
"If You Really Love Me"	1971	S. Wright S. Wonder

PRODUCER	POP CHART	R & B CHART	ALBUM	COVER VERSION
H. Cosby	26	11	*Signed, Sealed & Delivered*	—
S. Wonder	3	1	*Signed, Sealed & Delivered*	Soul Children Peter Frampton
Tom Baird Ron Miller	9	3	*Signed, Sealed & Delivered*	—
S. Wonder	13	3	*Where I'm Coming From*	The Beatles (Original)
S. Wonder	8	4	*Where I'm Coming From*	—

BIBLIOGRAPHY

Betrock, Alan, ed. *Girl Groups: The Story of Sound* (Motown sections written by Aaron Fuchs). New York: Delilah, 1982.

Brown, Geoff. *Diana Ross*. New York: St. Martin's Press, 1983.

Cruse, Harold. *The Crisis of the Negro Intellectual*. New York: William Morrow & Co., 1967.

DaSilva, Benjamin, Milton Finkelstein, and Arlene Loshin. *The Afro-American in United States History*. New York: Globe Book Co., 1972.

Deal, Terrence, and Allen A. Kennedy. *Corporate Cultures*. New York: Addison-Wesley, 1982.

Denby, Charles. *Indignant Heart: A Black Worker's Journal*. Boston: South End Press, 1978.

Drake, St. Clair, and Horace Cayton. *Black Metropolis: A Study of Negro Life in a Northern City*. New York: Harcourt, Brace & Company, 1945.

Eisen, Jonathan, ed. *The Age of Rock*. New York: Vintage (paper) 1969.

Fong-Torres, Ben. *What's That Sound: The Contemporary Music Scene from the Pages of Rolling Stone*. New York: Anchor Press, 1976.

Franklin, John Hope. *From Slavery to Freedom: A History of Negro Americans*, 5th edition. New York: Alfred A. Knopf, 1980.

Frazier, E. Franklin. *The Negro Family in the United States*, revised and abridged edition. Chicago: University of Chicago Press, 1948.

George, Nelson. *The Michael Jackson Story*. New York: Dell, 1984.

———. *Top of the Charts*. Piscataway, New York: New Century Education Corp., 1983.

Gillet, Charlie. *The Sound of the City*. New York: Dell, 1970.

Gordy, Sr., Berry. *Movin' Up*. New York: Harper & Row, 1979.

Guzman, Herbert G. *The Black Family: Slavery & Freedom, 1750–1925*. New York: Vintage, 1976.

Haskins, James. *I'm Gonna Make You Love Me: The Story of Diana Ross*. New York: Dell, 1980.

Haskins, James, and Kathleen Benson. *The Stevie Wonder Scrapbook.* New York: Grosset & Dunlap, 1978.

Hirshey, Gerri. *Nowhere to Run.* New York: Times Books, 1984.

Hoare, Ian, ed. *The Soul Book.* New York: Delta, 1975.

Klebanow, Diana, Franklin L. Jonas, and Ira M. Leonard. *Urban Legacy.* New York: Mentor, 1977.

Lieb, Sandra. *Ma Rainey: Mother of the Blues.* Boston: University of Massachusetts Press, 1981.

Louis, Joe, with Edna and Art Rust, Jr. *Joe Louis: My Life.* New York: Harcourt, Brace, & Jovanovich, 1978.

Meier, August, and Elliot Rudnicks. *Black Detroit and the Rise of the UAW.* New York: Oxford University Press, 1979.

Morse, David. *Motown.* New York: Collier Books, 1971.

Norman, Philip. *The Road Goes on Forever.* New York: Fireside Books, 1982.

Pareles, Jon, and Patricia Romanowski, eds. *The Rolling Stone Encyclopedia of Rock and Roll.* New York: Summit Books, 1983.

Peterson, Virgil W. *The Mob.* Ottawa, Illinois: Green Hill, 1983.

Report of the National Commission on Civil Disorders. New York: Bantam Books, 1968.

Ritz, David. *Divided Soul: The Life of Marvin Gaye.* New York: McGraw-Hill, 1985.

Shaw, Arnold. *Honkers & Shouters.* New York: Collier Books, 1978.

Tosches, Nick. *Dangerous Dance: Daryl Hall/John Oates.* New York: St. Martin's Press, 1984.

Vochman, Thomas. *Black and White Styles in Conflict.* Chicago: University of Chicago Press, 1981.

Walker, Alice. *The Third Life of Grange Copeland.* New York: , 1970.

Weinberg, Max, with Robert Santelli. *The Big Beat.* Chicago: Contemporary Books, 1984.

Wenner, Jann, ed. *The Rolling Stone Interviews,* vol. 2. New York: Warner Books (paper), 1973.

Westbrooks, Logan, and Lance Williams. *The Anatomy of a Record Company.* Los Angeles: Westbrooks, 1981.

White, Charles. *The Life and Times of Little Richard.* New York: Harmony Books, 1984.

Wilkins, Roger. *A Man's Life: An Autobiography.* New York, Simon and Schuster, 1982.

Young, Al. *Bodies & Soul.* San Francisco: Creative Arts, 1981.

INDEX

ABOUT THE AUTHOR

Nelson George, called by *Newsweek* magazine "perhaps the best black writer on black popular music in America," has been covering entertainment since 1977. His biography of Michael Jackson, *The Michael Jackson Story* (Dell), made every national bestseller list, sold 1.3 million copies in the United States, and was printed in several foreign languages. George's other books include *Top of the Charts* (New Century) and *Fresh, Hip Hop Don't Stop* (Random House). Born in Brooklyn, New York, and a graduate of St. John's University, he has served as *Billboard's* black music editor since 1982. Prior to that he was *Record World* magazine's black music editor and a staff writer at the *Amsterdam News*. His work has appeared in *The Village Voice, The New York Times, Musician, Rolling Stone, Black Enterprise, Essence,* and *Video Review*. George resides in Brooklyn.

WRITTEN
IN
STONE

Other P&R Books by Philip Graham Ryken

Art for God's Sake

Communion of Saints

Courage to Stand

Discovering God

He Speaks to Me Everywhere

My Father's World

When You Pray

REFORMED EXPOSITORY COMMENTARY SERIES

1 Kings

Galatians

Luke (2 volumes)

1 Timothy

BASICS OF THE FAITH SERIES

What Is a True Calvinist?

What Is Mercy Ministry?

What Is the Christian Worldview?

CO-AUTHORED

The Church

Give Praise to God

The Incarnation in the Gospels

Jesus on Trial

WRITTEN IN STONE

The Ten Commandments and Today's Moral Crisis

PHILIP GRAHAM RYKEN

PUBLISHING
P.O. BOX 817 • PHILLIPSBURG • NEW JERSEY 08865-0817

Printed in the United States of America

The Library of Congress has cataloged the first edition as follows:

Ryken, Philip Graham, 1966-
  Written in stone: the Ten commandments and today's moral crisis /
Philip Graham Ryken.
    p. cm.
  Includes bibliographical references and index.
  ISBN 1-58134-490-2 (alk. paper)
  1.Ten commandments—Criticism, interpretation, etc. 2. Law and
gospel. 3. Law (Theology). 4. Christianity and culture. 5. United
States—Moral conditions. I. Title.
BV4655.R95   2003
241.5'2—dc22
                                         2003015234

P&R ISBN: 978-1-59638-206-0